WEST AFRICA

THE FRENCH-SPEAKING NATIONS

Yesterday and Today

Richard Adloff

HOLT, RINEHART and WINSTON, Inc.

New York

Contemporary Civilizations Series

The design on the title page and at the beginning of each chapter is adapted from a mask of the Guro tribe, Ivory Coast.

Library of Congress Catalog Card Number: 64–25653

Preface

A striking chapter in the story of the transition of African lands from colonialism to nationhood is that which concerns the eight nations of former French West Africa.

Those eight countries—Senegal, Mauritania, Mali, Niger, Guinea, Ivory Coast, Dahomey and Upper Volta—were colonies of France from the late nineteenth century until 1946. That year marked the beginning of their rapid political evolution, which was to culminate in peaceful accession to full independence in 1960.

Despite their national frontiers, the eight states are the inheritors of a tradition of mutual cooperation, now being revived in common action through organizations whose keynote is African unity. The influence of France's cultural mission is also still widely evident, and French culture is accepted by many Africans of the new nations as a unifying factor.

Because French West Africa was, until recently, in many ways a single political, economic and social entity, the author has primarily dealt with it as such. It is his hope that this approach will aid in understanding the political and economic characteristics of the eight French-speaking West African countries. Africa, however, including West Africa, is in a continuing ferment, and anything that is written about it today risks being outdated tomorrow.

The author is indebted to many persons and several institutions for aid and source material. He wishes to thank particularly Dr. Gwendolen M. Carter, Africa specialist and professor at Northwestern University; Peter Duignan, Curator of the Africa Collection, Hoover Institution, Stanford University; and above all, his wife, Virginia Thompson Adloff.

Opinions and judgments expressed herein are entirely the responsibility of the author.

RICHARD ADLOFF served for eight years in the Department of State, Division of Research and Publication. Later he was engaged in publication work of the Treasury Department, the Tariff Commission, and the War Department (Military Intelligence Division). For some years, he has been a research associate of the Hoover Institution, Stanford University. Since 1953, he has made several study trips through French-speaking Africa south of the Sahara. With his wife, Virginia Thompson, he is co-author of *French West Africa* and *The Emerging States of French Equatorial Africa,* and they are at present writing a book on Madagascar.

VERA MICHELES DEAN, general editor of the Contemporary Civilizations Series, is professor of international development at the Graduate School of Public Administration, New York University. Mrs. Dean was research director and editor of the Foreign Policy Association, 1928–1961, and served as director of the Non-Western Civilizations Program at The University of Rochester, 1954–1962.

With the assistance of Harry D. Harootunian, Mrs. Dean prepared the anthology WEST AND NON-WEST: NEW PERSPECTIVES which is the basic reader in the Contemporary Civilizations Series.

Contents

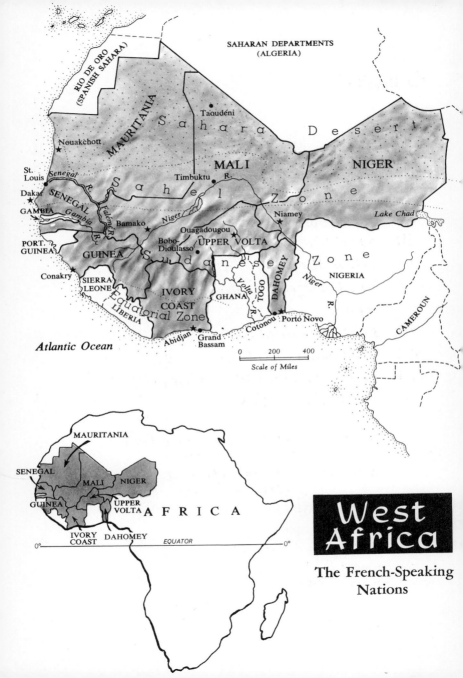

SAHARAN DEPARTMENTS
(ALGERIA)

RIO DE ORO
(SPANISH SAHARA)

S a h a r a   D e s e r t

MAURITANIA

Taoudéni

Nouakchott

MALI

NIGER

St. Louis

Senegal R.

Timbuktu

Dakar

SENEGAL

S a h e l   Z o n e

GAMBIA

Gambia R.

Falémé R.

Bamako

Niger R.

Niamey

Lake Chad

PORT. GUINEA

GUINEA

Ouagadougou

UPPER VOLTA

Bobo-Dioulasso

S u d a n e s e

Z o n e

Conakry

SIERRA LEONE

IVORY COAST

GHANA

Volta R.

TOGO

DAHOMEY

NIGERIA

Niger R.

LIBERIA

E q u a t o r i a l   Zone

Cotonou

Porto Novo

CAMEROUN

Abidjan

Grand Bassam

Atlantic Ocean

| 0 | 200 | 400 |

Scale of Miles

MAURITANIA

SENEGAL

MALI

NIGER

GUINEA

UPPER VOLTA

A F R I C A

IVORY COAST

DAHOMEY

EQUATOR

0°

0°

West Africa

The French-Speaking Nations

WEST AFRICA
The French-Speaking Nations

BECAUSE of its vastness, its inaccessibility and its mysterious ways of life, Africa has long exerted a magnetic attraction upon many people in the Western world. Although this great continent's remote past is still in many ways obscure, research during the last half-century has cast some light on its prehistoric era, and a good deal is now known about the historic period that preceded the coming of Europeans. During the nineteenth and early twentieth centuries, too, European explorers, administrators and missionaries spent much time and effort in studying the African scene, and their work is reflected in a sizeable body of literature.

Most of us who are accustomed to thinking of world areas as they appear on Mercator maps, which exaggerate the size of land masses toward the poles, cannot fully realize the immensity of the African continent. The best way to appreciate its enormous extent, as well as its relationship to the rest of the world, is to look at a world globe or one of the modern maps based on an "equal-area" projection of the earth's land and water masses.

Almost one-sixth of Africa was comprised in the French West African federation, which was formed in 1904. This federation included at first five and later eight colonies which after World War II were called territories. They were Senegal, Mauritania, Soudan, Niger, Guinea, Ivory Coast, Upper Volta and Dahomey. Although the political status of these eight countries has recently changed, the term French West Africa—usually abbreviated F.W.A.—will be used in this book for convenience in referring to the region as a whole. Its area of 1,831,272 square miles is nearly two-thirds as large as that of the continental United States and more than eight times that of France. To the north it extends into the central Sahara Desert and to the south it is bordered by the Atlantic Ocean and the Gulf of Guinea. Its western limit is the Atlantic and its eastern, Nigeria and Chad. This huge region's population of no more than 25 millions is small in relation to its area, and is very unevenly distributed.

During the summer of 1958, after the collapse of the Fourth Republic in France, a new constitution was drafted setting up the Fifth Republic and also providing for a Franco-African Community, which was planned to include France itself and all its overseas departments, establishments and territories. On September 28, 1958, this constitution was submitted to the vote of the populations of all the French possessions in a referendum by which they could choose either to remain associated with France in the Community by voting "yes" or to obtain immediate independence by a negative vote. Except for Guinea, all the West African territories and all other French possessions voted "yes." Guinea's "no" vote meant rejection of membership in the Community, and thus Guinea became with startling suddenness an independent country, a status for which it was ill-prepared both politically and economically.

Although, after the referendum, the other seven F.W.A. territories remained members of the Franco-African Community, their evolution toward independence was rapid. By the end of 1960 all of them attained complete political independence, although they continued to be more or less closely tied to France in economic and other ways through treaty arrangements. All of the eight states are now republics, and all have become members of the United Nations. They have adopted the names formerly applied to them as territories, except for Mauritania (which emphasizes its state religion by calling itself the Islamic Republic of Mauritania) and Soudan (now the Republic of Mali, a name borrowed from that of one of the ancient Negro empires of the sudanese zone, whose story is told in Chapter IV).

The Land

West Africa's history and ways of life, like those of the rest of the continent, have been deeply affected by environmental factors. Foremost among these has been its hostile climate, marked by extremes of heat and, in some areas, of rainfall. Another is the poverty of its soils, due to excessive heat and sunlight, as well as to the African custom of burning over land, and to torrential seasonal rains in the equatorial and sudanese zones. Still another is the centuries-long isolation imposed on it by natural barriers.

Although the burning wasteland of the Sahara to the north did not entirely shield sub-Saharan Africa from the raids of the medieval Muslim warriors, it did discourage European penetration from the north for many years. To the south, for hundreds of miles along the Guinea Gulf, an inhospitable unbroken coastline is guarded by offshore sandbars so that ships cannot approach the land. These land and sea barriers are the main reason why the interior regions, except in Senegal, were so little known before the late nineteenth century. And the adverse climate and soils go far to explain why the population is so meager and the Africans' resistance to disease so low.

The most difficult environments in F.W.A., for both men and domestic animals, are those of the equatorial zone along the southern coast and of the desert to the north. Both are marked by extremes of heat and by a physical setting that, for different reasons in each case, necessitates a constant struggle for survival by their sparse populations. Between these two zones lie two others in which both human beings and animals find it less difficult to live and move about: the sudanese or savannah zone, lying north of the tropical-forest region, and beyond it the *sahel,* with its scanty vegetation of thorny plants and trees, which merges into the barren reaches of the Sahara. It should be mentioned that these various climatic and vegetation zones bear no relation to the colonial boundaries that were arbitrarily defined by the European powers which competed in Africa in the nineteenth century and that largely still determine the frontiers of the new African states.

The Equatorial Zone

The equatorial zone (also known as the Guinea or tropical-forest zone) stretches east-west for some 800 miles along the coast of the Gulf of Guinea and the Atlantic Ocean. Extending inland to varying depths, it is widest—more than 180 miles—in the western region of Ivory Coast. Behind the sandy shores, marked by coconut palms, low sand dunes, lagoons and mangrove swamps, stretches red lateritic plain covered by forest, with few hills and no high mountains except those of Nimba on the Ivory Coast-Liberian border, where one peak rises to 6,000 feet. About 60 miles inland in Guinea is a rock-edged highland, the Fouta Djallon, where two great rivers—the Niger and the Senegal—have their source; it is mountainous, reaching in a few places over 4,000 feet, and its elevation gives it a climate and vegetation unlike those of the equatorial zone that adjoins it.

Much of the land surface in the equatorial zone consists of laterite, a porous substance formed by the decomposition of surface rocks under the action of heat and humidity. Because of its large content of aluminum and iron, it is blood-red or reddish-brown in color, and this has led some writers to call Africa the Red Continent as so much of it is covered by a lateritic layer. Laterite forms a thick, hard crust on which fertile earth cannot accumulate, for the torrential monsoon rains wash it away. In fact, soil erosion caused by those rains is a serious economic problem in the equatorial zone and to some extent also in the savannah. Laterite is useful in road-making, however, as it provides a firm surface, though one that is extremely dusty when dry.

In the equatorial zone, temperatures and humidity are high throughout the year. The average annual temperature is between 75° and 80° Fahrenheit, and humidity—higher at some coastal points than others—ranges upward from minimums of 55 per cent in January and 75 per cent in October. There are two rainy seasons—a "little" one in October–November and the principal one, brought from the ocean by the monsoon and lasting for several months in the late spring or in summer, depending on the locality. In an average year,

A village in the tropical-forest zone of Guinea. The footpaths are the only connecting link with the outside world.

for the zone as a whole, rainfall exceeds 60 inches, and near the shores of Guinea and Ivory Coast it is over 175 inches.

Violent winds are rare in this zone. There are two prevailing air currents, which come at different seasons: the more important of these is called the "southwest trades," which are scarcely more than sea breezes but bring ocean moisture over the land and thus are responsible for the so-called monsoon rains; the other is the *harmattan,* a dry wind, hot by day and cool by night, that blows from the Saharan regions.

Large areas of the equatorial zone are covered by the great tropical rain-forest, which, however, is not a continuous one, because it has been pushed back or cleared away in many places. In it grow a huge number of species of trees—at least 600, according to one French authority. So dense is this forest that the trees must engage in a life-and-death struggle as their long, bare trunks soar upward from tangled undergrowth as much as 150 feet, seeking sunlight and air. Among the most useful species are the oil palm, whose crushed kernels yield oil used as food and in many other ways, and many fine hardwoods such as mahogany. The humid equatorial zone is also favorable to the banana plant, which in some areas, especially in the Republic of Guinea, is cultivated on large plantations. Coffee and cocoa are important crops. Ivory Coast alone has more than 1.3 million acres devoted to coffee-growing and more than 590,000 acres to cocoa.

But apart from the plantations and the few cities and towns, the African of the tropical-forest zone has a hard time wresting a livelihood from the earth. The denseness of the forest greatly hinders not only communication but also the growth of villages, which are few in number and are connected, in most cases, only by footpaths. To clear ground for cultivation or construction is very difficult, and some of the Africans' energy must be spent on gathering wild products useful for food and for their clothing and hut-building.

The Africans of this zone are also greatly affected by diseases that are endemic in the hot and dank equatorial forest. Among them are fevers of various kinds, leprosy, filariasis caused by the Guinea worm, and sleeping-sickness for which the tse-tse fly is responsible. This fly is largely to blame for the fact that both men and livestock are scarce in the tropical-forest regions. Cattle, horses and dogs are unable to survive its attacks, and human mortality from sleeping-sickness is high. Neither the tse-tse fly nor the dense tangle of the forest, however, discourages such wild animals as the dwarf elephant, the hippopotamus, the wild buffalo, the leopard, the crocodile, the chimpanzee and many small monkeys—to name only a few.

The Sudanese Zone

Northward, beyond the edge of the tropical rain-forest, begins the sudanese or savannah zone, which is much friendlier to men and beasts. Topographically, it is a low plateau, most of it not more than 1,000 feet in elevation, sloping towards the north. Except for the desert, it constitutes the widest zone in West Africa in both the east-west and north-south directions. From a relatively narrow strip about 400 miles wide at the western extreme in Senegal and southern Mauritania, where it meets the Atlantic, it widens out to a broad belt more than 600 miles across, covering all of southern Soudan (Mali Republic), northern Ivory Coast, all of the Upper Volta Republic, northern Dahomey and southern Niger. Rainfall in the savannah zone, on a yearly average, ranges from 60 inches in the southern portion to 24 in the northern, and the number of dry months per year from four to seven, respectively. Consequently, although this zone is often hotter than the equatorial belt, it suffers much less from the humidity that makes the coastal regions almost intolerable for Europeans and even, at times, for Africans.

Thanks to its more favorable climate, the sudanese zone has a larger population than any other in West Africa, and it was the site of the old Negro kingdoms (or "empires") of Ghana, Mali and Songhaï, whose story is told in Chapter IV. These all flourished successively in and near, as well as to the west of, the region fertilized by the Niger River's yearly inundations.

It is the savannah or sudanese zone that is the true realm of African agriculture—of the peasant with his hoe, whose typical crop is millet but who also, depending on the region, cultivates corn, yams, manioc, peanuts, tobacco and rice. Every year vast areas of the savannah are burned over by the Afri-

A typical town of the sudanese zone—Sofara in Mali. Its houses are built mainly of banco (*mud-brick, or adobe*).

cans, who, in carrying out their traditional cycle of shifting cultivation, set fire to the brush so that its ashes will help to restore some fertility to the poor soils. The benefits of this procedure last no more than two to three years, after which the peasant must move on to another piece of land, where the cycle is resumed.

Because of the height of the brush that densely covers so much of the sudanese zone, the region is not suited to grazing, so that there is little herding on any large scale, and livestock is of secondary importance. There are few cattle and horses, and these animals are rather small specimens. Although the French administration in the Niger Valley region of Soudan (now Mali) tried for some years to introduce the use of bullocks as draft animals, especially for plowing, the Africans are not much inclined to adopt this practice. They prefer to cultivate their fields in the traditional way, bent over as they wield a short-handled hoe of the type that has been used for hundreds of years in Negro Africa.

In contrast to the scarcity of domesticated beasts in the savannah, wild life there is both very numerous and highly diversified—so much so that even a partial list is quite long: lions, panthers, wild-cats, elephants, giraffes, hyenas, gazelles, hippopotamuses, wart-hogs, baboons, red monkeys and horse antelopes, whose size is accurately indicated by their name. Most of these are hunted by the protein-starved Africans for food, and some because they are dangerous to men or crops. Because of the threatened extinction of many species, the French created a number of animal reserves in F.W.A. But the African hunter has been difficult to control even within the limits of the reserves, and besides, the African authorities of the new republics are little disposed to deny this source of food to their people. Consequently, the future of Africa's wild-life species is not bright.

Inevitably the peasants' brush fires destroy many useful trees along with the brush, and it is thought that the savannah, now characterized by isolated clumps of trees, was once covered by forest. Partly because rainfall is less here than in the equatorial zone, trees rarely reach more than about 60 feet in height. However, there is an astonishing range of species—some 370 have been identified. Outstanding among the useful kinds are the *karité* or shea (whose nuts yield a kind of butter) and the kapok (the silky fibers of whose seeds are a source of cash income for the Africans, although the labor involved in gathering them from widely scattered trees is disproportionate). There are also fine specimens of the baobab, a strange-looking tree that has been described by one writer as a "deformed colossus" or "a giant with arms that are too short." Despite its clumsy appearance, it is much valued by the Africans, who use its spicy leaves in flavoring their food, obtain flour and edible seeds from its fruit, and make rope from its bark. Decorative trees include the mimosas with their clusters of fragrant yellow flowers, and the flame tree, or *flamboyant,* whose brilliant red blossoms burst into bloom in the driest season of the year.

The Sahel

Along the northern limits of the sudanese zone, as it merges into the sahel, the soil becomes more sandy and the vegetation changes. Here the tall elephant-grass of the savannah gives way to short grasses, notably the *cram-cram* with its needle-pointed seeds, and to bushes bristling with spines. The widely scattered trees belong to a relatively few species of drought-resistant types, including the *doum* palm, thorny acacias, such as the gum-tree, and the baobab. "Sahel" is an Arabic word meaning "shore," for to the nomadic Islamized tribes of the Sahara, this zone—which, like the sudanese zone, is mainly low plateau—represented the shore of the desert, and its "ports" were such sub-desert cities as Timbuktu and Gao in Soudan and Agadès in the Niger Republic. Much narrower than the sudanese zone, the sahel is climatically a transitional belt lying between that zone and the desert, which steadily encroaches on it.

In the sahel, the harmattan blows for six months out of the year. Rain occurs only from July to September, when there are brief, violent storms, and ten successive months each year are dry. Rainfall averages less than 24 inches annually, and as it is concentrated in only two months, the period of drought is long and unbroken. Nevertheless, the sahel, compared with the Sahara, is verdant, especially during the early weeks of the rainy season, when the grassy plain and the trees seem to turn green and burst into bloom overnight. Because

A herd of zebu cattle in the savannah zone of western Senegal.

of the dryness of this region during most of the year, there are wide differences in temperature between winter and summer and between day and night, and for the same reason the heat causes less discomfort to animal life.

On the other hand, the scantiness of the rainfall is a barrier to extensive agriculture, although the sedentary Negro population succeeds in growing considerable amounts of millet and peanuts for their own subsistence. Irrigation projects installed by the French have redeemed large areas in the sahel for agriculture. These consist of the Richard-Toll project on the Senegal River in northwestern Senegal (see page 230), where large quantities of rice are grown, and the Niger project in north-central Mali Republic (see page 229), which produces some cotton and considerable rice.

Although ill-suited to agriculture, the sahel, with its vast areas of grassy land, is good country for animal husbandry.

There are large herds of humped cattle (zebus) and flocks of goats and sheep, and also, in the sahel regions of Senegal, Soudan and Niger, many horses and donkeys. These animals are mostly owned by nomadic or semi-nomadic "white" herders—by the Peuls, who have more or less Negro blood; by the Tuareg; and in the sahel of southern Mauritania and northern Senegal, by the Moors. These herders lead a nomadic existence not only because of their traditions and tastes, but also because they must be continually on the move with their animals in search of grazing areas and watering points. Even during the short rainy season, rain cannot be counted upon in any given sector of the zone, and it is the rain alone that determines the presence of new grass and supplies of water.

Wild life in the sahel, although less abundant than in the sudanese zone, is quite varied. Most of the animals that thrive in the savannah are to be found in the sahel as well, and this zone has in addition some that are especially characteristic of it, including the cheetah and the ostrich.

The Desert

To the north of the sahel, along a line beyond which animal life is very scarce and even the tough *cram-cram* grass no longer grows, lies the world's greatest desert, the Sahara. There neither agriculture nor animal husbandry is possible, except on a small scale in the widely separated oases. Throughout the Sahara, the camel—the "ship of the desert" —is the only animal useful to man that can survive other than the sheep and goats owned by the nomads, which must be kept for the most part at or near oases and watering points.

Of the F.W.A. countries, only Mauritania, northern Soudan (Mali Republic) and northern Niger contain true desert.

(Mauritania lies almost wholly within the Sahara.) Although the desert is marked everywhere by extreme aridity and therefore by the almost total absence of vegetation and animal life, it is by no means everywhere a monotonous, endless waste of sands, relieved only by rare oases. It differs greatly in appearance in various regions. Apart from the oases, the Sahara presents, broadly speaking, three types of landscape: vast areas of high, steep-sided sand dunes resembling waves, which change constantly in outline and position under the driving force of the wind (these dune regions are called *ergs*); sand-and-gravel plain (in Arabic, *reg*), also swept by the wind; and mountain masses, some of whose bare, jagged peaks rise thousands of feet above the plain.

In most of the desert zone, rainfall averages considerably less than 100 millimeters (3.9 inches) a year, and dew is nonexistent. Often the rain is so slight that it is impossible to measure it, and because of the heat, it may evaporate before it reaches the ground. Several years sometimes pass with no rain whatsoever. In these regions of F.W.A., only the mountainous terrain of the Adrar of the Iforas in northeast Soudan and the volcanic formations of the Aïr in northwest Niger Republic receive scanty rain each year at wide intervals.

Daytime temperatures in the desert are always high, but at night, especially in winter, they can fall very low. At Araouan in Soudan, on the salt-caravan route between Taoudéni and Timbuktu, the annual average temperature is 98° Fahrenheit, and during the day the thermometer has been known to climb to around 125° in the shade. The remote oasis of Bilma, however, in the dune region of northeast Niger, has an annual average of about 60° because of its wells and trees, and a January night temperature of 29° has been recorded there.

Although the Sahara now contains almost no plant life except in the oases, and very few wild living things other than some gazelles, desert foxes, birds, reptiles, scorpions and insects, there is considerable geological and archeological evidence to indicate that the prehistoric desert of north-central and west Africa possessed a far less arid climate, and that it had lakes and streams, cultivated and grazing lands, and thriving human and animal life. Some 8,000 years ago, in what is now the heart of the desert, neolithic man carved and painted on cliff faces and cave walls the figures of men and of wild animals that he hunted and that no longer exist in the Sahara—elephants, giraffes, ostriches, hippopotamuses. Many fossil fish have been found there, as well as stone-age weapons and tools in greater numbers than anywhere else in the world. In more recent prehistoric times, too, there evidently was much more abundant life in the Sahara than exists today, and the great climatic changes that created this desert probably began only a few thousand years ago.

The oases, with their springs and wells and the human and plant life that they make possible, are now the only remaining habitable parts of the Sahara. Widely separated from each other, often by hundreds of miles of burning plains or dunes, they once were the vitally important stopping points along the routes of the many camel caravans. These depended on the oases for supplies of the dates and cereals grown there and for water from their wells. For the same purposes, they are still vitally necessary to the few remaining caravans that ply the desert. It was from the oases, also, that the French Sahara—the region of F.W.A. that remained longest under military administration—was governed and controlled, and in Mauritania the oases still serve as centers from which military camel corps patrol the desert.

With the banning of the slave trade in the nineteenth century and the advent of motor vehicles and airplane services in the twentieth, the caravans lost much of their reason for being, and now few of them traverse the Sahara. One of the chief remaining caravans in F.W.A. is the famous one that moves, twice each year, between the salt mines of Taoudéni in the far-northern reaches of Mali Republic and Timbuktu on the Niger River. Each of these salt caravans (called *azalaï*) consists of several thousand camels, and its task is twofold: to bring salt from the Taoudéni mines to the sedentary Negro tribes of central Soudan, and to take back to the nomadic Tuareg such foods as millet, barley, peanuts and cooking fats. So long as nomads roam the desert, camels will probably continue to be used for carrying men and goods across the wastes of plain and dunes, for no other form of transport is as well suited to this hard and dangerous task.

The People

West Africa was peopled long before the dawn of history, but the origins of its inhabitants are largely veiled in mystery. The population of French-speaking West Africa today, estimated at about 25 millions, is extremely small for so vast an area and is very unevenly distributed. This imbalance is becoming more marked because, for economic and social reasons, the population of the cities is growing more rapidly than that of the countryside areas.

From time immemorial, Africans have been grouped in tribes, of which there are hundreds in West Africa today. The tribe is the matrix in which each individual is born, lives, and dies, and the ties of family and clan that exist within the tribal fold give him a sense of continuity and security for which nothing in modern life has proved to be a satisfactory substitute.

In former French West Africa, the two main population groups consist of the Negro tribes and the so-called "white" tribes, the Moors and the Tuareg. An intermediate group, the Peuls, consider themselves white but are almost indistinguishable from the Negro population.

Types of People

In East Africa, paleontologists have brought to light human remains and artifacts which seem to prove that that part of the continent was one of the cradles of humanity. In West Africa, however, although man or man-like creatures probably existed there in prehistoric times, evidence of this is scanty, aside from the rock carvings and paintings of the Sahara mentioned in Chapter I. Because of the damp climate and soils of the equatorial and southern sudanese zones, in which organic substances are rapidly broken down, such finds as have been made consist mainly of stone tools and weapons, along with remnants of pottery from the paleolithic (old stone) and the neolithic (new stone) age.

There is reason to believe that the people who inhabited West Africa before the coming of the Negroes and the Berbers were a race of pygmies, neither black nor white. Some of their descendants still live hidden away in the great equatorial forest, in central Africa as well as in West Africa's Ivory Coast, where they lead an animal-like existence as hunters and gatherers of wild products. The pygmies of Ivory Coast, even though they are much interbred with nearby

Negro tribes, still resemble their ancient forebears physically in many respects. They are short-legged dwarfs with sloping, narrow shoulders, protruding stomachs, and reddish-yellow skin.

Whatever the original inhabitants of Africa may have been, many present-day African Negroes believe that their remote ancestors came from "the east," particularly from Egypt. As for the "white" tribes of the desert, the Moors and the Tuareg, their Berber and Arab-Berber ancestors from the Mediterranean side of the Sahara had already penetrated as far as the sahel zone more than 2,000 years ago. The Peul herders of the sahel consider themselves to be of the white race, but are to varying degrees actually Negro-Peul, and are possibly of mixed Ethiopian-Negro-Arab stock. As a matter of fact, there is no ethnic African group in F.W.A., either white or Negro, that can be considered to be of unmixed blood, and all are dark-skinned, in many shades ranging from copper to black.

With the exception of the numerous Peuls, a handful of surviving pygmies, and the relatively small group of "Europeans" (that is, non-Africans), F.W.A.'s peoples fall under one or the other of two broad classifications. One of these comprises the Berber and Arab-Berber populations of the desert and sub-desert regions. They are Muslims, and the great majority are nomadic in their way of life. The other includes the Negroes of the savannah and tropical-forest zones, almost all of whom are peasant farmers and are described as sedentaries because they remain fixed in their respective localities. Most of them are animists, worshipping the spirits of their ancestors and the spirits of nature.

To the first group mentioned above, the nomads, belong the Moors of Mauritania and western Soudan and the Tuareg of eastern Soudan and the Niger Republic. Between this nomadic group and that of the sedentary Negro tribes come the Peuls. These are an intermediate group both from an ethnic standpoint and on the basis of their way of life. Because they are the great herders of West Africa, their life is predominantly nomadic, but it is tending to become sedentary under present-day conditions.

The second group, the sedentaries, which accounts for the bulk of F.W.A.'s population, consists almost entirely of the many Negro tribes. These in turn may be differentiated physically as being either of the savannah or of the forest type. Although the two types have characteristics in common, such as thick lips, kinky hair and wide, flat noses, the savannah-type Negroes are generally thinner and taller, whereas those of the forest zone tend to be rather short and stocky. The environmental and other influences that produced these anatomical differences probably also account for certain cultural dissimilarities. For example, it was in the savannah zone that there developed, during the Middle Ages, several complex, dynamic and powerful Negro states—the kingdoms or empires of Ghana, Mali and Songhaï. In contrast, the forest-zone communities, almost without exception, have always been small, disunited, static and relatively weak.

The Countries and Their Populations

As mentioned in the introduction, F.W.A.'s population of 25 millions is extremely small for so vast an area, and moreover it is very unevenly distributed. Taking the eight countries as a whole, the average population density is barely nine persons per square mile, but in and around the ports of Cotonou and Porto Novo in Dahomey, for instance, the rate runs as high as 268 per square mile. In the interior savannah belt, such as in Upper Volta (now the Republic of Upper Volta), the average density is about 30 per square mile. Mauritania, and parts of the dense equatorial forest zone near the Guinea Gulf coast, are distinguished for having the sparsest population, averaging less than one per square mile. In the Mauritanian part of the Sahara and the desert of northern Niger, tens of thousands of square miles are totally without inhabitants.

At this point, the reader might find it useful to consult the summary on the following pages containing basic information concerning the area and population of the eight former territories of F.W.A. The name that each formally adopted upon becoming fully independent in 1960 is given in parentheses. It should be noted that population figures are only approximate.

THE DRIFT TO THE TOWNS

More than 90 per cent of F.W.A.'s population lives in the countryside in villages or family groups, on communal lands. The people are chiefly farmers, herders, fishermen or hunters, sometimes combining two or more of these occupations. Although during the past 15 years or more there has been an increasing drift of country people to the towns and cities, this has not been in the direction of the old Negro towns of the sahel and sudanese zones—Timbuktu, Djenné and Gao, for instance—which are now only dusty and tumbledown relics of the past. None of the large urban centers of today existed before the Europeans came. It is such booming, European-created cities as Dakar, Conakry, Abidjan and Bamako that have tempted African peasant youths with their possibilities of wage-earning and their urban amusements and comforts. Their rapid growth since World War II, except in the case of Bamako, has been spurred by the massive export trade in such products as coffee, cocoa, peanuts, palm oil and hard-

French-Speaking West Africa
Areas and Populations

SENEGAL (REPUBLIC OF SENEGAL)

Capital, Dakar.

Area, 76,000 square miles, or about the size of the state of South Dakota.

Population, 3,109,840.

Principal ethnic groups:

Wolofs, 1,103,000; Peuls, 400,000; Sérères, 595,000; Tukulors, 422,000; Diolas, 120,000; Malinkés, 84,000; Sarakolés, 40,000; Moors, 30,000; Europeans and other foreigners, 61,700.

MAURITANIA (ISLAMIC REPUBLIC OF MAURITANIA)

Capital, Nouakchott.

Area, 418,810 square miles, or almost the size of Washington, Oregon, California and Nevada combined.

Population (estimated), 1,000,000.

Principal ethnic groups:

Moors, 800,000; Tukulors, 75,000; Peuls, 45,000; Sarakolés, 35,000; Bambaras, 2,500; Europeans and other foreigners, a few hundreds.

SOUDAN (REPUBLIC OF MALI)

Capital, Bamako.

Area, 464,752 square miles, equivalent to the combined area of Texas, Oklahoma, Arizona and New Mexico.

Population (estimated), 4,300,000.

Principal ethnic groups:

Bambaras, 1,011,000; Peuls, 345,000; Markas (Sarakolés), 280,000; Songhaïs, 230,000; Malinkés, 200,000; Tuareg, 240,000; Senoufos-Miniankas, 370,000; Dogons, 150,000; Bobos, 90,000; Moors and Arabs, 110,000; Tukulors, 60,000; Bozos, 55,000; Europeans and other foreigners, 7,400.

NIGER (REPUBLIC OF THE NIGER)

Capital, Niamey.

Area, 490,000 square miles, somewhat more than Texas, California and Louisiana combined.

Population, 3,127,565.

Principal ethnic groups:

Hausas, 1,350,000; Songhaïs (Djermas), 600,000; Tuareg, Arabs and *bellah,* 330,000; Peuls, 440,000; Europeans and other foreigners, 6,000.

GUINEA (REPUBLIC OF GUINEA)

Capital, Conakry.

Area, 95,000 square miles, about the same as that of Oregon.

Population, 3,000,000.

Principal ethnic groups:

Peuls (Fulani), 900,000; Malinkés, 625,000; Susus, 275,000; Kissis, 185,000; Guerzas, 150,000; Tomas, 85,000; Kurankos, 70,000; Europeans and other foreigners, about 7,000 in 1958 (this foreign element shrank to about 2,200 by early 1960).

UPPER VOLTA (REPUBLIC OF UPPER VOLTA)

Capital, Ouagadougou.

Area, 105,811 square miles, equivalent to that of Colorado.

Population, 4,280,000.

Principal ethnic groups:

Mossi, 1,700,000; Bobos, 275,000; Peuls, 200,000; Gourounsis, 180,000; Lobis, 100,000; Samos, 90,000; Markas, 80,000; Senoufos, 40,000; Dioulas, 20,000; Hausas, Tuareg and *bellah* (no data); Europeans and other foreigners, 3,000.

IVORY COAST (REPUBLIC OF IVORY COAST)

Capital, Abidjan.

Area, 127,500 square miles, slightly more than that of New Mexico.

Population, 3,500,000.

Principal ethnic groups:

Agnis-Ashantis (including Baoulés) ; Mandé tribes, including Malinkés, Dioulas, Markas and Bambaras; Senoufos; Dan-Gourou tribes; Koua tribes; Voltaic tribes, including Bobos, Lobis and Foulbés. No census figures or reliable estimates for this mosaic of African tribal populations are available. Europeans and other foreigners are estimated to total about 12,000.

Dahomey (Republic of Dahomey)

Capital, Porto Novo.
Area, 44,290 square miles, or about the size of Pennsylvania.
Population, 2,050,000.
Principal ethnic groups:

Fons, 800,000; Adjas, 250,000; Baribas, 175,000; Yorubas, 170,000; Sombas, 90,000; Peuls, 68,000; Europeans and other foreigners, 5,500.

woods, to list only the principal ones. As for Bamako, it owes its expansion to the fact that it is situated at the center of the populous savannah zone of Soudan (Mali Republic) and that it has rail connections with Dakar and the Atlantic Ocean on the west and with the Niger River's longest navigable stretch on the east. Another reason why people are drawn to all of the capital cities of the new republics is their hope of getting government jobs, even if very menial ones.

Although the inhospitable desert and northern sahel regions could scarcely sustain more than their present sparse nomadic population, other parts of F.W.A. might easily support more inhabitants than they now have. As a matter of fact, much of the savannah belt and the northern forest zone once contained far more people than they do today, with a few exceptions such as the densely populated Mossi country. The shrinkage of F.W.A.'s population, and its failure to regain a normal rate of growth, had several causes, the most important of which was the slave trade.

EFFECTS OF THE SLAVE TRADE

The traffic in able-bodied Negroes was originally carried on by the Arabs with the aid of some unscrupulous Negro chiefs. It continued from about the eighth century until the coming of the Europeans in the sixteenth and seventeenth centuries. It did not reach massive proportions, however, until the eighteenth century, during which an average of 100,000 slaves were shipped out of Africa each year. Besides these, perhaps as many more Negroes died after their capture, during forced marches to the coast or in slave depots. Even though the slave trade was outlawed by a treaty between the

Slaves on their way to a coastal market, to be sold by Arab slave traders. This was a common scene in West Africa in the eighteenth and early nineteenth century.

European nations in 1815, and though slavery was officially abolished in the French colonies in 1848, its suppression was very slow and was not fully effective until many years later. In fact, this trade is reported to be still carried on secretly between sub-Saharan Africa and Saudi Arabia, where—until 1963—slavery was still legal and slaves were common in princely and wealthy households. Considering that the majority of the captives were young men and women, their removal from Africa obviously affected the birth rate there disastrously, as well as the continuity of family and tribal life and the production of foodstuffs.

Other Factors Limiting Population Growth

Besides the slave trade, three other handicaps to normal population increase should be noted: disease, alcoholism and malnutrition. In pre-European days, Africa already had what might be called indigenous diseases, such as sleeping-sickness, malaria and leprosy, which took a heavy toll. But the European occupation brought with it a wide range of formidable new ailments—venereal disease, tuberculosis and others—which greatly increased disability and mortality among the Africans. The struggle by the French administration and the missions against both tropical and European diseases is described in Chapter IV.

As for alcohol, although alcoholic beverages of African invention have existed since time out of mind, the palm wine and millet beer made by the Negroes are not so harmful as was the cheap and poisonous "trading alcohol" introduced by the slavers. Nevertheless, the consumption of these native alcoholic concoctions in large amounts is undeniably damaging to the Africans.

Much more to blame than alcohol for West Africa's retarded population growth is the chronic malnutrition—in part a consequence of the poor soils and harsh climate—that afflicts vast areas, causing high infant mortality, a low rate of life expectancy and lack of resistance to disease. This malnutrition is traceable to both imbalance in diet and irregularity in food supply. Throughout the savannah zone, the staff of life of the African peasant is usually boiled millet, occasionally boiled corn, sweet potatoes, and in some areas, manioc or rice. In the forest regions near the Guinea Gulf, the diet consists mainly of yams, manioc, corn and bananas, at times augmented by meat brought in by the hunters. When available, tomatoes, onions, salt and spices are added to the starchy foods mentioned above to make them more palatable. Africans are fond of fresh meat and fresh, dried, or salted fish, but there is by no means a steady supply of these, nor can the Africans often afford to buy them when they cannot be obtained through hunting or fishing. Then, too, the Negroes as a rule lack the foresight to lay aside enough food to tide them over the gap between crops (called in French the *soudure*), so that often for several months at a time they suffer from hunger, and occasionally even famine. During the *soudure,* the majority of Negro peasants keep body and soul more or less together by gathering and eating wild grass seeds, roots of various wild plants, lizards and similar things to which they are driven out of sheer desperation. In prolonged droughts, even such substitutes are scarce.

The "White" Tribes

The two main "white" tribes living in former French West Africa are the Moors and the Tuareg. Both groups are descended from Berber and later, Arab-Berber, ancestors who lived along the Mediterranean and penetrated south many centuries ago. The Moors call themselves *Beidan*

(Arabic for Whites), or Bedouins, but they are not to be confused with the Arab Bedouins, people of purely Arabic stock.

THE MOORS

Mauritania, as already noted, is one of the largest of the eight states in area but has the smallest population. Widely scattered throughout Mauritania and in the desert and sub-desert regions of the northern reaches of the Mali Republic, as well as along the northern fringe of Senegal, live the restless Moors. Totaling about 475,000 in these regions, they are divided into numerous rival tribes. One of their sub-groups, the Zenaga, settled many centuries ago near the Senegal River, whose name was derived from theirs. The strongly Islamic Moors resisted French control for many years.

Moorish society is marked by a rigid caste system, in which the warriors and the *marabouts* (learned religious men) are the ruling elements. The lower castes are those of the *griots,* freed slaves who are the tribal minstrels; and the blacksmiths, who make arms, tools and jewelry, and whose wives make leather articles such as saddles, weapon sheaths and amulet boxes. Some of the *marabouts* have earned Mauritania the reputation of being F.W.A.'s chief center of Islamic learning. In the past, *marabouts* from that territory carried their religion—along with trading activities—as far south as Ivory Coast, though they have been slow to make converts among a good many of the animist (fetishist) Negro tribes of the equatorial zone. Many of the Negroes are inclined to mistrust these missionaries because for so long the Moors were active in the slave trade and kept Negro slaves themselves, and because they still look upon the Negroes as inferiors and show contempt for them.

The Moors have the reputation of being intelligent,

quarrelsome, crafty and cruel. Although they claim to be a white group, they have intermarried extensively with Negroes during the course of centuries. However, almost all of them retain the distinctive Moorish appearance—a narrow, oval face, with dark, fierce eyes; a thin, hooked nose; black, wavy hair standing out in a bushy halo around the head; and a dull skin of rather indeterminate color much darkened by sun and dirt, for the Moors are reputed never to wash, but only to rub themselves occasionally with sand. With their downcast eyes and their flowing if ragged robes, they seem like characters out of the Bible. Their bones are fine and their muscular bodies are thin to the point of scrawniness, but they are tough. Their needs are simple, and they can live for long periods on a frugal diet of millet, dates and camel's milk. In short, they are well adapted to the hard life of the desert nomad.

Except for a relatively small number who are fishermen along the northern part of the Mauritanian coast, the Moors are nomadic herders, living in much-patched camel-hair tents and wandering from one waterhole and sparse pasturage to another. In the torrid months of April through June, the extreme heat drives them south with their herds of sheep, camels, and goats to find grazing lands and water. At that time, too, they go to the markets of Dakar and St. Louis in Senegal, to Bamako in the Mali Republic, and to other towns of the desert fringe. There they barter their animals, along with salt from the desert deposits and dates from the oases, for local and imported foodstuffs (rice, millet, corn, dried fish, tea and sugar) and such useful manufactured articles as kerosene lanterns and stoves, tools and cooking utensils. This trade is quite large, and the Moors thus play an important economic role in the life of both Senegal and Mauritania, and to some extent of Mali.

THE TUAREG

The Tuareg are the other Berber element of F.W.A.'s "white" African population. (Tuareg is the plural form of their name, Targui the singular.) Driven out of North Africa in the seventh century and later by the Bedouin invasions from Arabia, they took refuge in the Adrar region of Soudan and in the Aïr mountains of Niger. Although they were converted to Islam many centuries ago, they are only lukewarm Muslims. The two main Tuareg groups in F.W.A. are the Iforas of the Mali Republic, who nomadize in the region of Timbuktu and the Niger River bend, and the Kel Aïr and Oulliminden, whose country is the mountainous Aïr region and the vicinity of Agadès and Tahoua, in the Niger Republic. They speak a Berber dialect called *tamachek;* its alphabet, *tifinar,* is the only written form of Berber now in use. Like the Moors, the Tuareg long fought against French dominance, but later some of them allied themselves with the French in military ventures, and many Frenchmen have a great admiration for them.

In the Mali Republic and the Niger Republic, the Tuareg and their dependents are estimated to number about 500,000. This figure includes, besides the warrior nobles, their vassals called *Imrad,* as well as a *marabout* caste similar to that of the Moors, and a class of Negro serfs known as *bellah,* who are slaves or descendants of slaves. The *bellah* are the herders of the Tuareg animals, and some of them are artisans such as blacksmiths and tanners.

Tuareg nobles are tall, graceful and haughty, but though superior in some ways to the Moors, are likewise quarrelsome and thieving. Unlike the Moors, however, they are noted for keeping their word. The men wear a turban-like headcloth; a veil (called the *litham*) covering all of the face below the eyes as a protection against sandstorms and sun; and indigo-

Tuareg of northern Mali in an encampment.

dyed robes. They carry a large, straight sword in a scabbard strapped to the waist, a shield, and usually a lance. Because the dye from their robes stains their normally copper-black skin, they are sometimes called "the blue men." The warrior nobles ride camels, most of which are of a long-legged racing breed, and the Targui saddle is handsomely decorated and has a distinctive cross-shaped pommel. This pommel cross, and the cross design that ornaments their shields, are thought to be survivals of a remote period when the Tuareg were Christians, before the Arabs converted them to Islam.

In Tuareg society, which is mostly monogamous, women

have much freedom—it is significant that they do not wear veils as do many Muslim women—and they usually participate in tribal councils. Although they are often beautiful when young, usually they soon grow very fat because of overeating and their inactive life in the tents. This is encouraged by the men, who consider fat women more attractive than thin ones.

Although most of the Tuareg are still desert nomads, there is a tendency among them to turn to a sedentary way of life. Some entire groups have settled down as farmers and animal-breeders in the sahel zone of central Niger Republic and the Mali Republic, even going so far as to live in stone or mud-brick houses instead of the traditional tents. Those who have remained nomads keep large herds of camels, horses, sheep, goats and sometimes cattle, and with them move from place to place according to a schedule dictated by the seasons and the rains. The various Tuareg tribal groups have what might be called movable squatters' rights to predetermined circuits. Their habits of mobility and their intimate knowledge of the desert make the nomads, both Tuareg and Moors, very hard to control, because they can always slip away into inaccessible and remote parts of the Sahara.

FEATURES OF NOMAD SOCIETY

Certain factors affecting the lives and relationships of all the desert nomads, both Moor and Tuareg, should be mentioned. An outstanding one is the extent to which this nomadic society is split up because of such physical conditions as the scarcity of water and grazing land, and such social ones as the suspicious jealousy existing between the various chiefs as well as between the groups of their followers. This splintering is carried still further by the rigid separation that exists within each nomadic subgroup because of the caste system. All these factors make for a disunity that is characteristic of Moorish and Tuareg society from top to bottom, so that neither tribal nor national unity has ever been attained or even sought by West Africa's nomadic tribes. And the deeply ingrained anarchy of the desert nomad's character leads him also to resist all efforts to modernize him, whether in the field of education, in that of administration, or in any other aspect of his life.

The quarrelsome nature of these nomads, and the vitally important part played by water supply in their lives and those of their herds, are responsible for another crucial element bearing upon their activities. These are the conflicts, often bloody, that have occurred since time immemorial in regard to use of water holes between rival desert nomad groups, and between the nomads on the one hand and the sedentary or semi-sedentary farmers of the sahel and northern savannah regions on the other. Hostility between the peasants and the desert nomads has been heightened by the damage caused by the famished herds, which often trample and eat crops.

The French government years ago started to develop dry-zone water resources in West Africa. After World War II, its program was resumed on a much larger scale in the hope of eliminating, or at least reducing, nomad-peasant clashes by providing ample water for both the nomads' herds and the peasants' fields. To some extent this effort was successful; between 1949 and 1954, more than 600 wells were dug in Mauritania, Soudan, Upper Volta and Niger, and some 200 irrigation dams were built. In those years, for example, about 50 wells were dug along the main nomadic herding routes in the Ferlo desert of north-central Senegal. But there the new water supply attracted sedentary settlers, and once again there was fighting with the nomads over its use and that of the land. Such heated encounters have often taken place elsewhere in the sahel zone as well, and only the progressive settling down of the nomads offers hope for more peaceable relations between them and the sedentary farmers.

THE PEULS

In an intermediate position between the desert nomads and the Negro sedentaries of the savannah and forest zones is the huge so-called "white" group known as the Peuls, who have inter-married to a great extent with the Negro tribes. Like the Moors and the Tuareg, the nomadic and semi-nomadic Peuls are resistant to any control.

The Peuls and the Negro-Peul tribes closely related to them make up together what is probably the largest single element of F.W.A.'s population. Totaling some 2.7 million, they are widely scattered from the Atlantic Ocean to Lake Chad. (In their language, *poular,* the word "peul" means "scattered.") Of that total, a considerable number of Negro-Peuls called Tukulors (or Toucouleurs)—roughly ·estimated at about 450,000—live in Senegal, Mauritania, Mali and Guinea; this tribe is described in more detail below. Of the countries of former F.W.A., the Guinea Republic has the largest Peul population (900,000), most of whom have settled among the Fouta Djallon mountains of west-central Guinea. There they are called Fulani or Foulas. Besides the 2.7 million Peuls and Negro-Peuls in F.W.A., there are approximately two million more in former British Nigeria and in Cameroun.

Taciturn, meditative and aloof by nature, the Peul is tall and distinguished in appearance. Like other Islamized Africans, the Muslim Peul wears a long robe, white, indigo-dyed, or brown; his headgear is usually a large conical hat of braided straw. Animist Peuls are not averse to semi-nudity— an animal skin tied around the waist is regarded as sufficient clothing—though they also favor the huge straw hat. The

A young Peul girl with the facial scars of her initiation into her age group.

Peul's way of life is very simple, and often he is undernourished and more or less toothless. The nomadic Peul shelters himself in a low hut, round or oblong, made of straw mats or tree branches. Those who have turned sedentary live in more solid houses of mud-brick. Polygamy (or more correctly, polygyny, which is the custom of a man's having two or more wives) is common among the Peuls, but many of them have only one wife. The women, often very beautiful, dress their hair in a distinctive crested form, and like other Muslim women south of the Sahara, do not veil their faces. Although many Peuls are Muslims, in their case their religion is not very pure, being much diluted by animist or fetishist practices such as the wearing of *grigris* (magical amulets) around their necks.

The origin of the Peuls is obscure. Some French authorities on this tribe believe, however, that they may be related to the Masai of East Africa, who also are predominantly herders. After many centuries of cross-breeding with Negro tribes, the Peul is very difficult to define ethnically. Only in the sahel zone do a few Peuls of unmixed blood remain, and in the vast majority of the peoples known as Peul, Negro blood is predominant. Nor is the *poular* language—which is related to that of the great Negro tribe of Senegal, the Wolofs—a deciding factor in defining the Peul, because some Peul groups contain up to 80 per cent of *poular*-speaking serfs who are of pure Negro blood. One possible definition is of an intangible kind: there is a distinctive Peul psychology based on the mystical devotion of the Peul herder to his idle and mostly useless cattle. In other words, being Peul is a state of mind.

Although originally most of the Peuls were nomads whose dwellings were frail straw huts, more and more of them have settled down in fixed locations with their herds and live in rectangular, flat-roofed sudanese-style houses of mud-brick. This trend, especially strong among the large population of Peuls (or Fulani) in Guinea's Fouta Djallon region, has been accentuated by the French water-supply program mentioned above, which has even encouraged some Peuls to turn to farming.

The vast majority of Peuls are herders, though the cattle may either be their own or belong to Negro peasants. The Peul is contemptuous of the Negro who employs him as cattle-herder, and never takes part in Negro dances or other festivities. His life is centered on supplying the needs of the beloved animals under his charge—he literally lives for them and in order to serve them. Besides feeling a mystical bond with the cattle, he regards them as a form of capital and—except for consuming their milk and using them to pay the bride-price—never puts them to any use whether as meat or as an aid in agriculture.

The Negro Tribes

Aside from the Moors and the Tuareg, and to some extent the Peuls, all of whom are fairly homogeneous peoples, F.W.A.'s African population is so complex that it is almost impossible to catalogue its tribes accurately. Only the more important ones, therefore, are described in the following pages. Some Negro tribes can be defined in a broad sense by physical characteristics, some by religion, and some by language, but none of these factors can be taken as a sure indication in the case of any of the hundreds of related tribal groups.

LANGUAGES

As to languages, for instance, a French specialist has counted 126 principal ones, but there are literally hundreds of dialects, some spoken widely but most of them limited to isolated villages or groups of peasants. Among the Ivory Coast tribes alone, at least 80 different languages and dialects are in use, and in certain dense forest regions of the south, the inhabitants of neighboring villages cannot understand each other's dialect. Moreover, except for a few north Guinea tribes which have their own alphabet, the Negro languages and dialects of F.W.A. are oral, without recognized written forms and therefore without any literature. Some effort has been made, however, especially by missionaries, to establish written forms of a few of them, using the Latin alphabet.

Most Africans, therefore, find it convenient to use one or another of the three or four most widely spoken African tongues as a second language. From the meridian of Ouagadougou in Upper Volta, westward as far as the Senegal coast, Bambara is the great common language. Eastward from Ouagadougou, the Hausa language—used by the Hausas, the Dioula traders and the *marabouts*—is understood by a large part of the population. The language of the Peuls, *poular,* is spoken and understood very widely in the savannah zone from Senegal on the west to the Niger Republic on the east. And throughout F.W.A., French has been for many years the indispensable *lingua franca* among educated Africans. It is the official language of all of the eight new nations of former F.W.A. except Guinea, and for practical purposes it is the official language there also, even though this is not specified in Guinea's constitution as it is in those of the other seven countries.

THE TUKULORS (TOUCOULEURS)

With the Tukulors, despite the fact that they form part of the Negro-Peul world already mentioned, we enter into contact with the great mass of F.W.A.'s population, which is Negro and agricultural. Most of the 450,000 Tukulors live in Senegal, though Mauritania has about 75,000, there are some 60,000 in western and central Mali Republic, and 15,000 or more live in the eastern part of Guinea's Fouta Djallon region.

No distinctive Tukulor type exists, because they are so much interbred with Wolofs, Bambaras, Mandingos and other tribes. The only unifying factor among the Tukulors is that they all speak the Peul language. Their feudal and stratified society resembles that of other Muslim Negro-Peul groups and is even more complex than some others. Beneath the Tukulor aristocracy, in descending levels of social status, there are numerous castes and classes engaged in such occupations as farming, fishing and artisanry.

THE WOLOFS

By far the most important of the Senegal tribes is that of the Wolofs, who number around 595,000. Tall, fine-featured and very dark-skinned, they are highly intelligent and adaptable and are one of the most "evolved" tribes in F.W.A. Wolof society is divided into five castes, ranging from the free aristocratic families through the blacksmiths, the jewelers, the shoemakers and the *griots* (despised but influential entertainers) to the descendants of slaves. The top caste forms an elite group, and Wolof merchants, contractors and government employees are to be found in all the important towns of the eight countries of former F.W.A.

Almost all Wolofs are Muslims, although animist practices survive among them. Most of this tribe are mediocre farmers, but in the late nineteenth century some Wolofs organized a religious sect called the Mourides, among whom agriculture was made a pre-condition of salvation. In their case, agriculture meant peanut culture. The Mourides *marabouts* won many followers and became very rich, thanks to the work of their unpaid farm laborers, who colonized abandoned regions in eastern Senegal.

THE SÉRÈRES

A tribe related to the Wolofs is that of the Sérères, whose 422,000 members all live in western Senegal. Their language has many elements in common with that of the Wolofs and also with *poular,* the language of the Peuls. Physically they resemble the Wolofs, though their features are coarser, and

Children of the Sérère tribe of Senegal puzzling over a French primer.

their caste system is also similar, but it is even more complex than that of the Wolofs. In contrast to the Wolofs, however, only the two highest Sérère classes—the chiefs and the warriors—are Muslims; the rest of this tribe fiercely resists Islam. Moreover, the Sérères, unlike most of their relatives the Wolofs, are proud of their farming ability as well as of their livestock-breeding. The thatched huts of their villages are surrounded by fields where the hard-working Sérère peasants engage in mixed farming. They are producers of large quantities of peanuts, which is Senegal's most important export crop.

THE MANDINGO TRIBES

Widespread in the western Niger River valley and in northern Ivory Coast is a large and important family of tribes known as the Mandingos, whose ancestors formed the main population element of the empire of Mali in the thirteenth to sixteenth centuries (see pages 111–112).

The Mandingos, who are also called Mandés, are credited with having created, several thousand years before Christ, one of the four great agricultural civilizations of human history. The list of useful food plants which they developed from local wild growths is astonishing and includes many of the foods that are basic in tropical Africa today—fonio, pearl millet, sorghum, yams, watermelons and a number of others. These tribes, which today account together for about 2.5 million of the population of F.W.A., include the Malinkés, the Sarakolés, the Bambaras, the Dioulas and numerous minor groups not described in this book. Their languages, which have many elements in common, form a link between them. Generally speaking, they are all Muslims except the Bambaras, who are animists, and the Malinkés, who are divided between Islam and animism.

The Malinkés. The Malinkés are actually a group of tribes having different names but all speaking the Malinké form of Mandingo. Their 800,000 to 900,000 members are widely scattered from Senegal on the west through Mali and into upper Guinea and upper Ivory Coast. Those in the western regions are mostly Muslims, but the animist Malinkés in the eastern sector outnumber them.

The Sarakolés. The Sarakolés—called also Soninkés or Markas—number about 360,000. They are found primarily in the Mali Republic, but some 75,000 live in Senegal and Mauritania. Tribes related to them linguistically, but having other names, are to be found in Mauritania, Senegal, Upper

Volta, Guinea and northern Ivory Coast. Altogether the Sarakolé-speaking tribes account for close to 500,000 persons. The Sarakolés proper are descended from the oldest Negro peoples of F.W.A., were formerly warriors, and were probably the founders of the ancient empire of Ghana. Later they turned to peaceful occupations, becoming farmers, cattle-breeders and merchants. Many of them are far-ranging traders, and in vast areas of F.W.A. they compete with the Dioulas, who are described below. Their chief stock in trade is kola nuts, a stimulant much sought after by Muslims, to whom alcoholic drinks are forbidden. Besides their legitimate activities, they have long engaged in smuggling along the frontiers of Gambia, Portuguese Guinea and Sierra Leone. And along with trading and smuggling, they have been active in trying to spread Islam among the animist tribes.

The Dioulas. The Dioulas, an offshoot of the Sarakolés, are noted for being fervent Muslims and clever merchants. Although less numerous than the Sarakolés—there are only some 200,000 Dioulas—they are well-known throughout the sahel and sudanese zones. They combine missionary zeal with commerce in their extensive wanderings, during which they strive to convert the pagan tribes to Islam while at the same time they trade cloth, as well as dried fish from the Niger, for kola nuts. The Dioulas are so noted as itinerant traders that the word "dioula" has come to mean "merchant" among many African tribes.

The Bambaras. The huge tribe of Bambaras, of whom there are well over one million, is concentrated mostly in the Mali Republic, although some also live in northern Ivory Coast and southern Mauritania. Almost all animists, the Bambaras are peasant farmers and are also artisans in metals, cotton cloth and wood, in which work they show a striking artistic ability.

THE BOZOS AND THE DOGONS

In central Mali Republic there are two tribal groups, the Bozos and the Dogons, who are probably the residue of the old tribes which occupied that region before the coming of the Bambaras. The Bozos number only about 55,000; they are Niger River fishermen of the Macina region. Although they are now Muslims, their tradition links them with the cliff-dwelling animist tribe called the Dogons, numbering some 150,000, who live in the vicinity of Bandiagara, east of Macina. There this naked tribe, said to be the oldest in Soudan, builds strange, fortress-like houses on the almost vertical cliffs.

THE SONGHAÏS

An interesting Islamized tribe whose 230,000 members live in a dense community in the Niger River bend area of Mali is that of the Songhaïs, also called Sonraïs. Centuries ago in approximately the same region, this tribe formed the powerful Songhaï empire, described in Chapter IV. In the great days of the trans-Saharan caravans, the Songhaïs were noted caravan-drivers, especially in the *azalaï* (salt caravans) to and from the Taoudéni salt mines in the southern Sahara. They still take part in the *azalaï,* but most of them have turned to farming, fishing and trade. The western Niger Republic contains a branch of this tribe known as Djermas, of whom there are nearly 600,000.

THE VOLTAIC TRIBES: THE MOSSI

Upper Volta and southern Mali, particularly the former, are the home of the so-called Voltaic tribes, a grouping based on language. They have special dialects, all belonging to the Voltaic family of languages; they are marked by complicated ritual scars (sometimes called tattooing); and some live in strong, easily defended dwellings made of sun-dried mud brick, though the majority are housed in high-walled thatched huts.

By far the largest and most important of the Voltaic tribes is that of the Mossi—this name being the plural form of Moro—of whom there are about 1.7 million in Upper Volta. Although the great majority of the Mossi live in Upper Volta, that country is poor and overpopulated, hence their young men go in tens of thousands each year as seasonal laborers to Ghana and Ivory Coast. There they earn a little money on the coffee and cocoa plantations, or in factories. In addition, because of population pressure on the farmlands of the Mossi country, some 500,000 of this tribe have emigrated southward, mostly to Ghana, where they have settled more or less permanently. The Mossi population of Upper Volta is densest in the central regions, particularly around Ouagadougou, the capital. However, they are essentially a rural people, and fewer than 200,000 of them live in towns. The Mossi farmers cultivate mainly millet, sorghum and peanuts; their cattle are cared for by Peul herders.

The Mossi, whose early history is given in Chapter IV, long possessed one of the most highly developed tribal administrations in French-speaking West Africa. Together with their military organization, this enabled them to withstand many attacks by neighboring tribes in the past. Their country is divided into three feudal states headed by despotic chiefs, all three of whom are descendants of the founder of the Mossi dynasty. The principal chief, usually called "the emperor," is the Moro Naba of Ouagadougou, who is the 34th ruler in his dynastic line. The two minor ones, the Yatenga Naba and the Tenkodogo Naba, rule over smaller segments of the Mossi population, respectively northwest and southeast of Ouagadougou. These chiefs once had absolute powers of life and death over their subjects, but after the French gained control of the country their powers were greatly reduced. Nevertheless, they continue to maintain courts at their "palaces," and their subjects look upon them with awe, respect and even fear. This feeling still persists among many of the Mossi, even though the Nabas—like most other paramount chiefs as well as lesser ones in West Africa—have been deprived of their power. The policy of all the new governments of French-speaking West Africa is to suppress the traditional chieftaincies, and the present Nabas, who already have been reduced to figureheads, will have no successors.

The chiefs, and the caste of nobles and warriors who surround them, are Muslims, but the mass of the peasant population are animists. Catholic missionaries have made many converts among the animist Mossi, as well as among the Bobos, described below.

OTHER VOLTAIC TRIBES

Smaller tribes of the Voltaic group are those of the Senoufos of southern Mali Republic, western Upper Volta and northern Ivory Coast, who number some 600,000; the Bobos of western Upper Volta (275,000) and eastern Mali (90,000); the Gourounsis of Upper Volta (180,000); and the Lobis (over 200,000), about equally divided between southwestern Upper Volta and northeastern Ivory Coast. The people of these four animist tribes are peasant farmers, hunters, artisans and metal workers, and like most animists, wear little or no clothing. Some Bobos, however, as mentioned above, have been converted to Catholicism. The Lobi tribe especially is typical of the most loosely organized communities in former F.W.A., for they have no central authority or communal life, no chiefs or councils of elders and live in dispersed family groups.

THE HAUSAS

In the Niger Republic, seven groups of tribes with very mixed Negro-Peul-Berber blood together form a part of what has been called the Hausa world. They are a branch of the predominant Hausa people of former British Nigeria, but there is no unity among the Hausa tribes except for a common language. The majority of the 1,350,000 Hausas in former F.W.A. are Muslims, although many groups of animists among them still cling to their fetishist traditions. The main occupation of the Hausas is trade, and the itinerant Hausa merchants, wearing big, wide-brimmed, conical straw hats and carrying bundles of goods, are familiar figures throughout large areas of West Africa.

THE BAOULÉS AND THE AGNIS

Ivory Coast's bewildering mosaic of tribes includes two outstanding ones—the Baoulés, of whom there are some 500,000, and the Agnis, who number about 100,000. These two inter-related tribes speak the same language, derived from the Ashanti tongue of Ghana. According to Baoulé legend, that tribe was led into the Ivory Coast region from the east by a heroic queen. Because of their intelligence and enterprise, the Baoulés and Agnis have provided most of the present-day political leadership of Ivory Coast. They are also good farmers, raising coffee, cocoa, bananas and taro, and for a long time some of them have panned gold in certain streams of eastern Ivory Coast. The Baoulé men are outstanding artisans and artists, skilled in designing and making gold objects and bronze statuettes. They have also won a reputation for themselves as impressive consumers of yams and palm wine. Like most of the other Ivory Coast tribes, the Baoulés and Agnis are animists.

THE KRUMEN

Another Ivory Coast tribe, or rather group of tribes, is known collectively as the Krumen (probably a corruption of the English words "crew men"). Living on the shores of the Guinea Gulf in western Ivory Coast and in adjoining Liberia, the Krumen (about 400,000) are fishermen and boat-builders, as well as skillful and fearless boatmen. They have a virtual monopoly of the loading and unloading of cargo ships across the maritime sandbar that parallels the entire Guinea Gulf coast.

FONS AND OTHER DAHOMEY TRIBES

Dahomey is the country of several important equatorial-zone tribes: the Fons, the Adjas, the Baribas and the Yoru-bas. The Fons, also called Dahomeyans, numbering around 800,000, formed the population of the famous kingdom of Abomey or Dahomey, which, as told in Chapter IV, once dominated the present-day southern Dahomey (pages 120–124). Fierce warriors until the French defeated their army in 1893, they have become peaceable farmers but continue to take pride in the tradition of the Abomey kings, even though most of these rulers were cruel and bloodthirsty. The Fons have always been strongly animist, although many have been "converted" to the Catholic faith and some to Protestantism. In Ouidah on the coast, the snake-fetish temple and the Catholic church face each other across the town's central square. Fetishism is a distinguishing element of Fon society even today, and Islam has had no success among this tribe. Because of their quick intelligence, they often acquire a good education and special skills, and many of them work in European commercial houses. During the French regime, Fons held many government positions in various southern territories of F.W.A.

The Fon tribe was an offshoot of the Adjas, whose 250,000 members have settled as farmers along the Mono and Couffo Rivers in southern Dahomey.

The Baribas, totaling around 175,000, cultivate *karité* (shea) trees and kapok trees in the savannah zone of northern Dahomey.

In eastern and southern Dahomey live about 170,000 animist Yorubas, mostly farmers, but some of whom are engaged in trade. The forebears of this tribe came from British Nigeria, where the greater number of Yorubas still live.

THE SOMBAS

In northern Dahomey there is an interesting tribe called the Sombas, practically all of whose 90,000 members are

An elderly Somba on the roof of his "tata," where corn and peanuts are dried and stored.

animists. (Sombas are also found in the regions of northern
Togo and southern Upper Volta that adjoin Dahomey.) Both
the men and the women of this tribe, who are very black, live
in a state of near, and quite often total, nakedness. The
Somba men combine the occupations of farming and hunting,
and always carry an array of farm tools and hunting gear
hung from their shoulders and waist. These include a short-
handled hoe, a heavy knife, bow and arrows, and a lance,
besides a long-stemmed pipe for smoking the local tobacco.
The unique Somba houses of mud-brick, hidden away in the
tall brush, resemble miniature castles, with thatched turrets
at the corners. They are two or even three storeys high; the
livestock are sheltered on the ground level, the family live on
the floor above (which they reach by climbing a notched tree
trunk, through a hole in the ceiling), and grain is spread out
to dry on the flat rooftop.

Europeans

Turning to the European element in F.W.A., we find the
smallest of all its population components, which totals only
about 100,000, or approximately 0.5 per cent of the whole.
Locally the term European means non-African, except, of
course, for the few individuals of Far Eastern origin, who are
in a different category. The label of European is applied not
only to persons of European origin or descent but also to
Syrians and Lebanese, to half-castes, and even—before Senegal's independence in 1960—to Senegalese Negroes having
full French citizenship. (This special status given to some
Senegalese under the French regime is explained in Chapter
VI.)

Unlike the situation in, for example, Algeria (which, until
the exodus of whites resulting from Algerian independence

in 1962, had a white-settler population totaling over one million), no large-scale white settlement has ever taken place in former F.W.A. Generally speaking, only the handful of French foresters and coffee and cocoa planters of Ivory Coast can be considered settlers. Except during the nineteenth-century period of conquest and military administration, the white "Europeans," who have probably never numbered more than a few tens of thousands at any given time, have been for the most part either businessmen or government employees, and with few exceptions have been town-dwellers.

A large proportion of the so-called European element has always consisted of Syrians and Lebanese. Although they are sometimes referred to disparagingly as "the Chinese of West Africa," they have played a useful role in the economy of the country as small traders and moneylenders. Often their shops, in remote country areas, are the only available agency for the sale of African products and the purchase by Africans of needed imported articles. Whether in city or country, the Syrians and Lebanese live in a more or less closed community, and they seem to have little regard for comfort or hygiene. Although they are closer to the Negro population than to the white, they are unpopular with both. Nevertheless, being astute businessmen and economical by nature, they have made a solid place for themselves, and they often finance the migration of their compatriots to West Africa.

Social Institutions

Despite the vast area of French-speaking West Africa, the many African languages and local dialects that are spoken there, and the differing ways of life in the three principal climatic and vegetation zones, certain common denominators exist among its peoples.

Outstanding among them is the Negro social structure—the family and extended family as the basic unit, next the clan, then the village community and finally the tribe. (The social structure of the nomadic "white" groups, the Moors and Tuareg—which differs in some essential ways from that of the Negro population—is explained in Chapter II.)

Traditional Negro society is closely knit at the family, clan and village level, and also demands tribal loyalties. Under this system the individual is bound in total obedience to the authority of the family head and must pay respect to the spirits of the ancestors and of nature. At the same time, he is protected by them and derives strength from the community of which he is a unit.

In recent years, the formerly unshakeable position of the institutions just described has been impaired to some extent by the drift of young peasants away from their villages to the towns and by the influence of alien religions—Islam and Christianity. Motives for the townward migration include the desire to escape from traditional authority and to earn money. The result has been the development of both individualism and an urban proletariat. Still another force that has undermined the old social order is education, which has caused Africans to question age-old institutions and beliefs.

West Africa's population, for many years virtually stationary in numbers, is now tending to increase because of better health care and other factors. In time this may give rise to economic and social problems that will have to be dealt with by the new national governments.

The Family

In Negro Africa, as in most other parts of the world, the family is the basic unit of society. But in the greater part of sub-Saharan Africa, the word "family" means something rather different than it does, for example, in Europe and countries with European traditions and customs. It consists of all the living, as well as the dead, descendants of a common ancestor who live in the same small area or have close contacts with each other. The family thus constitutes a much larger group than simply a household made up of the husband, the wife (or wives), and their children; and the authority of this larger family and its head, the patriarch, over individual members is very extensive.

Members of the group who have died are considered its real chiefs. They watch over tribal customs and their observance. Through the patriarch the dead ancestors reward or punish their descendants, depending upon whether or not the latter have properly fulfilled the traditional rites and customs. Absolute conformity with the rules of the group, whether family or clan, is required, and the individual is wholly subordinated to the group. No one dares isolate himself from it by breaking those rules or defying the patriarch—in fact, to be so isolated is inconceivable to the African Negro. His worst misfortune is to be banished from his group, thus losing its protection and being exposed to both physical and spiritual dangers.

In traditional African society betrothals are arranged between the families involved, often without consulting either of the two persons directly concerned. (By a decree of June 1939 issued by the French Minister of Colonies, the consent of the girl was necessary if the marriage was to be valid, but this was largely ignored in Negro Africa. Not until after World War II did improved economic conditions, social evolution and new ideas begin to accomplish this change, and marriages are now often contracted without reference to the respective families.) Sometimes the betrothal takes place while the prospective wife is still a child, so that years must pass before she reaches marriageable age. As custom requires that the intended husband contribute to the support of his future wife's parents, he may be saddled with this burden for some years before he can marry the girl.

After her marriage the wife is considered to be still part

of her own family, and in depriving it of her services the husband must pay the family a sort of indemnity, sometimes called the bride-price. This "price" is usually paid in the form of animals, cloth or money, sometimes of service, but such a payment does not mean that the wife becomes the property of her husband. If the marriage breaks up the wife goes back to her family, who as a rule must refund to the ex-husband the amount of the bride-price he had paid, or its equivalent. If they have had children, the children either stay with the father, or go with the mother, or are divided between them, depending on the circumstances of the divorce.

Polygyny (the marriage state in which a man has two or more wives) is the rule in Negro Africa, between 80 and 90 per cent of the continent's Negro households being polygynous. The existence of this custom, which is strongly reinforced both by tradition and by economic forces, is one of the reasons why Christianity has made comparatively little progress south of the Sahara and why Islam, which permits polygyny, has been more successful in converting animist Negroes. Under this system, which has its firmest supporters among African women themselves, no woman need lack for a provider, and she is always certain as to her position in the household. When there is more than one wife, there is almost always a baby-sitter or helper at hand if one is needed, and the work, which is often hard (such as pounding millet), is shared. The wives, at least in theory, are treated with equal consideration, each has her separate dwelling, and each receives an endowment of animals and land. As a result, there is usually little friction among them.

The extended-family household is more typical of Negro Africa than is the independent one of husband-wife-children. Housed under a single roof, or more often in a close-knit group of huts surrounded by a protective wall or a thorny barricade, the extended family comprises two or even several families of different generations related by blood.

Such a household is subject to the authority of one family head—usually the patriarch, or oldest member of the group. He holds this authority, however, only by consent of the group, and it may be taken from him if he shows himself incapable or unworthy. The patriarch is responsible for keeping order and harmony among the group, which usually numbers at least 20 individuals and sometimes adds up to 100 or more. He has many other duties as well: he is spokesman of the household in relation to other family groups; he is member of the village council; and he is priest of the family worship. In the last-named capacity he acts as intermediary between the worshippers and the family divinities—the souls of the ancestors and the spirits of nature. At the beginning and end of each farming season, he must offer sacrifices to these forces, first to beg their help and later to thank them for it.

The Clan

The next step beyond the family is the clan. It is a sort of enlarged or dispersed family all of whose members have the same common ancestor, but which has split up for one reason or another—often because the original family lands have become insufficient to support the number of people living on them, but sometimes because of a quarrel between one part of the family and the rest. The group that goes off to find other lands sets up a new family, headed in turn by a patriarch, but it continues to be attached by blood ties to the family from which it separated and remains part of a single clan with it.

Clans are distinguished from one another particularly by taboos (totems), each clan having its special one, which usually is based on a legend associated with the ancestor who set up the clan and gave it its name. For instance, the taboo or totem of the Diara clan of the Mandingos is the lion; their legend tells that the founding ancestor of this clan was saved from starving while a baby by a lioness which gave him milk when his mother was unable to feed him. However, the clan does not worship its taboo animal nor regard it as magical, though its members are forbidden to harm, kill, eat or touch that animal.

The Village Community

The clan relationship may or may not form the basis of the typical community of Negro Africa—the village. More often the village comes into existence to protect the common interests of unrelated families living near each other. It has a simple, compact administrative life and communal authority based upon the solidarity of the interests of the villagers and their observance of its internal rules of conduct.

The village is a form of community that is well suited to the needs of the Africans. Most of them are peasant farmers and herders and hence must live near or among their fields, flocks and herds. Besides being in close proximity to lands suitable for farming, the village usually is situated at a point where roads or paths meet and, whenever possible, near a well or stream.

In the old days before peace was established in West Africa by the European administrations, villages—especially in the sudanese zone—had to serve as centers of defense against enemy raiders and conquerors, both Negro and Arab. At that time, they were ringed by walls which, like those of medieval fortresses, were pierced by slits through which the defenders could launch spears or arrows. After raids and tribal wars became things of the past, the walls crumbled away and the villages, no longer cramped, were able to spread more widely. As a result, the huts of the villagers are now often dispersed among fields and barnyards.

SUDANESE-ZONE DWELLINGS

Throughout the sudanese zone, the houses are so typical of the dwellings in which the great majority of rural West Africans live that it might be worthwhile to describe them.

The hut has a circular wall, usually low but in some regions higher than a man, which is built of *banco* (sun-dried mud-brick). On the outside, this wall may be decorated with geometrical designs. In northern Guinea these are cut into the wall (incised) while the *banco* is still wet; in other regions, they stand out in relief, and in still others, they are sometimes painted, in red and black. Atop the wall and more or less overlapping it is a conical roof of braided or thatched straw, laid on a frame of saplings or bamboo. As a rule, the door is rather narrow and low, so that at night it can be more easily barred to animal or human intruders. The huts are placed—in the older villages—close together in a haphazard arrangement, according to the whims of the builders, and village pathways are almost always narrow and twisting. Westerners who visit villages of the savannah zone are often much impressed by the cleanliness and neatness of the huts with their beaten-earth floors, as well as the areas surrounding them, both of which usually are kept well swept and free of debris. Near the huts are communal granaries for storing millet and corn. These round, mud-brick structures, which resemble enormous jugs six or eight feet tall, are raised above the ground and have a top opening with a lid, through which the dried grain is passed. Often there is a communal oven likewise made of the ever-present *banco*.

A one-family thatched house built of banco, and its Somba owners, in the country northwest of Natitingou, Dahomey. Often of two storeys, the rooftop of this house can be seen in the picture on page 49.

The Negroes of some regions of the sudanese and sahel zones (particularly in the Mali Republic) have built for centuries in a distinctive kind of architecture known as the sudanese style. Houses of this type are quadrangular, with flat roofs made of long logs covered with the same *banco* as is used for building the rest of the house. Not infrequently the houses have two storeys, and some have interior courtyards, which probably reflect North African influence.

HUTS OF THE FOREST ZONE

In forest-zone villages, the hut is usually rectangular, with a long, low, pitched roof of palm-leaf thatch or corrugated metal. The walls here are higher than those of many of the round huts of the sudanese zone, and are more varied as to material, some being of mud-brick, others of branches or palm leaves covered with *banco,* still others simply of palm leaves or mats attached to a framework. In some cases a mud-brick house wall is given a coat of white paint outside and then adorned with crude frescoes in color—two boxers with their fists up; a smiling lion; a large snake following a man on a bicycle; and many other similar subjects. These creations, usually applied for a trifling sum by an itinerant "artist," are more curious than artistic, but seem to serve as a sort of African status symbol in the country areas.

SOCIAL ORGANIZATION IN THE VILLAGE

Within the African village, society is highly organized, primarily on the basis of the two sex groups. Because of the specialization of tasks traditionally performed by men and women, and for physical reasons as well, there is a separation of sexes that occasionally goes so far that a village may have a "men's house" and a "women's house," although this is rare. More often it means that while the husband goes hunting or works in the field, the wife remains at the hut to attend to such household tasks as preparing the food (pounding of millet takes hours each day), washing clothes or spinning cotton. She has help in this work if her husband has taken another wife or two, as mentioned above. She may not weave cotton, this task being reserved to men. The woman usually has the right to a small field of her own, which she tends at times when she is not performing communal or household tasks, and she may sell its products for her own benefit. For this purpose she goes to the market, which in most villages is held one day each week and which represents one of the most important social as well as commercial elements of village life.

The bustling market place of Bamako, Mali.

THE AGE CLASSES

Village society is characterized also by having age classes or fraternities, ranging from small children through the oldest group of adults, each of which has its duties and responsibilities. Adolescents are not considered to have reached adulthood until after a long period of instruction which culminates in a ceremony of circumcision.

There also exist age classes or fraternities with secret rites calculated to test physical courage, including the cutting of incisions on the face and body to produce traditional tribal scars (sometimes called tattooing). When the candidates are considered to be properly prepared to fulfill their role in the community, they undergo impressive ceremonies of initiation in which each is symbolically buried and then resurrected, thus becoming a different person, who receives a different name. Secrets are then revealed to the initiate under a vow of silence, and he begins his education in tribal laws and customs, farming techniques, and other matters, which may go on for several years in a sanctuary or a sacred forest. The young women go through a similar process at the hands of older ones in the secret fraternities for women, although their education is different. For them it comprises learning the proper attitude of a wife, child care, household duties, and such novel subjects of education as how to seduce men, deceive husbands and lovers, and bring about abortion.

The role of the age fraternities is made stronger and more lasting because it continues throughout the life of the initiate, who from time to time must undergo supplemental training. Each member of the various age classes has special communal obligations, and this helps to give cohesion to the life of the village.

THE CONFRATERNITIES

Aside from the age fraternities there exist certain organizations with secret rites also but with different objectives, which might be called "confraternities" to distinguish them from the age fraternities (age classes). In some cases the age fraternities have been replaced by the confraternities. Membership in these is not automatic or involuntary, as is the case with the age classes, but must be conferred and consented to. Many of their practices and rules resemble those of the age fraternities, but they differ from the latter in some respects, such as their concern with law, order and morality in the village, their role in winning favor with the supernatural beings who protect or harm crops, and sometimes their aesthetic activities in developing dances, music, singing and sculpture. The confraternities own property and collect dues, and thus are able to help out needy members.

It should be mentioned, however, that besides those just described there are sinister confraternities which engage in cannibalism and ritual murder. Ivory Coast, Guinea and southern Senegal have had many of these. They are not, however, confined to former F.W.A., but have existed also in other countries along the Guinea Gulf. Of a similar type are the societies of Leopard Men, Crocodile Men and others which from time to time have received considerable publicity.

CASTES AND CLASSES

West African society embraces a complex system of castes and classes, which is reflected in the life of each village. Castes may be those of social rank (nobles, free men and slaves, as among the Peuls and Wolofs) or of occupation (blacksmiths, weavers, wood-carvers, etc.). Caste status is hereditary and unchangeable—the son or nephew of a blacksmith inevitably takes up that trade and can never rise above his caste or marry a woman of a higher one, nor may a noble marry anyone of a lower caste. Class, on the other hand, is determined by material possessions (wealth in the form of cattle, for instance), which give their owner the chance to acquire many things, even power and prestige.

The occupational castes grew up in Negro Africa long ago under the protection of kings and nobles, very much as artists and artisans of the medieval and Renaissance courts in Europe were supported and encouraged by them. They have tended strongly to come together in local associations grouping all the members of families of the same occupational caste, and these associations have both a caste and a class status. Each of them is characterized by specialization of task, by relative rank, and by restrictions on intermarriage. Among certain Tukulor clans, for example, there are three categories of occupational-caste groups:

1. Musicians, weavers, shoemakers, ordinary blacksmiths and workers in precious metals; these may all intermarry.
2. Artisans who make wooden objects and canoe (*pirogue*) makers; these also may intermarry.
3. The lowest caste, that of the feared and despised singing *griots,* who are not allowed to marry anyone belonging to the first two categories.

The members of all these occupational castes are more or less regarded with contempt, notwithstanding their recognized usefulness, and they are also greatly feared. Contempt is felt for them because of the nature of their work, which may involve handling and skinning dead animals (the shoemaker-tanner), working with iron-bearing earth (the blacksmith), and the like. Their dependent position also provokes contempt. They inspire fear for various reasons. One is their apartness—generally each caste tends to live apart from the rest of the village and develops a special language intended to keep its techniques secret. Blacksmiths are particularly feared because they work with fire, using it to compel the "earth mother" to surrender iron, so that they are believed to possess powers of black magic.

The Tribe

Although many anthropologists disagree as to the meaning of the word "tribe," an eminent German anthropologist defines it as "an agglomeration of groups and individuals, not necessarily related, who form a cultural and political unity through living in a common territory, having a common leader, one language, and similar customs and usages." These factors determine what makes the tribe a special entity, and from this it follows that the rules which the tribe establishes will determine the way of life of each member of it. Thus whether meat is eaten or is not, whether fishing is carried on, who cares for the children, what is the bride-price, what ancestors are worshipped, will all vary from tribe to tribe.

Great diversity exists among the nomadic and sedentary tribes of former French West Africa, as indicated in Chapter II. However, whether large or small, strong or weak, each tribe is ruled by a chief, usually a paramount chief, whose authority assures the maintenance of law and order. Loyalty to the chief, and through him to the tribe and its ways, is strong among the Negro peoples. It is recognized by the new governments of French-speaking West Africa as a barrier to the creation of national loyalty among the population. This is the main reason for the moves which have been undertaken to suppress the chieftaincies and to re-direct the loyalties of the people (see page 171).

Tribal authority has been highly centralized and pervasive among the sedentary Negro population. It is much looser among the nomadic Moors and Tuareg of the sahel and desert zones. Because of their migratory way of life, they are fundamentally anarchic, and their tribes are broken up into many factions which often are mutually hostile.

As mentioned in the introduction to this chapter, the forces of modern life have begun to undermine African Tribalism.

The Land and Land Rights

The African Negro has quite a different point of view regarding land rights and land use than the one to which we are accustomed in Western countries. In sub-Saharan Africa, land belongs to no living person and cannot be bought or sold, either by an individual or a group. The same is true of vacant and apparently ownerless land, although for many decades this fact was not grasped by the French officials of West Africa. In consequence, hard feelings and even clashes resulted from the administration's occasional attempts to cede land. By Negro tradition, all their lands belong to ancient divinities who—in return for offerings or sacrifices—granted the use of such lands long ago to the first families which arrived on them, and this right or privilege is then handed down in the same family.

With the enlargement of families into sizable ethnic groups in the course of many generations, the number of individuals sharing the collective right to use a particular land area may become very large. Therefore it is necessary that someone be charged with the responsibility for use or division of the land and for maintaining good relations with its divinities. The man who holds this position is called the Master of the Land, and is usually the oldest member of the oldest family among the descendants of the original family. As a rule, he is assisted by a Council of Notables (the elders of the village). Among his duties is that of assigning tasks on the land to each family of the village, and later that of dividing the crop. He enjoys a prestige almost equal to that of a political chief, and in some ways his power is greater, for without his cooperation the land cannot be allotted, and it can even be removed from use if he does not carry out the ritual sacrifices to its divinities. The Master of the Land, however, may be replaced—like the family patriarch referred to above—if he proves to be incompetent or abuses his powers.

Forces of Change

To appreciate the importance that village life has held in F.W.A. and to grasp some of the changes that are taking place in it, we might consider the situation in two of the countries, the Niger Republic and Ivory Coast.

Although the Niger Republic has a population of 3.1 million, its area is so huge that it has a very low average population density (about three inhabitants per square mile). There is only one center that can properly be called a city—Niamey, the capital, which has some 42,000 inhabitants. The country has only three other towns with more than 10,000: Zinder, Tahoua, and Maradi. But there are over 7,000 villages, mostly in the central and southern parts of the country, the north being pre-desert or desert, thinly populated by nomads and by small groups of oasis-dwellers.

Ivory Coast's population totals some 3.5 million, but its average density of about ten per square mile is likewise low. Abidjan can count at least 247,000 inhabitants, having grown at a tremendous rate since 1950, when it became a deep-water port thanks to the completion of a canal connecting its lagoon with the ocean. Aside from Abidjan, only four of the country's towns can claim a population of more than 10,000, and there are six others containing from about 8,000 inhabitants down to 3,000. All of the cities and towns mentioned account together for no more than about 500,000 of the country's population. The remaining three million live in many thousands of small villages and groups, principally in the savannah country of the central and northern parts of Ivory Coast, beyond the tropical forest.

In both Niger and Ivory Coast the chief cities have exerted a strong attraction on many young people of the villages, especially the young men. Visions of an exciting life in the large towns, the hope of earning money and being able to buy fascinating imported items such as cork helmets, fountain pens, sun-glasses and other novelties—and above all, the prospect of shaking off family and village duties, obligations and

Town life offers certain attractions not found in the villages. A barber shop and a beauty shop in Bobo-Dioulasso, Upper Volta, display the latest hair styles.

prohibitions—have caused a minor invasion of Niamey and Abidjan by peasant youths. Dakar has had the same kind of invasion on a big scale, and Bamako, Conakry, Cotonou and Porto Novo have all been more or less plagued by it.

These young men who drift to the towns form an unstable and in certain respects disquieting element, for they become detribalized when they are so far removed from family contacts and the influence of traditional restraints. Often they are unable to support themselves and therefore live on the charity of relatives in the town, become public charges or turn to petty crime. Moreover, their rebellion against tribal authority is undeniably beginning, along with other influences, to weaken the structure of village and family life that for centuries has imbued the African with a sense of shared dangers and shared protection.

Other factors playing their part in altering the social framework are the improvement of roads and of transport (automotive and plane) and the spread of mass media of communication (radio-broadcasting and motion pictures). This is a trend which is bound to be accentuated by the strong desire for modernization that is so potent an influence in the newly independent African states, some of which have already gone far toward reducing or abolishing such institutions as the chieftaincies.

In still another sphere of his life, that of religion, the West African Negro has met with forces that have disturbed the traditional order of things. Two of these are themselves religions, Islam and Christianity. A third is that of education, which by providing young Africans with rational explanations of natural phenomena and introducing them to a wider world, has made at least a beginning in liberating them from their age-long burden of fears and superstitions. Still another potent force is represented by modern medical knowledge, which through the work of doctors, hospitals and traveling clinics has proven to the Negro that many of his ailments are curable and need not be stoically endured as punishments for some supposed offense against his ancestors or the spirits of nature.

There is another and rather regrettable side to this picture, however. The foreign religions, the education and the medical care which help to free the Negro from his traditional fears often deprive him of the sense of security that arises from his complete immersion in African pagan society, in which family and tribal life, and the unseen world of natural and ancestral spirits, are so closely inter-related.

Traditional Beliefs

To the outsider, the pagan world of Negro Africa may appear primitively simple, but in actuality it is an intricate one. For its inhabitants, the spiritual and the material aspects blend into each other at many points. This world has a way of life which in some aspects resembles that of certain ancient Far Eastern civilizations, for the aim of the pagan Negro is to live in harmony with nature, not to try to dominate or oppose it as does the European. The African Negro feels that he is truly a part of nature, subject to both visible and invisible forces on which his life and all his activities depend.

The age-old religion of the African Negro is one that permeates all his waking and sleeping hours, and embraces not only communal worship of natural forces but also family ceremonies and beliefs aimed at gratifying and influencing the spirits of the ancestors. Often this religion is called animism or fetishism, but though "animism" is partly correct, "fetishism" tends to be misleading. Fetishism implies worship of a thing—a statue, or rock, or tree, for example. The inanimate fetish, however, actually serves only to represent a spirit or to provide a temporary stopping-place for it, and it is the spirit that is worshipped, not the fetish. Animism denotes a body of beliefs which may vary in detail from region to region, but which all have certain basic elements in common: the world was created by a single god; however, this god is not worshipped directly—because he is too remote and indifferent —but only in the form of spirits, which are masters of the persons and things that they enter and which possess intelligence and will.

WORSHIP OF THE ANCESTORS

The spirits of the ancestors of the family and the tribe are given special worship in order to induce them to protect and not harm the living, and this involves persuading them to enter into a material inanimate object, such as a statue, a rock, or a stick of wood, which becomes a fetish and has its household altar. By propitiating the ancestors through family or communal rites, the worshippers insure good crops in their fields and shield the family against disease and other harmful outside influences. Having become divinities, the ancestors wield great power in both the supernatural and the natural worlds—which to their living descendants co-exist and are indistinguishable.

It is among the Dogon tribe of the Mali Republic that the mythology of divine ancestors is most elaborate, and in their religion it is the outstanding element. Their greatest ceremony lasts 24 days and is performed only at intervals of 60 years, when by tradition the time comes to renew the Great Mask which is the dwelling-place of the tribe's founding ancestor. The Great Mask is in the form of a long wooden snake, and to make the ancestor's soul pass into the new mask

Fetish of the tailors' guild, in its enclosure marked with symbols, at Abomey, Dahomey.

A fetish priest of Ivory Coast with some of his followers.

a dog and a chicken are sacrificed. There is much beer-drinking, and many masked dances are performed, the carved wooden masks representing animals, birds, people and even houses. Betweentimes, the masks are kept on altars devoted to rites of fertility and rain.

THE SPIRITS OF NATURE

Besides the cult of the ancestors, led by the family head and the village chief, West African paganism includes the worship of natural forces personified in the spirits of things—the sky, the stars, water, fire, wind, thunder, lightning and many others. This worship is in the charge of special fetish priests, each of whom devotes himself to a particular nature spirit, and it takes the form of public or private ceremonies. Dances and sacrifices are performed, in which all the followers of the fetish participate. It is in Dahomey that fetishist practices, especially among the important Fon tribe, are the most colorful and deeply entrenched and are strongly tinged with fear.

WHITE AND BLACK MAGIC

African belief in spiritual forces whose goodwill must be won and whose vengeful anger must be turned aside finds its group expression in religion, as described above, through the intercession of the family or clan patriarch and the fetish priest. But the individual—or the group when it must deal with certain other forces—may turn for help to white magic or may have to fight black magic.

For white magic, which is frequently called upon to foretell the future, one consults the soothsayer, who usually also acts as a healer. Besides telling fortunes, he supplies *grigris* (amulets) to wear and prescribes procedures such as taboos to observe, which will cure sickness, protect against sorcerers, bring rain, arouse love, etc. To cause the rain to fall is one of his most important functions.

Belief in black magic is widespread, and with it the dread of sorcerers and witches, who are considered the principal causes of sickness and death. The sorcerer, who sometimes does not know that he is one, is a public enemy who must be found out and punished. Usually the suspected person must undergo an ordeal, such as swallowing poison; if he survives, he is innocent. Confessed sorcerers are invariably put to death.

Islam in West Africa

In magic as in the worship of the ancestors and of nature spirits, symbols are constantly at hand to make the invisible

visible, and from this springs the importance of ceremonies. When Islam spread into Negro Africa from the north and west during the Middle Ages and later, these symbols and ceremonies were simply modified in details and were more or less taken over by Negro "converts" into the new faith.

Throughout former F.W.A., except among the devout Moors, the Muslim religion exists in watered-down form, far different from the fierce fanaticism of many Muslims of the Near and Middle East. In West Africa south of the Sahara, Islam has proven to be an adaptable creed, and almost all of its "converts" there still continue to wear *grigris* and to venerate the ancestors and the spirits of nature.

Conversion itself is a simple process—to become a Muslim the Negro has only to recite the formula, "There is no god but Allah and Mohammed is his Prophet." He is required to make few changes in his way of living, except to recite the five prayers each day, to renounce intoxicating drinks, and to put on a long robe (*boubou*) if he has hitherto gone naked or semi-naked. The last-mentioned requirement has caused resistance to Islam among some pagan tribes, who feel, with some reason, that their sketchy costumes are better suited to the climate and to their labors than is the cumbersome *boubou*. Islam's campaign of conversion in Negro Africa has been a centuries-long battle between Muslim modesty and pagan nudity.

Islam was the first foreign religion to take the field against traditional African religious beliefs, which had been sheltered from the outside world for thousands of years by the ocean and by the Saharan Desert barrier. In the eleventh century, an Arab missionary from Morocco made the first conversions in West Africa, and these converts, who became known as the Almoravides, were puritanical and warlike. The advance of Islam eastward through the sudanese zone during the

A mosque at the village of Akka, Mali, on the banks of the Niger. Built of banco, it has not yet been repaired after the damage caused by seasonal rains.

Middle Ages, which began with the Almoravides' holy war, forms part of the story of the Negro empires of that zone, which is told in Chapter IV.

In modern times, during the period of French administration, the Muslim missionaries, whether *marabouts* or Dioula or Hausa traders, have been greatly aided by two factors: the pro-Islamic policy of France in F.W.A., and the peaceful conditions resulting from French rule, which have made it possible for them to circulate easily and safely through the country.

Nearly 50 per cent of former F.W.A.'s total African population are nominally Muslims, most of them being in the sahel and desert zones and in the northern savannah regions, except for certain parts of southern Senegal and central and northern Guinea, where there are also large Islamized areas. The Islamic Republic of Mauritania, where Islam is the state religion, is almost solidly Muslim, as is the vast majority of the population of the Niger Republic. In Senegal, at least 70 per cent profess Islam. The Mali Republic, however, has many animists who have resisted conversion, and barely 50 per cent of its population are Muslims. The countries where Islam has penetrated least are eastern Guinea, Ivory Coast, Upper Volta and Dahomey, where animism is still a strong force and where the Christian missions have been most successful. Among the Mossi tribe of Upper Volta, Islam has gained some converts but has met with stiff competition from the Christian missions.

Generally speaking, the Muslim missionaries are winning far more so-called converts in F.W.A. than are the Catholic and Protestant missionaries combined. As already indicated, however, these conversions—both Christian and Muslim— are often superficial, because of the underlying strength of animist beliefs which are so closely interwoven with Negro traditions and family and tribal life.

The Role of the Christian Missions

Christianity did not arrive in F.W.A. until the 1600's—six centuries after the Islamic warriors called the Almoravides began their drive of conquest and conversion eastward from the Senegal coast. The first Christian missionaries were Portuguese Catholics, but their attempts to install permanent missions on the coast of Senegal and the Guinea Gulf failed.

CATHOLIC

It was not until 200 years later, in the early nineteenth century, that French Catholic missionaries gained a shaky foothold in Ivory Coast and a somewhat firmer one in Dahomey. Senegal continued to be an Islamic and animist stronghold until the Fathers of the Holy Spirit established a mission on the island of Gorée, near Dakar, in 1845. For many decades, Christian missions made little or no impression among the Islamized Peuls of Guinea, and until the end of the nineteenth century they failed totally to penetrate the great West African hinterland, where for centuries Islam had been the religion of the sahel and also much of the sudanese zone.

As the French conquest of F.W.A. was rounded out in the last two decades of the ninetenth century, the Catholic missionaries, and also French Protestant ones, found their activities greatly facilitated, and they made better progress in Senegal and Dahomey and eventually in Ivory Coast. But the Catholic missions were dealt a blow in 1905 when separation of church and state in France put an end to government cooperation in their work, which had been conspicuous in the educational and medical fields as well as in evangelism. Although misunderstandings and mistrust followed for a long time, especially as to the relationship between missionaries and their converts and its effect on the business of government, the atmosphere between the missions and the French government distinctly improved after World War II. During the 15-year span after that war, until the F.W.A. territories became independent nations, all the missions, both Catholic and Protestant, received government subsidies for their educational and medical work.

The Catholic missions have not made spectacular progress in converting F.W.A.'s Negroes. They have been faced with the tenacity of animism in some regions and with the severe competition of Islam, whose simple worship appeals much more to country Africans than do the puzzling rituals and dogmas of Roman Catholicism. (In 1958, the Apostolic Delegation of Dakar vaguely claimed that there were one million Catholics—an improbably high figure—among F.W.A.'s population, which at that time totaled between 18 and 19 millions.) Moreover, at least until recently, little effort was made to train an African Catholic clergy, and as of 1957 there were fewer than 100 Africans in training for the priesthood. Not until 1956 was the first Negro Catholic bishop of the Federation consecrated.

However, in terms of influence on the African scene, the Catholic missions have produced more impressive results. Many of the outstanding leaders of the new French-speaking West African nations, especially certain Guinea Gulf states, are Christians, and most of these are Catholics, the majority of whom received at least a large part of their education in mission schools.

PROTESTANT

Although Protestant missionaries came to Ivory Coast as early as 1848, to Dahomey in 1843, and to Senegal in 1862, there have never been many of them, and in the early years they confined their work to a few places. For many years the Protestant missions in Ivory Coast concentrated on the British Africans who came there to cut mahogany logs or gather wild rubber, and their influence was restricted mainly to prosperous, middle-aged, non-indigenous Africans.

Not until 1913–14, when a Liberian "prophet," William Harris, began making thousands of converts in lower Ivory Coast, did the government's indifference to Protestantism give way to alarm. Harrisism and similar cults are described in more detail below. Harris preached obedience to authority, not subversion, but the war was on and he was an alien, as were the British and American Protestant missionaries then in the federation. The "prophet" was deported in 1915, but for the time being, the British and American missionaries—being nationals of France's allies—were left undisturbed. They were nevertheless regarded with suspicion by the Federation government as being possible forerunners of Anglo-American imperialism in the French African territories.

Later, during the inter-war period, various government decrees sharply limited mission activities of fund-raising and laid down such educational requirements for missionaries as the holding of a degree from a French institution, teaching only in French, native languages or Latin, and following a government-approved curriculum. These moves hit the English-speaking Protestant missionaries much harder than they did the French Catholic ones, and before World War II, many of the Protestants had given up and gone to other, more hospitable parts of Africa.

After the end of that war, as mentioned above, relations between the French government and the Catholic and Protestant missions improved, and with government subsidies they were able to expand their work. However, evangelism continued to be the main activity of the Protestant missionaries in West Africa. As of 1953, the Protestant missions claimed to have made upward of 116,000 converts in F.W.A. and French Togo together—hardly an impressive showing after a century of evangelical labors. Perhaps because in F.W.A. the American Protestant missions have stressed evangelical effort instead of education and medical service, no better showing has been made by the American missions there than by those of other countries. This is true despite the fact that nearly half the Protestant missionaries in the federation—over 100 —have belonged to one or another of four American mission societies, and that their financial resources have been larger and their material equipment better than those possessed by the British, Canadian, French, Dutch and Swiss Protestant missionaries who also have been working in former F.W.A.

AFRICAN "CHRISTIAN" SECTS

Besides having to fight what seems a losing battle against the steady inroads of Islam by way of its thousands of itinerant *marabouts* and Dioula and Hausa missionaries, both the Catholic and the Protestant missions are confronted with two basic handicaps to the development of organized and conventional Christianity in F.W.A. One is that Christianity came to Africa as the white man's religion and thus is associated with colonialism in the minds of Africans. The other is the tendency of Black Africans to adapt to the point of deformation any and every alien religion they take over.

Christian missionaries in F.W.A. have gone out of their way to be tolerant of African customs and traditions, but they have felt that they must draw a line somewhere. Both Catholicism and Protestantism have drawn that line at polygyny, and their refusal to sanction this time-honored African institution has been the greatest single stumbling-block in the path of Christian conversion in the F.W.A. countries.

As a result, pseudo-Christian, wholly African sects which sanction polygyny have sprung up and won a large following, especially in Dahomey and Ivory Coast. One of the earliest of these to appear in F.W.A., as mentioned above, was launched in 1913 by a Liberian Negro, William Harris. After his mission as prophet was revealed to him in Liberia, as he claims, by the Angel Gabriel in 1910, he began preaching in and around Monrovia. In 1913, he went to lower Ivory Coast, which then was passing through a spiritual crisis. Traditional society was disintegrating, crude fetishism was supplanting true animism, and the Christian missions had made only a handful of converts.

The coming of Harris seemed a miracle to the coastal tribes. One Catholic missionary described his advent as follows: "At the sound of his voice, the fetishes turned to dust, the pagan priests renounced their false gods, and whole villages embraced his religion. . . . He moved forward leaning on a long stick topped by a wooden cross, and was followed by six women, dressed like him in white, whom he called his 'disciples.' He spoke of God in a thunderous voice, using a pidgin English which had to be translated to his listeners. His preaching was accompanied by the shaking of gourds filled with seeds. He commanded the fetishers to touch his cross, and when they did so they rolled on the ground screaming; he calmed them and sent them off to burn their own fetishes. More than 100,000 Negroes were converted by him as he moved along; he baptized them by placing the Bible on their heads and pouring a little water over them. He also cured the sick by means of the Bible."

Harris' doctrine, in no way subversive, was the rough and simple one of the Old Testament: a fierce God demanding observance of his commandments; the virtues of labor; obedience to authority; one day a week of absolute rest; moderation in the use of alcohol. Nevertheless, under the tensions of World War I the government became uneasy because of the agitation among his followers, and he was deported. Some of his converts were taken over by the missions, especially the Protestant ones, but many were rejected because they clung to the polygyny permitted by Harris' teachings. These followers of Harris set up churches based on his doctrine, which have continued to this day to attract large numbers of Africans. In fact, since World War II, the growth of "neo-Harrisism" in Ivory Coast has been very marked.

Ivory Coast has harbored more pseudo-Christian African cults, such as Harrisism, than any other F.W.A. country. One was the religious movement started by the "prophet" Adae who baptized with perfumes, condemned fetishes, and issued his own ten commandments, including "Thou shalt not damage the plantation of thy next of kin." Another such prophetic cult began after the introduction of universal suffrage into Ivory Coast in 1946, when a woman, Marie Lalou, launched a movement called Deima, which had great popular success. In her temples, Jesus and the cross played a part, but magic was also practiced. Unknown to him, the well-known African leader, Félix Houphouët-Boigny—who is now president of Ivory Coast—was made a divinity in the Deima cult, and he did not learn of this for some time. Only at his urgent request was he demoted from this position.

Dahomey, too, especially since World War II, has had half a dozen or more pseudo-Christian religious societies whose success can be attributed to the African liking for group activity, high-sounding titles and colorful costumes. Among them are the Eledja Church, the Native African Union, the Eternal Sacred Order of Cherubim and Seraphim, and the Organization of Celestial Christians.

Thus, in much the same way as "converted" African Muslims have clung to traditional animist practices, African Christians are now adapting Catholicism and Protestantism to suit their psychological needs, their traditions and their folklore. Only time will tell whether Christianity's basic creed will be so distorted that it will no longer be recognizable by the parent churches.

Education

In the field of education, as in that of religion, African customs, psychology and superstition have had a profound and adverse effect. Other barriers to progress in this direction have been the nomadic way of life of a large segment of the population, the vast number of African languages and the extreme poverty of most of the countries.

WORK OF THE MISSIONS

Catholic missionaries of various religious orders pioneered in educational work in F.W.A. They founded the first non-Koranic schools for boys, as well as schools for girls and for mulattoes, at St. Louis in Senegal early in the nineteenth century. No Federation-wide school system was organized until after the separation of church and state in France in 1905, and up to that time the Catholic missions provided almost all the formal instruction given in F.W.A.

The mission schools were mostly in Senegal until near the end of the nineteenth century, when a number were also set up in Soudan (Mali Republic), Guinea, Ivory Coast and Dahomey. In lower Dahomey, by 1900, there were 20 or more well-attended mission schools. It is in the Guinea Gulf region, generally speaking, that the missions have been most successful in promoting education as well as in winning converts, for unlike the Muslims of the more northerly zones, the animist coastal peoples are eager for education. There have never been mission schools in Islamic Mauritania, very few exist in the Niger Republic, and they are weak in Senegal and Mali.

Both Catholic and Protestant missions suffered a setback in losing government subsidies in 1905. Nevertheless, most of the former and a few of the latter managed to keep operating, and when they again began to receive French financial aid in the early 1950's, they more than recovered the ground lost. During the academic year 1955–56, in the Federation as a whole, 88,557 students were enrolled in Catholic mission schools, 23,379 of these being girls. Catholic secondary and normal classes had an enrollment that year of 2,096 boys and 1,067 girls. In addition, more than 25,000 children were learning to read and write French in the catechism schools.

THE GOVERNMENT SCHOOL SYSTEM

As for the state school system, the aim of the French government from 1904 until its responsibilities below the university level began to be shifted to African administrations in 1958, was to provide—so far as was possible under local conditions—education for Africans that would meet the same high standards of quality as those in France itself. To begin with, instruction was carried on in the French language from the earliest years. It was recognized, however, that African needs required special consideration, and for many years official policy stressed the development of primary, technical and vocational education. Increasing attention was given to training in agriculture and animal husbandry, health and hygiene, and African arts and crafts, despite the opposition of some of the Negro elite, who wanted the government schools to prepare Africans for white-collar jobs.

As of January 1, 1957, French West Africa had a total of 2,546 public and private—that is, mission—educational institutions. Of these schools, 2,339 were primary, 128 technical and 75 secondary, and there were four higher institutions, the most important of which was the University of Dakar. At that time, the number of students enrolled in public and private schools totaled 379,186, of whom 24 per cent were girls. It should be mentioned that although primary, secondary and even technical education in F.W.A. under the French regime was free, it was not compulsory at any age.

PRIMARY SCHOOLS

The extent and nature of education offered in F.W.A., as

well as school attendance, have varied widely from one territory to another. For example, with regard to children of primary-school age, the proportion actually attending such schools, both public and private, in 1958 was as follows: in Dahomey, 29 per cent; Ivory Coast, 27 per cent; Senegal, 25 per cent; Soudan (Mali Republic), 8 per cent; Upper Volta, 7.8 per cent; Mauritania, 7 per cent; and Niger, 4 per cent. (Because of Guinea's break with France in 1958, as told in Chapter VI, statistics are not readily available for that country.)

NOMAD SCHOOLS

As can be seen from the school-attendance percentages given above, the two lowest are to be found in Mauritania and Niger. These two countries are poor, vast and underpopulated, and are peopled mostly by Muslim nomads. The nomads have long been indifferent and even hostile to education of the Western type, although some nomad boys have attended mediocre Koranic schools where they learn to recite the Koran and to read a little Arabic.

An interesting if partial solution to this problem—which to some extent confronts Mali as well as Mauritania and Niger—was worked out by the French in the form of nomad primary schools. A few of these schools were tried out for the first time in 1924, but they have been more successful since World War II than they were in the 1920's and 1930's, when it was very difficult to round up the children and to keep them in school when they were brought there. *Goumiers* (African police, usually mounted on camels) had to bring the children in from the tribal tents and then guard the school to prevent them from slipping away.

In Mauritania, the school tent and the teacher move with the tribe, to which they are permanently attached, and school hours and methods are adapted to Moorish and Muslim customs. A difficulty which it took many years to overcome was the hostility of the nomads to the Negro teachers who were sent to run the schools because no Moorish teachers were available. It was not solved until Moorish teachers could be trained and assigned to the schools. Now the teacher is a member of the tribe to which he is assigned, and is chosen by its chief. There has been a big increase in the number and attendance of Mauritania's nomad schools in the past few years. In 1954, the country had only 12 such schools (with 241 pupils), but by 1959 there were 88 of them in operation. By that year, Mauritania had a total of 156 primary schools,

A class in a nomad school of the Trarza region of Mauritania. Such schools move with the Tribal groups as they wander through the desert.

both fixed and nomadic, with an attendance of about 7,500.

In the Mali Republic and the Niger Republic the main barrier to nomad education is less the hostility of the Tuareg tribes than the problem of getting enough suitable teachers. Mobile schools for Mali's nomads exist in only a few areas; in the rest of the country, as well as in Niger, which is too poor to afford mobile ones, schools for nomad children have been created at fixed points. The sites of all of Niger's 11 nomad schools—which in 1954 had 560 pupils—were carefully chosen along the main caravan routes so that parents could see their children. Pupils in these schools have been left as free as possible, with a flexible school routine, and an effort has been made to reproduce, in somewhat improved form, the conditions of their tribal life.

A secondary school for nomads—the first of its kind—was opened at the town of Agadès in Niger in June 1962. It is hoped that this will influence the course of nomad education in such a way as to encourage and make possible greater nomad participation in the political life of Niger.

SECONDARY SCHOOLS

In recent years, secondary schools have multiplied very rapidly in F.W.A. From a total of only 23 in 1953, when they had about 5,000 students, they increased within four years to 75 schools with some 20,000 students, as of January 1957. Because of this growth in high-school facilities, along with improvement of their curricula and standards of performance, fewer Africans have had to go to France for secondary education. Moreover, graduates of the F.W.A. schools can enter higher institutions in France on the same footing as students from the French *lycées* (which are about equivalent to the last two years of an American high school plus junior college).

An ultra-modern secondary school built by the French at Niamey, Niger, in 1953.

HIGHER EDUCATION

Until recently, the only institution of university level in F.W.A. has been the University of Dakar—an outgrowth of an institute comprising colleges of medicine, law, science and liberal arts which were established at Dakar, Senegal, after World War II. This university was inaugurated in September 1957, in impressive new buildings on the western shore of Cap Vert peninsula. In 1963–64, its enrollment totaled 2,000. On January 31, 1964, a university was inaugurated at Abidjan in the prosperous republic of Ivory Coast, with 1,150 students.

With the facilities provided since 1957 by the University of Dakar and since early 1964 by that of Abidjan, French-speaking African students can now pursue higher studies without leaving Africa. From 1946 until 1957, however, hundreds were sent each year to France, on grants that enabled them to live and study at Paris, Montpellier, Grenoble and other university centers.

From several points of view, that system turned out to have serious drawbacks. For years the African students and their organization in Paris were at loggerheads with the Ministry of Overseas France. This Ministry gave them their monthly allotments, which they denounced as inadequate, and had general supervision over their welfare and activities, another feature which they resented. Then, too, a large proportion of them found life in France so glamorous that, after completing their university work at the expense of the French administration, they resisted returning to their home territories, where they were badly needed. Sometimes they simply disappeared. Most disturbing of all, in the eyes of both the Paris government and that of the federation, were the extreme left-wing tendencies shown by many African students, over whom the French Communist party gained a strong influence. This radicalism is clearly reflected in the programs of a few of the new French-speaking nations of West Africa, particularly Guinea and Mali.

Mass Communications Media

Education and also the lack of it have greatly influenced the evolution of mass communications media in F.W.A. First among them, in order of seniority, is the press (including both newspapers and periodicals), which has long played an important role as an educational medium. In recent years, African political parties and now the new governments have used it increasingly as a propaganda tool. Next is radio-broadcasting, comparatively a newcomer in West Africa, which already commands a huge public, much of it illiterate and therefore largely beyond the reach of newspapers. The third mass medium, one that is very popular with African Negroes, is the motion picture. As for television, which was introduced in Abidjan and Ouagadougou in 1963, it does not yet reach more than a minute percentage of the population and hence cannot be considered a mass medium in either case.

THE PRESS

F.W.A.'s newspapers fall into two categories—those that are owned by Europeans and aimed at the European community and the African elite, and those that are run by and for Africans. The great majority of all the newspapers are in the French language.

The oldest daily paper, which has been published for a quarter-century, is *Dakar-Matin,* formerly called *Paris-Dakar,* founded by a Frenchman who owned a newspaper chain as well as the African illustrated monthly, *Bingo. Dakar-Matin*'s estimated circulation is around 15,000 copies, but these pass through many hands and it is probably the most widely read newspaper in former F.W.A. About 60 per cent of its readers are Africans, the rest Europeans. Another interesting European-owned newspaper is the weekly, *Afrique Nouvelle,* published at Dakar by the Catholic mission of the White Fathers, which stresses social and civic questions more than political ones. Its circulation is upward of 7,000 copies— large as African papers go—is spread throughout former French Negro Africa, and most of its readers are Africans. The first truly indigenous newspaper (no longer published) was *L'Eclaireur de la Côte d'Ivoire,* founded in the mid-1930's by two Ivory Coast Africans.

Both before and after World War II, many newspapers,

both European and African, were launched, but for various reasons the mortality rate among them has been high. Most of them were started on a shoestring by individuals who wanted to air their opinions or grievances. Almost none of them has had a circulation of more than a few thousand, and until recently there was little revenue to be gained from advertising. Many of them were therefore unable to meet expenses. Censorship has been another handicap, and it promises to become, if anything, more strict under the new national governments than it was during the French regime. Since the rise of numerous African parties began in 1946, many African-owned newspapers have been launched as party propaganda organs. With the present trend toward one-party government in many of the new African states, the newspaper of the dominant party tends to become the government's mouthpiece, and the papers published by opposition parties are suppressed along with the parties themselves.

Nevertheless, despite censorship and other troubles, the local press in most of the countries will probably continue to develop if the literacy rate and purchasing power of Africans continue to rise. Already its impact is much greater than circulation figures indicate. A few years ago, for example, a market survey in F.W.A. by Paris advertisers showed that a single copy of a newspaper was often read aloud to hundreds of illiterates, and that the African public in general was well up on the daily news contained in the local press.

RADIO-BROADCASTING

Radio-broadcasting has made the most sensational advance of any of F.W.A.'s mass media of communication. As recently as 1938, only about 2,000 receiving sets, all short-wave, existed in the whole of F.W.A., and almost all were owned by Europeans in Dakar. The federation had no broadcasting station until one began operating in Dakar some months after World War II began in 1939, and not until 1948 and later were transmitters installed in some of the territorial capitals. During the 1950's, however, radio-broadcasting made a spurt and receiving sets multiplied enormously. By 1953, around 75,000 receivers were in operation, and that year, too, the government distributed about 1,000 sets for installation in rural communities which otherwise would hear no broadcasts. Later in the decade, with the aid of a French government agency abbreviated as SORAFOM, many more broadcasting stations, as well as village receivers and town public-address systems, were installed throughout F.W.A.

Every one of the eight capital cities now has at least one transmitter, even if low-powered, and three countries can now boast of 100-kilowatt stations: Senegal, Guinea and Ivory Coast. Senegal's 100-kw short-wave transmitter went into operation in June 1960. Guinea's big station was built in the spring of 1962 by technicians from behind the Iron Curtain as part of Communist-bloc aid to that nation. And Ivory Coast's powerful Abidjan transmitter, built with French help, began broadcasting early in 1962. In each of the eight countries, the stations that were being operated by SORAFOM before 1958–60 have been taken over by the new national governments for propaganda purposes. However, the broadcasts of the older stations as well as the new ones still include varied programs of news and educational talks in French and various African languages, as well as a good deal of music, both classical and popular.

MOTION PICTURES

An attractive and outstanding characteristic of most African Negroes is their delight in being amused and in finding distraction from the monotony of their lives. Motion pictures have done a great deal to fill this need, especially since World War II, although naturally they are still confined to cities and towns and the relatively few villages where electricity is available. Experience has shown that the productions that rural and small-town African audiences seem to like best are American comedies or Wild West films. The entire audience usually talks, laughs and shouts throughout the showing of a film. Documentary films, no matter how expertly made or even how related to African everyday concerns, find very little favor with them, and animated cartoons of the Disney type, surprisingly, leave the Africans cold.

During the five years 1947–52, motion-picture audiences in F.W.A. trebled in size, and between 1947 and 1954, movie houses—almost all of which are outdoor affairs, because of the climate—increased in number from 40 to 110. More recent data are not available, but it is certain that both attendance and projection facilities have greatly increased during the past few years in most of the eight countries of the former federation.

Health Services

Turning to the problem of health and medical care—both curative and preventive—in former F.W.A., it is evident that the eight new states which have been granted their independence there have at the same time received a precious tangible gift from France. This gift consists of a great medical network of modern hospitals, mobile health clinics, research and serum-producing laboratories, maternity centers, and trained doctors, medical assistants, midwives and other medical personnel. F.W.A.'s public-health organization was created for the most part in the 15 years between the end of World War II and the birth of the new nations. Its beginnings, however, go back at least a half-century to the time when the French conquest of the West African colonies was being completed.

The army doctors who came in with the French troops were the pioneers of public-health work in the colonies. They and their successors established two of its basic principles—that medical treatment in F.W.A. be free of charge and that the health services should concentrate on sanitary and preventive measures. The Africans still receive free medical care, but the health services and Pasteur Institutes are now trying by prophylaxis and hygiene measures to control and eradicate diseases as well as to prevent their spread.

Treating without charge all the Africans who came to them for medical examination, the French army doctors of the early 1900's found themselves both overwhelmed with patients and unable to cope with the many and dread diseases, both epidemic and endemic, that were decimating West Africa. They therefore began to stress sanitation and prevention, special attention being given to maternal and child welfare. Many of these doctors were transferred to Europe during World War I, so that after 1914 the work of the health services was seriously hampered. A step to remedy this was taken in 1918, with the founding of a medical school at Dakar. For many years that school trained African doctors (who were also called "junior doctors"), pharmacists, nurses and midwives, totaling about 90 a year. The Africans who underwent medical training there have made outstanding contributions to the health of the population. Dakar University (of which the medical school has become a part) is now able to graduate full-fledged African doctors whose degrees are accepted as the equivalent of those conferred by French universities. However, to this day the vast majority of fully trained doctors and surgeons in former F.W.A. are army

A village boy of Upper Volta guides two blind men, victims of "river blindness," a disease spread by a black fly.

officers, many of whom, since the withdrawal of French armed forces as required by most of the new governments, are working under contract with those governments.

MOBILE HEALTH CLINICS

For many years the health services offered medical care only at fixed centers located in the cities and towns, but finally it was realized that no more than a small part of the population could be reached in this way. In 1934, the first mobile medical clinics were created at Ouagadougou in Upper Volta, by an army doctor who formed such teams to track down and treat sleeping sickness in the rural districts of the territory. These were so successful in reaching the scattered peasant population that mobile units were put into action to deal with many other endemic diseases, such as leprosy, malaria, bilharzia, yaws and syphilis.

Although the mobile units have brought to light many cases and have made heroic efforts to bring these diseases under control if not to eradicate them, their success has been uneven, partly because the cooperation of the Africans as to hygiene and treatment has been often inadequate. Cautious hope has been expressed for the eventual eradication of venereal diseases in F.W.A., but the elimination of leprosy— of which 500,000 cases have been diagnosed in the eight countries—appears to be far off. Smallpox, too, although its incidence has been reduced, is giving way very slowly, mainly because of the human factor—failure to appear for vaccination, improper vaccination techniques, or lack of follow-through. Malaria—responsible for 15 per cent of infant mortality besides many deaths and much incapacity among adults —is also evading control, partly because the anopheles mosquito has developed resistance to most known insecticides. On the credit side, such epidemic diseases as yellow fever, plague and cholera have been almost wiped out. And sleeping sickness has been largely brought under control: by the end of 1957, 450,000 victims of this disease in F.W.A. had been treated, and more than 300,000 had been cured.

Besides the many mobile clinics, each of the eight countries of former F.W.A. has at least one up-to-date hospital in its capital, and there are medical posts in all the main territorial centers. Scattered throughout the countryside are dispensaries, which, like the mobile units, send cases they are not equipped to treat to the medical posts or to the big hospitals in the capitals.

THE PASTEUR INSTITUTES

A tremendous contribution to the health and welfare of the West African and also Central African peoples has been made over the years by the Pasteur Institutes of Dakar (Sene-

gal) and Kindia (Guinea), which are branches of the famous
Institute at Paris. The work of the Dakar laboratory dates
back to 1896 and the Kindia one to 1924.

Both the Dakar and the Kindia Institute carry on far-
ranging research with regard to tropical diseases of men and
animals and prepare serums and vaccines for use throughout
West Africa. The Dakar Institute has earned a wide fame for
developing the most effective technique of yellow-fever inocu-
lation, and the yellow-fever serum made there is regularly
distributed in F.W.A. and is also sent to former French
Equatorial Africa, Cameroun, France, and some foreign countries. In addition to research and serum-manufacture, the
Kindia Institute provides monkeys, especially chimpanzees, for
research laboratories in France and also supplies all of West
and Equatorial Africa with antivenin made from the venom
of various poisonous snakes kept in captivity for this purpose.

MISSION MEDICAL WORK

In the medical field, the Catholic missions, and to some
extent the Protestant ones, have made a contribution to African welfare which, though much less extensive than that of
the public-health services, has been appreciable. Three of the
Catholic orders—the Fathers of the Holy Spirit, the Society of
Missionaries of Africa (the famous White Fathers) and the
African Mission of Lyon—soon after World War II were
operating 70 dispensaries in F.W.A., which together were
giving roughly 1,750,000 consultations a year. Most of the
medical work of the missions has been concerned with treating cases of leprosy.

PROSPECTS FOR DISEASE-CONTROL

As mentioned earlier, the new governments of former
F.W.A. have inherited the equipment and techniques, as well

as numerous personnel, with which to fight and perhaps in time wipe out many of the diseases that take such a heavy toll among their peoples. Most of the new states are also assured of the continued financial and technical cooperation of France and such international agencies as the World Health Organization. It remains to be seen whether they will continue the work that has been so well begun or whether the progress that has been made in curing and preventing disease in West Africa will suffer a setback.

A step in the right direction seems to have been taken by many of the new nations of F.W.A., on the international level, by the formation in April 1960 of an Organization of Cooperation and Coordination for the Fight against Great Epidemic Diseases. The members of this organization are Ivory Coast, Dahomey, Upper Volta, Mali Republic, Mauritania, Niger and Senegal—in other words, all of the former F.W.A. countries except Guinea.

Arts and Crafts

No portrayal of Africa's peoples, particularly its Negroes, should be concluded without at least some comment on their arts and crafts, which are deeply rooted in the traditions and daily life of even the most primitive of them.

Specialists on Africa, especially in the field of ethnology, have long argued among themselves as to whether the masks, statuettes, ornaments and other objects of wood, ivory, gold or bronze which have been produced by Africans are "artistic" in the conventional Western sense of the word—that is, whether they have been made by artists consciously aiming to create objects that will be "decorative" or "beautiful" in conformity with their aesthetic standards.

However, it should be emphasized that the creation of the

best African Negro art has most often not been motivated by the need or the desire to produce an object intended for decoration but for a specific use, either in religious ceremonies or in ordinary everyday activities.

Most of the masks and statuettes that are now eagerly sought by collectors of primitive art were originally destined to be used in animist rites or dances or in connection with the worship of the ancestors, or occasionally as offerings to rulers. The artist whose hands formed these pieces did not consciously aim to produce something beautiful. What he was aiming at was the representation of an idea, bound and regulated by the conventions of tribal custom and religion. The influence of these conventions can be seen in the exaggeration of eyes, lips, nose or other features in masks, or in the symbols used in decorating them, or in physical distortion in statuettes, such as over-long torsos, short legs, relatively huge heads and arms held rigidly against the body. Their beauty, when it exists, is thus a by-product of the artist's sensitivity to rhythm and form and line, which is instinctive and often sure. Masks, statuettes and similar ritual objects are as a rule jealously and fearfully reserved by Africans for ceremonial use. Only if they lose their magical properties are they regarded with indifference and either thrown away or allowed to pass into the hands of strangers to the tribe.

Because of the destructive effects of the African environment on such substances as wood, iron and textiles, very few examples of older West African Negro art have survived. Almost all pieces now in existence that were produced in that region are less than 100 years old. However, a number of bronze, stone and pottery masks, statuettes, and articles such as bowls and pitchers intended for religious use, dating back some hundreds of years, have been found. Among the best known and most prized of these are the bronze and ivory masks and statuettes of the old kingdom of Benin (now part of Nigeria). Many of these were made in the fifteenth and sixteenth centuries, and examples of them form prized parts of the African collections of certain museums in Europe and the United States.

In more recent times, the outstanding artists of former F.W.A.'s Negro tribes have been those of the Baoulés of Ivory Coast, the Bambaras of Soudan (Mali Republic), and the Fons of Dahomey, although other tribes also have produced much fine work. The Baoulés, who create masks, statuettes and other pieces for animist ceremonial use, are noted as well for their carved-ivory bracelets, necklaces and the like, and for the strikingly beautiful gold ornaments (many in the form of miniature masks) which they make by casting gold, using the ancient method called *cire perdue*. The distinctive products of the Bambara wood-carvers are the tall head ornaments worn by masked dancers. These carvings, inspired by the graceful head and upswept horns of the antelope, are fertility symbols connected with the worship of the earth and of natural forces.

Among the animist Fons (Dahomeyans), much of the output of forged iron, cast brass and decorated pottery consists of objects used in fetishist ceremonies and observances. Although the art of wood-carving is tending to die out in Dahomey, there is still a considerable production of striking painted masks intended for fetishist uses, and a few wood-carvers—said to belong to only one family—still turn out unique furniture handsomely carved from solid blocks of *iroko* wood. Such furniture was formerly made by private wood-carvers employed by the Abomey kings, and its use was reserved to the kings and their courtiers. More recently, however, the few available pieces could be bought. Some years ago, the royal palace of Abomey became a museum,

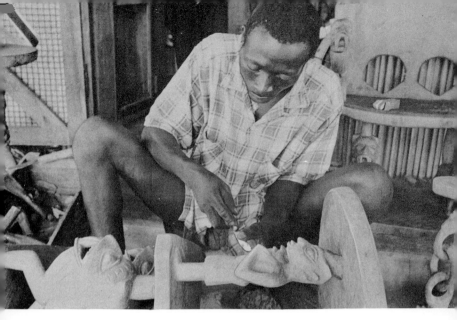

An artisan of Abomey carving a table from a solid block of iroko *wood. This is a dying craft, now carried on by a single family.*

and it contains many striking examples of Fon arts and crafts.

Although French administrators made considerable efforts in certain regions of F.W.A. to encourage African artists and craftsmen to continue producing work of high quality, economic and other pressures have undoubtedly caused a decline from former standards. The reduction of the powers and revenues of the chiefs has forced these local art patrons to reduce or discontinue their support of artists and craftsmen. The advance of Islam is gradually submerging animist observances along with their colorful array of masks and statuettes, and in Islamized communities the artist has little outlet for his talents because of Muslim prohibitions against representation of living things. And the growing demand by undiscriminating souvenir collectors has inevitably spurred the wholesale output of inferior masks, statuettes and other articles for sale either by the makers or by itinerant Hausa traders, or for export. It is to be hoped that the new African governments, which are keenly conscious of their heritage of African culture, will attempt to reverse this trend.

Life in the Past

In ancient times, before the coming of the Arab invaders from the east and later, of European traders, sub-Saharan West Africa was almost totally isolated from the rest of the world. Such scanty contacts as existed were those made by nomadic Berber traders from North Africa with the Negro tribes of the northern sudanese zone. It was not until the Arab invasions, which began in the seventh century, that the historical period of the region later known as French West Africa can be said to have begun. These campaigns to convert the pagan Negroes to Islam and to capture gold and slaves continued until the eleventh century. From that time on, the Arabs devoted their warlike energies mainly to the conquest of Spain, and the Islamic penetration of sub-Saharan West Africa was carried on by converted Negro empire-builders and holy men (*marabouts*).

Several centuries before the earliest Arab invaders appeared in West Africa, the first of that region's ancient "empires," Ghana, was founded by a tribe of Berbers, a white people of North Africa. Ghana fell successively under the domination of a Negro tribe and that of the Muslim Almoravides, an Arab religious group founded in Senegal in the eleventh century. In the thirteenth century, it was succeeded by another Negro "empire," called Mali. After a relatively short existence, this powerful and wealthy state declined, and by the end of the fifteenth cenury almost all of its territory had been taken over by the third and last of the great West African states of the pre-European era—the Songhaï empire. This "empire" was also short-lived, for before the end of the sixteenth century it had been conquered by a Moroccan army.

From the seventeenth century to the nineteenth, there rose and fell in the western sudanese zone such minor kingdoms as the Bambara states and the Peul kingdom, which controlled relatively limited areas in the Niger River valley. The Peul kingdom, which for 400 years after its founding in 1400 A.D. was a vassal state, enjoyed only a few years of real power after its defeat of the Bambara king of Ségou in 1810. It was overthrown in 1862 by El Hadj Omar, a Muslim conqueror from central Senegal who belonged to the Tukulor tribe. Then, beginning in 1872 and for nearly 30 years, West Africa was plagued by the slave raids and devastation caused by a notorious Sarakolé conqueror, Samory, grandfather of President Sékou Touré of Guinea.

In French West Africa's eastern sudanese zone and Guinea Gulf region, respectively, arose the Mossi kingdoms of Upper Volta and the kingdom of Dahomey. The Mossi dynasty, whose last remaining shreds of authority will end with the death of the present "emperor," the Moro Naba of Ouagadougou, has a long and interesting history going back to legends about its founding in the eleventh century. And the able but cruel rulers of the Dahomey kingdom, the origins of which are traced to the twelfth or thirteenth century, wielded great power over the southern tribes of that country until they were overthrown by a French army in 1892.

Before the Dawn of History

For thousands of years, until the Arabian Bedouins, who had already invaded North Africa from east of the Red Sea, began to invade and pillage the sahel and sudanese zones of sub-Saharan Africa 12 centuries ago, the Negro tribes there—farmers, fishermen and hunters—had been leading their lives with little or no contact with the world outside. The isolation of the sub-Saharan peoples was caused mainly by the drying up of the vast region which became the Sahara Desert. Conquering peoples such as the Carthaginians and later the Romans did not dare to venture beyond the limits of their North African lands, which were protected by the Atlas Mountains.

Even before the collapse of Roman rule in North Africa in the fifth century, however, the nomadic desert Berbers had been trading with the Negro tribes to the south for at least a century, thanks to the camel. The camel caravan was already a familiar feature of the desert trails in the fourth century, but it was not always a peaceful one for the nomads also used camels in making slave raids on the Negro tribes.

Much of the trading of those days betwen the Berber nomads and the Negroes took the form of what has been called "the silent trade." This curious method of trading, which seems to have been practiced in Africa as long ago as the time of Herodotus (fifth century B.C.), continued through the Middle Ages and as late as the seventeenth century. It involved mostly the barter of sudanese gold (and later, slaves) against salt and manufactured goods such as cloth and beads.

The traditional procedure of the "silent trade" was described by El Yakut, an Arab geographer of the twelfth century. The caravans of the gold-traders from North Africa, bringing cheap goods, especially glass and coral beads, and also salt, went into what is now southeastern Mauritania to Kumbi, the capital of Ghana—a sudanese-zone empire whose history is recounted below. From Kumbi their local agents continued with them southwestward and crossed the Senegal River into the region of its tributary gold-bearing streams called the Bambuk and the Falémé. Large drums were beaten to attract the attention of the Africans, who were described as being naked and living in holes in the ground—which probably were the pits where they dug the gold. However, the Africans never showed themselves so long as the traders were visible, so the latter placed their goods in piles near the river and then moved away out of sight. When they had done this the Africans approached the goods, left some gold beside those they wanted, and then disappeared. The traders returned, and if they were satisfied with the quantity of gold offered, took it and went away after beating their drums again to indicate to the Africans that their offers had been accepted.

The isolation of the tropical-forest zone of the Guinea Gulf and the south Senegal coast continued much longer. In ancient times, the small sailing ships of the Carthaginians and the Romans were discouraged from trying to explore the coast of that region because of the contrary winds that prevailed off the western capes of the continent. Neither did the Arab invaders who appeared later attempt to penetrate the dense and hostile forest from the north. Thus the coastal regions, from Senegal southward and along the Gulf of Benin, did not begin to emerge from obscurity until the Portuguese traders came in their caravels in the fifteenth century.

During the many centuries when it was shielded by the desert and the ocean, Negro civilization apparently underwent comparatively few changes, and even today some Negro tribes are still at a stage of development that must be very similar to what it was at the time when the Pharaohs ruled Egypt several thousand years before the birth of Christ. The new stone (neolithic) age in West Africa drew to a close during the two or three centuries preceding the Christian era as a result of the introduction of iron and of methods of extracting it from ore by white Saharan tribes who were the ancestors of the Berbers. Iron-bearing ores, especially laterite, were abundant in some of the sub-Saharan areas, and stone tools and weapons gradually gave way to iron ones, except in the inaccessible forest zones of the Guinea Gulf region.

At about the same time the horse was introduced into the sahel and northern sudanese zones by Saharan tribes. The camel, however—a later arrival—was the animal that was destined to revolutionize desert transport in West Africa and, in fact, to alter the whole course of history in that region. This bad-tempered but sturdy beast was first brought to North Africa from Arabia during the third century A.D., and it increased greatly in numbers during the next several centuries. In the course of those centuries the nomadic tribes of the desert, especially the Berbers, were able to intensify their raids on the Negro tribes as well as to develop camel-caravan trade with them. Camels were used also by the Arabs in their holy war against the North African lands of the short-lived

Byzantine empire, Rome's successor there, lands which were conquered in the last half of the seventh century. And camels made possible the first Arab invasion of the western Soudan in 734 A.D., when, as described below, Arabs from Morocco attacked the empire of Ghana.

Beginnings of West African History

Although vague and mostly inaccurate details regarding parts of Negro Africa in ancient times have come down to us from the Greek historian Herodotus as well as from the astronomer-geographer Ptolemy, who lived in Alexandria, Egypt, in the second century A.D., the historical period of West Africa south of the Sahara did not really begin until the Arab invasions of the seventh and eighth centuries. These invasions had two aims: to spread the Muslim faith and to obtain gold and captives, who were sold as slaves. The fierce Arab warriors were unable to penetrate the tropical-forest zone, which sheltered elusive animist tribes, but they devastated the sahel and the savannnah. Nevertheless, they also introduced into Negro Africa many worthwhile elements of Arab civilization such as their architecture and written language, as well as new plants, including rice, cotton, sugar cane, and lemon trees. Their commerce also brought to the Negro tribes various goods of the Mediterranean area, such as cloth, copper and brassware and beads, and above all the much-prized salt of the Sahara, which was one of the most valuable burdens carried south by the camels. (At one period, a pound of salt was traded for an ounce of gold.) In exchange for these goods the Arabs obtained the famous gold of the Soudan and also slaves, but it was the Soudan's gold which was the basis of Arab power in the Middle Ages. From the fifteenth century on, when the sudanese gold supply began to dwindle, the traders bargained mainly for slaves, but they dealt also in ivory, ostrich feathers and ebony wood.

The Empire of Ghana

Most of the knowledge we possess regarding West Africa as it was in the Middle Ages was handed down by a few Arab historians, of whom an outstanding one was a Spanish Muslim named El Bekri. His book, *A Description of North Africa,* which was written in 1068 A.D., gives a vivid picture of West African life at that time. In it he tells of the trans-Saharan trade, of sudanese-zone agriculture, and of the rise of the power of the Almoravides, the Islamic sect of warriors described below. El Bekri also gives many details regarding the capital of the Ghana empire, Kumbi, which was attacked and captured by the Almoravides a few years later. Kumbi actually consisted of two towns several miles apart—one was inhabited by Muslims and had 12 mosques, and the other contained the palace of the king, who was an animist, and the houses of his court officials, as well as fetishist temples surrounded by a sacred grove of trees. Although the exact location of Kumbi is not known with certainty, excavations earlier in this century indicate that it was probably in the extreme southeast corner of what is now Mauritania.

The empire of Ghana was founded in the fourth century of the Christian era by a Berber tribe, the Zenagas. (It should be noted that present-day Ghana, formerly the British colony of Gold Coast, does not correspond either geographically or tribally to the old Ghana empire; the modern nation adopted the name of Ghana simply because of its historic fame.) Thanks to the Zenagas' camels, which gave them a military advantage, this empire grew during the next 400 years until it spread from the Atlantic Ocean to the Niger River and from deep in the desert to the country south of the Senegal River, where it controlled the gold-bearing streams called the Falémé and the Bambuk. Sometime during the latter part of the seventh or the early eighth century, power in Ghana passed into the hands of a Negro tribe related to the Sarakolés. In 734 A.D. the Arabs sent a raiding expedition from Morocco against Ghana, mostly in hopes of discovering and capturing the source of its gold. Although the expedition's attack on Ghana failed, it did obtain quantities of the precious metal.

The empire of Ghana reached the peak of its power during the ninth and tenth centuries, and began to break up when the Almoravides under Abubekr ben Omar launched a holy war against it in 1061 A.D. This war ended in 1076, when the Almoravides captured Kumbi and forced the Sarakolé ruler to pay tribute and to become a Muslim. Although the rule of the Almoravides lasted only a relatively short time, the empire steadily disintegrated because of their pillaging and of later raids by the neighboring Sosso and Mandingo tribes in the early part of the thirteenth century. The Mandingos of the empire of Mali finally destroyed Kumbi in 1240 A.D. Another cause of the decline of Ghana and the dispersion of its people seems to have been the drying up of the region and the resulting famine. By the end of the thirteenth century, Ghana no longer existed as a country, and even the remains of its capital had disappeared beneath the sands.

The Almoravides

Ghana was destroyed by the warriors of the Almoravides sect of Muslims, one of the most dynamic and colorful outgrowths of the seventh-century Arab invasion of North Africa. In the eleventh century, Ibn Yacin, a *marabout* of the Lemtuna tribe of Mauritania, founded an Islamic convent on an island in the lower Senegal River, which was the nucleus of this fierce body of warriors. It attracted large numbers of fanatical and turbulent Muslims, who before long found pretexts for attacking Morocco (then called Moghreb al Aksa). By 1063 A.D., the Almoravides had conquered Morocco, from which they soon launched a war against the Christians of Spain. By 1102 A.D., they controlled all of Spain as far north as the Ebro River, which they held for a long time thereafter. But in Africa south of Morocco, they showed little liking or ability for politics and administration. Moreover, they were so weakened by constant war that when their ruler, Abubekr ben Omar, was killed in 1087 A.D. during a revolt in the Adrar region of northern Soudan (now the Mali Republic), the tribes of Soudan succeeded in freeing themselves, and Almoravide rule there quickly came to an end.

The real mission of the Almoravides—and one which had far-reaching effects—was religious conversion. It was they who won over to Islam the sudanese tribes which have furnished, ever since that time, the most zealous Muslim missionaries in that part of Africa—the Tukulors, Sarakolés, Dioulas and Songhaïs.

The Empire of Mali

Ghana's successor was the empire of Mali. Its origins are somewhat obscure but by the mid-fourteenth century it had become as powerful as Ghana had been in its day. Mali's people were the Mandingos, who before the Almoravide period, had been subjects of Ghana. Although the Mandingos were then animists, their chief had by 1050 A.D. been nominally converted to Islam and had made a pilgrimage to Mecca.

A century and a half after the death of the Almoravide ruler of Ghana, the chief of the Mandingos, Sundiata, was able in 1235 A.D. to defeat the Sosso kingdom, which had earlier been conquered by Ghana but which had become independent. Five years later, Sundiata captured and destroyed the capital of Ghana and established his rule over the ruins of that empire, including the gold-producing areas of Gangara and Bambuk.

In time the Mali empire covered all the western sudanese zone from the desert on the north to the tropical forest on the south, and from the country of the Tukulors in the west to the lands of the Songhaïs and the Mossi in the east. In the fourteenth century, Mali's ruler, Gongo Musa, conquered the Tukulors and the Songhaïs, and during his reign (1307–1332 A.D.) Mali reached the height of its power. It was known throughout Africa, Europe and Asia at that time for the splendor of its court and for its enormous resources of gold. In 1324, Gongo Musa made a sensational pilgrimage to Mecca. His caravan was said to have been preceded by 500 slaves carrying staffs of solid gold, and the Arabs were astounded by the prodigality with which he gave alms. During Gongo Musa's reign, Islamic conversion of the sudanese tribes reached its most active phase since the holy war of the Almoravides some 250 years earlier.

The Mali empire began to decline in the last decades of the fourteenth century, and as time went on, it was torn by the quarrels of rival princes and by revolts of the tributary tribes, especially the Songhaïs. By the beginning of the sixteenth century it had already lost most of the lands that had been conquered by Gongo Musa, and though the "empire" survived in reduced form until the seventeenth century, power over the Soudan had long since passed into the hands of the Songhaïs.

The Songhaï Empire

At the end of the ninth century the Songhaïs had come from the region of the town of Ansongo in the central Niger River Valley and settled around Gao, in what is now the Mali Republic. There they built up a thriving caravan trade with the North African Berbers and with Negro tribes to the south. As already mentioned, they fell under the rule of the Mali (Mandingo) empire in the early 1300's, but in 1465, under the leadership of their prince, Sonni Ali, they revolted against the Mandingos. In 1468, Sonni Ali captured and pillaged Timbuktu—then a center of Muslim learning as well as of the caravan trade—and a few years later captured the old city of Djenné, also famous for its scholars and commercial activity. Soon he had brought the whole Macina region of the Niger Valley under his control. Although Sonni Ali was a Muslim, he is said to have been a brutal conqueror and to have shown little mercy to the learned Muslims of Timbuktu, many of whom were massacred. Besides controlling much of the middle region of the Niger River valley, he pushed his conquests westward as far as Walata in eastern Mauritania.

After Sonni Ali's death in 1492 there began at Gao a new Songhaï dynasty, that of the Askia kings, who were pious Muslims and who ruled over the Songhaï empire for a century. The first Askia king, Mamadou Touré—better known as Askia Mohammed—reigned for 35 years and was the most outstanding of the Songhaï princes. He made great efforts to promote Islamic literature and learning and to bring prosperity to his kingdom. Like the Mali emperor Gongo Musa a century and a half earlier, Askia Mohammed made a pilgrimage to Mecca in 1495 accompanied by a brilliant court, and was lavish in giving alms. Legend has it that he gave away 300,000 gold-pieces for pious works in the holy city.

The tomb of the Askia rulers of the old Songhaï empire, at Gao, Mali. It is now also used as a mosque.

The Askia kings who succeeded him were much less able than he, and when in 1590 the Sultan of Morocco—envious of the Songhaïs' valuable salt mines and gold holdings—sent an army equipped with firearms across the desert, the Askia empire soon collapsed. Although fewer than 1,000 of this 3,000-man army survived the crossing of the desert, their firearms plus the element of surprise overwhelmed the Songhaïs. Within a year the Moroccan army, many of whom were Spanish renegades, had taken Timbuktu. They occupied that city, as well as Gao and Djenné, for nearly 70 years, until 1660, during which time the Songhaï lands were ruled by a governor sent by Morocco's Sultan.

From the mid-seventeenth to the mid-eighteenth century there was a period of anarchy and of defiance of the Sultan's authority by the Spanish-Moroccan adventurers whose center was Timbuktu. This ended when the last of these minor tyrants were wiped out at Timbuktu by the Tuareg. By 1780, most of the lands of the old Songhaï empire had passed under the control of pagan chiefs—the Peul king of Macina and the Bambara king of Ségou.

Lesser Sudanese-Zone Kingdoms

The era of most aggressive Islamic conversion of the sudanese Negroes came to an end with the collapse of the empires of Mali and Songhaï. Muslim missionary activity experienced a setback because of the prosperity that developed among such animist tribes as the Mossi, the Dogon and the Sérères and because of the rise of several new non-Muslim states.

Two of these new states were created in the mid-seventeenth century by the Bambara tribe. One had its center at Ségou on the Niger River in central Soudan (Mali Republic) and the other, called Kaarta, farther west. The life of the Bambara kingdoms was comparatively short, however, and they never controlled such vast areas as those covered by the Negro empires of the Middle Ages.

As for the Peul kingdom of the Niger's Macina region, it was no more than a vassal state for four centuries, beginning in 1400 A.D., when its dynasty of the Diallo family was founded. This kingdom paid tribute successively to the Mali and Songhaï empires for 200 years; then, beginning in 1591, it became a vassal of the Moroccan *pashas* (governors) of Timbuktu; and after 1670 it paid tribute for more than a century to the Bambara kings of Ségou. During all that time the Peuls of Macina, who were animists, were regarded as oppressors of the Muslim Negroes of their region, pillaging their towns and forcing them to pay tribute. These Muslims finally united, in about 1810, under the leadership of a Peul *marabout,* Hamadou Bari, and they defeated an army sent by the Bambara king of Ségou, to whom the chief of the pagan Peuls had appealed for help. Hamadou Bari then proclaimed the independence of the Macina, thus ending Bambara rule there. Hamadou then set out to make some conquests, captured Djenné and Timbuktu, and before he died in 1844, organized his country thoroughly. In 1862, his grandson— who had allied himself with Hamadou's former adversaries, the Bambaras of Ségou—had to fight the army of El Hadj Omar, the Tukulor conqueror, and was defeated. Until the French troops arrived in the Macina region in 1893, the former Peul kingdom remained under the domination of the Tukulors.

The Exploits of El Hadj Omar

El Hadj Omar's career as a fanatical Muslim conqueror, though it lasted less than 15 years, was colorful. Omar Tal (his name until he made the Mecca pilgrimage in 1820 and thus was entitled to call himself El Hadj) was born in 1797 to a Tukulor family of the Senegal valley, near the town of Podor. After 18 years at Mecca, he returned to his country with a great reputation for learning and piety, and a few years later settled, as a *marabout* of the Tidjaniya sect of Muslims, in north-central Guinea.

In much the same way as the Almoravide warrior sect had grown up in Senegal many centuries before, El Hadj Omar's disciples soon became so numerous that he was able to form a powerful army and in about 1850 to proclaim a holy war against the Mandingo and Bambara infidels. After capturing the Bambara capital of Nioro in 1854, his army moved southwestward to attack the Senegal province of Khasso, then a French protectorate. Khasso's capital, Medina, was defended by a small garrison made up of some 50 French and Negro soldiers, who for four months were able to resist the assaults of El Hadj Omar's 25,000 Tukulors. They were rescued by French troops under General Faidherbe, who forced the besiegers to withdraw. After another unsuccessful attempt against a French post—Matam on the Senegal River—El Hadj Omar resumed his campaign against the pagan Bambaras and Peuls of the Niger Valley region. He captured Ségou in 1861 and the Macina region in 1862, but the Peuls did not surrender, and they continued to fight him. He died near Bandiagara in the central Soudan in 1864. However, as mentioned earlier, his Tukulors kept their grip on the Macina region until they were subjugated by the French in 1893.

The Last African Slaver: Samory

During the latter part of the nineteenth century, after El Hadj Omar disappeared from the scene, many regions of F.W.A. were devastated by the wars and raids of the last of its slave-hunters, a Muslim named Samory.

Samory was born in about 1830 to a poor Sarakolé family in upper Guinea. As soon as he was grown he seems to have acquired a taste for pillaging as a member of a bandit gang of his region. By the time he was 35 or 40 he had recruited a band of followers, and then captured Sanankoro, his birthplace, of which he named himself "king" in 1872. As his power increased, he extended his raiding activities to the north and west of the Niger River, where, from 1880 on, he met with increasing opposition by French army units which were progressively occupying the Niger Valley. About this time, despite the fact that he could scarcely read the Arabic language, he assumed the title of Imam (or Almamy), usually applied only to scholarly religious chiefs. Until 1898, when he was finally captured, clashes continued between his followers and the French.

Samory showed considerable ability as an organizer, both of the administration of lands he conquered and of his army, but these talents were overshadowed by his cruelty and by his complete devastation of the regions through which he passed during his raids. Above all, his reputation as a dealer in slaves of his own race has not yet been forgotten in West Africa, even though West African nationalism—especially in Guinea, whose president, Sékou Touré, is Samory's grandson—has in the past few years prompted efforts to refurbish his reputation.

The Mossi Kingdoms

As told above, the central and western sudanese zone of F.W.A. for many centuries was dominated successively, and for brief periods simultaneously, by the empires of Ghana, Mali and Songhaï, and during part of the nineteenth century was scourged by the followers of the Muslim conquerors El Hadj Omar and Samory. Near the beginning of the eleventh century, when Ghana was still powerful, the eastern part of the sudanese zone saw the birth of certain less powerful kingdoms that deserve attention, partly because of their outstanding political, military and economic organization and partly because they have continued to exist, in the same region and in name at least, until our own day. These are the Mossi kingdoms of what is now the Upper Volta Republic. (An account of the present-day Mossi tribe and its chiefs, the three Nabas, is given in Chapter II, pages 44–46.)

A romantic legend surrounds the founding of the Mossi dynasty. Early in the eleventh century, a king of the northern Gold Coast region led pillaging expeditions into nearby areas,

The Moro Naba, "Emperor of the Mossi," of Upper
Volta, at his wedding to his second wife, a young
Paris-educated Moro.

including the vicinity of Tenkodogo in southeastern Upper
Volta. One of his warrior groups was under the command of
his daughter, Yennenga, who one day rode deep into the
forest. There she met a young hunter, Riare, married him,
and in time bore a son. In honor of the horse that his mother
was riding when she met the hunter, this son was given the
name Wedraogo (or Ouedraogo) still current as a family
name in Upper Volta, which means "stallion." Yennenga
and her family after a few years rejoined her father, and
when Wedraogo grew to manhood he conquered Tenkodogo
and the region around it, some of whose inhabitants were
expelled and many of whom were absorbed by the conquering
tribe.

The Mossi, who later became a huge tribe, grew out of this

mixture of human elements, among them a tribal group called the Nyonyosé. The latter are still regarded by the Mossi as the original owners of the land, so that one of their descendants invariably holds the high position of Master of the Land in the Moro Naba's court, where he sits next to the emperor.

After the Tenkodogo kingdom became firmly established, it extended its rule northwestward, absorbing the regions of Ouagadougou and Yatenga, which in time became separate Mossi kingdoms. In the fourteenth and fifteenth centuries the Mossi attempted to conquer parts of the Niger River valley to the west, but were defeated and each time had to retreat to their own country. At the end of the fifteenth century King Askia Mohammed of Gao declared a holy war against the Yatenga Naba, and his Songhaï warriors pillaged the Mossi country in 1497–98. This war dragged on for half a century until the Songhaï empire finally collapsed.

Since their unsuccessful expansionist moves of the fifteenth century, the Mossi have been content to remain peaceably in their three kingdoms of Ouagadougou, Yatenga and Tenkodogo. For over 400 years they have kept mostly unchanged their tribal identity, their ancestral territories, their kingly institutions and their customs. The mass of the people have long been resistant to outside influences, including Islam, and their obscure history during the several centuries preceding the arrival of the French seems to have been concerned primarily with maintaining the economy of their kingdoms, which have long had too large a population for their poor lands and meager resources.

The Kingdom of Dahomey

In striking contrast to the dispersion and anarchism of almost all other tribal groups of the equatorial zone of F.W.A. was the strongly organized kingdom of Dahomey, whose first ruler, Dako, reigned from 1625 to 1650 A.D.

The origins of the Dahomey kingdom, also known as the kingdom of Abomey after its capital, go back to a much earlier period, somewhere in the twelfth or thirteenth century. At that time the Adja tribe founded a little kingdom called Ardra, near the coast. The town of Allada, its capital, still exists. (It should be noted that the Fon tribe of the present day are closely related to the Adjas.)

As a result of quarrels among members of the Adja royal family, some of them left Allada and established chiefdoms at Porto Novo on the coast and in the area north of Abomey, but they remained in contact with the Allada court and continued until the sixteenth century to acknowledge its sovereignty. This situation changed, however, at the end of the sixteenth century, when European slave-traders began to come in numbers to the coast of the Dahomey region, which soon acquired the unhappy name of the Slave Coast. The slave trade was so profitable that each of the Adja chiefdoms began acting like an independent state and no longer regarded itself as tributary to Allada. The Abomey chiefdom—which had become the kingdom of Dahomey under Dako in 1625 as mentioned above, soon dominated all the surrounding area, but its rivalry with the Porto Novo kingdom continued. Dako's successors carried forward his work of enlarging the Abomey realm, which was rounded out by the conquest of Ardra in 1727, and shortly thereafter, by the occupation of Savi, just north of the coastal town of Ouidah where the Portuguese had built a fort in the sixteenth century.

The Dahomey kingdom fell on evil days from 1738 until Ghézo came to the throne in 1818. First it was invaded by the Yorubas from the east, who captured Abomey in 1738 and demanded annual tribute, which they continued to exact until the mid-nineteenth century. The kings who reigned from 1775 to 1797 were unable to shake off the Yorubas, and the country was troubled by other attacks from outside and by revolts. From 1797 until Ghézo became king in 1818, his elder brother acted as regent, but committed such atrocities against his own people that he was finally poisoned and all his descendants were killed.

Shocking stories of the cruelty of most of the Dahomey kings have come down to us. They were greatly addicted to human sacrifices and showed no mercy toward captives, including their chiefs. Still displayed in the museum of Abomey are the thrones of a number of the kings which are mounted on the skulls of slaughtered enemy chiefs. Tradition has it that the dark-red walls of the palace of Abomey were built of mud-brick made by mixing the clayey laterite soil with the blood of captives.

As a ruler Ghézo showed remarkable ability, and during his long reign of 40 years he made Dahomey a powerful state. He restored internal order and built up a large army, which included a famous corps of Amazons whose exploits in war furnished the story of a dance still performed by women of the court of Abomey. Toward the end of his reign, Ghézo defeated the Yorubas, who from that time on were no longer paid the annual tribute. Meanwhile, being a good administrator, he provided Dahomey with an efficient state organization copied from those of the European nations. And it was during his reign that activity in the arts and crafts reached its highest level.

Beginning in 1727, the power of the Dahomey kings and the prosperity of their courts were based to a large extent, unfortunately, on the slave trade. This continued until after the middle of the nineteenth century despite the international agreement of 1815 banning the slave trade. Ghézo, thanks to the raiding expeditions of his army into the interior, was continuously provided with great numbers of captives which he sold profitably to European slave-dealers on the coast. This grim record of the Dahomey kings is only slightly offset by the fact that they laid the foundations of their country's outstanding economic resource—its oil-palm groves. This tree was introduced into the Slave Coast in the fifteenth century by Portuguese navigators who brought it from Indonesia. To cultivate it, the forest had to be cleared away, and this process went on for several centuries under the encouragement of the kings, so that Dahomey's equatorial zone now has only thin patches of what was once forest. But the oil yielded by the kernels gathered from the palm groves has continued to this day to be Dahomey's principal asset in its foreign trade.

The "Dance of the Amazons," performed by the young women of the court of Abomey. It enacts a legend of Amazon defeat of the king's enemies.

Ghézo's successors on the throne of Abomey were handicapped not only because they lacked his ability but also because they were compelled to deal with strong external forces, especially the French. Gléglé, who reigned from Ghézo's death in 1858 until 1889, experienced difficulties with both his neighbors and the French. Béhanzin, who followed him on the throne, began hostile actions against the French establishment at Ouidah on the coast. In 1892 a French army was sent against him and was about to capture Abomey when Béhanzin set the town afire and went into hiding. Before doing so, he transferred his powers to Ago li-Agbo, who reigned from 1893 to 1900 and was the last king of Dahomey. Thereafter the French, who for several years had been in control of the region, placed some administrative duties in the hands of descendants of the royal line, who were named chiefs of cantons.

The Emergence of
French West Africa

France's relations with West Africa from the middle of
the sixteenth century until the end of the nineteenth
can be divided into two principal phases. The first and longer
of these was commercial in character. It was concerned chiefly
with the promotion of French trade along the coastal areas of
West Africa and with the slave traffic which provided
laborers for the French West Indian islands and the American
continent. This phase lasted from 1564 until slavery was
abolished in the French possessions in 1848.

The second phase, that of colonial expansion, began in the
mid-nineteenth century. This turning point was marked by
the first large-scale efforts of European nations to acquire

colonial possessions in Africa. During the half-century that followed, European competition to win territories in Africa grew steadily keener. By 1900 all of West Africa south of the Sahara, except Liberia, had been brought under the colonial rule of one or another West European power— France, Great Britain, Germany, Portugal and Spain. Holland, an early contender, had been eliminated from the race long before.

French penetration of West Africa in this period took place along two main geographic lines. The first of these was from west to east, and it began with the establishing of trading posts in the Senegal Valley and later the Upper Niger valley region as far eastward as Lake Chad. The second was along the coasts of Senegal and the Guinea Gulf regions, where French military as well as trading posts were founded and where French protectorates later were set up, usually by treaty arrangements with local chiefs.

For a number of years the difficulty of crossing the forest zone lying inland for hundreds of miles, with its jungles and hostile tribes, prevented links from forming between the French on the coast and those in the sudanese zone to the north. It was not until 1889 that a French expedition from Soudan, after a voyage of two years by way of the Niger, Volta and Comoë rivers, reached the Guinea Gulf in Ivory Coast.

In 1895, the French government established an over-all administration for the French colonies in West Africa: the Government-General, with headquarters at Dakar in Senegal. This was the forerunner of the federation of West Africa, which was to last for more than 60 years. At first the powers of the Government-General were very limited, but its centralized control over the various colonial administrations was strengthened by later decrees from Paris.

The nineteenth century brought greater changes to West Africa (and to Africa in general) than any other comparable period in the past. Almost all of Negro Africa fell under the control of European nations and until very recently did not enjoy political independence. But it must be remembered that for centuries the Negro tribes had been plagued by anarchy. They had been oppressed and slaughtered by local despots, decimated by Arab and Negro slave raiders and tormented by almost incessant tribal warfare. The conquest and partition of West Africa by Europeans were undeniably marked by misdeeds, but it is hard not to conclude that the long-run benefits of pacification outweighed its abuses. Above all, the security and other advantages, such as education and health measures, that European rule brought to the African peoples made possible the evolution of their countries toward independence and the nationhood which almost all of them have now achieved.

Early Exploration and Trade

It was by sea—not overland from the Mediterranean, across the perilous desert—that Europeans made their earliest contacts with West Africa. And the first who really explored the African coast, beginning about the year 1400, were the Portuguese in their caravels—the same type of ship as those in which Columbus and his men sailed to the New World near the end of that century. Until 1460, Prince Henry of Portugal, known as "the Navigator," held a monopoly of the African coastal trade in which ships of his countrymen were engaged. Before the end of the fifteenth century, their captains had charted some 5,000 miles of African coastline and rivers as

far as the eastern Guinea Gulf and the lower reaches of the
Congo River. Portuguese mariners pushed far to the south
and east of the continent and were the first to round the Cape
of Good Hope, in 1487. Within a few years thereafter, Vasco
da Gama had extended Portuguese influence to the East
African coast as far as Mozambique, Zanzibar and Mombasa,
and by 1505 all these places had passed from Arab control to
Portuguese dominance. Although Mozambique is still ruled
by Portugal, Mombasa was recaptured by the Sultan of Muscat
(Arabia) in 1727, and the Portuguese soon also lost Zanzibar
to the Arabs.

Inland exploration of Africa by the Portuguese was more
extensive south of the Equator than in West Africa, where
they made few attempts to push into the hinterland and confined themselves mostly to setting up coastal trading posts.
In the seventeenth century they did send one large expedition
from the Guinea Gulf coast northward with the aim of reaching Timbuktu, then a great trading center, a fanatical Islamic
stronghold and a meeting-place for sudanese and Saharan
caravans. The expedition had to turn back, however, long
before nearing that legendary and mysterious city on the edge
of the Sahara Desert.

With the decline of Portuguese wealth and power in the
late sixteenth century, Dutch, English and French merchants
and companies, backed by their governments, began to crowd
the Portuguese traders out of West Africa, and by 1650 the
latter had lost control of all the West African coast north of
the Equator except for the small colony which became known
as Portuguese Guinea, south of the Gambia River. Nevertheless, during the 1600's a few Portuguese missionaries were
still to be found in certain places along the shores of Senegal
and the Guinea Gulf region, and were making converts
among the African tribes there. Later in the seventeenth cen-

tury, Portugal regained a slight political and economic foothold on the Guinea Gulf coast by building a fort on a few acres of ground at Ouidah, a village then controlled by the African kingdom of Abomey. This pocket handkerchief of land remained a Portuguese enclave until it was seized by Dahomey's new African government in 1961.

THE FRENCH TRADERS

The French trailed the Portuguese in African exploration and trade. A Norman sailor-adventurer, Jean de Bethencourt, conquered the Canary Islands about 1405 (although very soon afterward they were lost to the Spaniards of Castille). About the same time he landed on the northern part of the West African coast, probably in what is now Mauritania, where he captured some slaves. This fleeting touch with the continent was not followed up by the French until 1564. From then on, for 50 years, trading ships sent by Norman merchants of Dieppe made frequent voyages to the little port of Rufisque (Senegal) and to Boulombel (now Sierra Leone) and other Guinea Gulf points.

During the reign of Louis XIII (1610–1643), Cardinal Richelieu, Louis XIII's chief minister, became convinced of the necessity of firmly establishing French power not only in Europe but also on the high seas in order to checkmate the strength of Spain in America and the Indian Ocean. Closely tied in with his political aims were economic projects designed to strengthen and enrich France. He had been much impressed with the commercial success of the British chartered East India Company launched by Queen Elizabeth and a similar one formed by Holland, the famous Dutch East India Company.

With the object of promoting French trade with West Africa, as well as with India and other Indian Ocean countries,

Richelieu, in 1633 and later, granted overseas trading monopolies to several private chartered companies. They were called chartered companies because they operated under royal charter. The best-known of these was the powerful French East India Company. Such companies were assisted financially and otherwise by the French monarchs and were allowed to exercise many rights of sovereignty, including fitting out warships, maintaining armies and dealing with local rulers in the king's name. In return, they were expected —aside from their trading activities—only to aid missionary work and colonization and to provide a steady supply of slaves for France's American colonies. The first of these obligations was not fulfilled with nearly as much enthusiasm as the second, for the slave trade soon became the most profitable element in the companies' operations.

Many commercial voyages were made by private French ships to Senegal and Guinea. These vessels carried cloth, firearms, brandy, glassware, household utensils and other goods to be exchanged for slaves, vegetable gum ("gum arabic"), and to some extent such tropical products as pepper, ivory, palm oil and ostrich plumes. Very soon the trade in slaves overshadowed all the rest, although the gum trade continued to be important and was the cause of troubles with the Moors—who tried to control it—and of international incidents involving the French with English and other competitors.

It was in 1638 that the first French trading post was established in Senegal, at the mouth of the Senegal River. In return for the regular payment of fees called *coutumes* (literally, customs), local chiefs granted French traders the right to establish and maintain such trading posts. These posts were actually forts protected by stockades and flew the French flag.

Before Cardinal Richelieu had chartered the private companies, and without royal support at the time, a group of merchants in the northern French cities of Dieppe and Rouen had formed in 1626 an enterprise to carry on trade with West Africa that came to be known as the Norman Company. In 1633, Richelieu granted it a ten-year monopoly of French commerce on the Senegal and Gambia rivers and Cap Vert. However, Richelieu's successor, Cardinal Mazarin, who from 1643 to 1661 was prime minister of the Queen Regent, Anne of Austria, was too preoccupied with European politics to give much thought to promoting overseas ventures. But after Louis XIV took up the reins of government in 1661, his finance minister and navy secretary, Colbert, adopted a colonial policy similar to Richelieu's. He felt that the king's political power must be reinforced by profitable trade ventures overseas. Therefore, while carrying on a war with Holland in Europe, he gave strong support to French commerce with Senegal in an effort to oust the Dutch, who had maintained garrisons at Gorée and two lesser coastal points since 1629. Under Louis XIV and Louis XV, charters were granted to a series of companies—12 in all—similar to the pioneering Norman Company. These included the Cap Vert Company in 1658, the West Indies Company in 1664, the Africa Company in 1679, the Senegal–Guinea Coast–Africa Company in 1681, and the Royal Company of Senegal in 1696.

Soon after 1763, when France lost almost all its overseas possessions in North America and India as a result of the Peace of Paris ending the French and Indian War (Seven Years' War), the last of the French chartered companies was dissolved. Rightly or wrongly these so-called "privileged" companies were blamed in part for the loss of India and Canada. They were charged with having involved France in disastrous and expensive military ventures, and were also criticized for being almost always insolvent. Philosophers and economists of the period condemned them as infringing on the rights of the people and retarding economic progress. The Duc de Choiseul, Louis XV's prime minister at the time, decided that the government must take direct control of France's colonies, and he therefore put an end to the practice of granting charters to private companies.

Compared with the brilliant accomplishments—political as well as commercial—of the great East India companies sponsored by England, Holland and France, none of the French chartered companies operating in West Africa was properly financed, well managed or durable. Nevertheless, they made huge profits in the slave trade, and this trade throughout a long period was a key element in royal policy and a main cause of the almost incessant warfare between France and England for many decades, during which their African and various other overseas possessions changed hands repeatedly.

The French in Senegal

In the early history of French relations with West Africa, two dates stand out as especially important. One is 1659, when the fort of St. Louis-du-Sénégal—named in honor of the "Sun King," Louis XIV—was built by the Norman Company on a coastal sand-bar island at the mouth of the Senegal River. The other is 1677, when the island of Gorée, close to the African village of Dakar on Cap Vert, was captured from the Dutch, who had held it since 1629.

During the nineteenth century, the St. Louis fort served as the starting point for almost all the military expeditions which gradually extended French rule through the Senegal Valley, the Soudan, the upper Niger River valley, and the region east of it as far as Lake Chad. And Gorée, soon after it was taken over by the French, became a naval center and was for 200 years the base of seaborne ventures that carried the French flag to most of the West African coastal regions bordering the Atlantic, south of Cap Vert, and to the Guinea Gulf countries. Gorée also rapidly gained sinister fame as a very active depot from which, when the slave trade was at its height in the eighteenth century, tens of thousands of Africans were shipped to the New World to spend the rest of their lives laboring on plantations.

In the middle of the eighteenth century, through its defeat in the French and Indian War, referred to above, France in 1763 lost to Great Britain not only Canada and India (except for a few small parcels of territory) but all its West African holdings aside from the island and fort of Gorée, and some scattered minor trading posts such as Rufisque near Dakar and Albreda in Gambia, to the south. When the American Revolution compelled Great Britain to send a large part of its army and navy to the Western Hemisphere between 1776 and 1783, France hoped to profit by this to recapture many former overseas possessions, including those in coastal Senegal. But these hopes were doomed to disappointment, for the French were greatly handicapped because of financial and human losses in the French and Indian War of 1754–63, and they were to be still further weakened by their own revolution of 1789 and the help they gave to the American colonists. After the disastrous conflicts with Great Britain in the late eighteenth century and the first years of the nineteenth, the French flag temporarily disappeared from West Africa.

Early in the nineteenth century most of France's West African lands were restored to it by the treaties of 1814 and 1815 which ended the Napoleonic wars. But it was not until 1817 that the English actually turned over these territories to the French. At this time another factor entered the situation. The rise of liberalism in Europe caused a change in French policy with regard to Africa: most important of all, in this respect, was the formal abolition of the slave trade in 1815 by agreement between the Great Powers. With its disappearance, Europe's relationship with Africa entered a new phase.

For over a century Gorée had been a notorious slave depot, and its prosperity had been built on the trade in captive Africans. With the suppression of the slave trade, Gorée lost its chief reason for being. It was overpopulated, with 5,000 inhabitants of whom only 500 were employed, and it had no cultivable soil. While agricultural land and trading opportunities both lay close at hand on the Cap Vert peninsula, the French were unable to install themselves freely on the mainland. Although in centuries past they had not looked on African territory as land to be conquered and absorbed into the empire but simply as a field for private commercial enterprise, with the abolition of the slave trade the situation was altered. This was reflected in schemes involving settlement to which the Africans were usually opposed. Difficulties with the Lebou tribe on the Cap Vert peninsula were a case in point. By a treaty of 1765, the Damel (king) of Cayor—the region of which Cap Vert was a part and in which the Lebous lived—had ceded to the French "in perpetuity" the coastal lands including Cap Vert. But for 40 years after the treaty was signed, the French had made no attempt to take possession of Cap Vert, and meanwhile the Lebous had revolted against the Damel and set up a sort of republic. When the French returned to Gorée in 1817 and tried to assert their rights under the old treaty, the Lebous refused to consider it as binding. Disputes and clashes took place between the French and the Lebous for forty-two years before the French were able to settle peaceably on the peninsula.

Meanwhile, Louis XVIII, who came to the throne in 1815 after the defeat and exile of Napoleon, believed that there was a great future for peaceable agricultural development in the Senegal Valley. Unfortunately, he must have ignored or been misinformed about the hostility of the Moors and certain Negro tribes to such activities by Europeans. Evidently he also failed to take into consideration other serious handicaps, including an exhausting climate, various crippling and killing diseases, and the age-old African customs relating to the ownership and use of land (see pages 65–66).

So Louis XVIII set his prime minister, Baron Portal, to work out the details of his project. Beginning in 1817, Senegal's Governor Schmaltz tried to put Portal's plans into effect by bringing in colonists from France. Some 200 of them were installed on Cap Vert, but this settlement was soon abandoned. A new attempt was then made to found an agricultural colony made up of immigrants from France about 300 miles inland on the south bank of the Senegal River, near Bakel. The Tukulors of this region were paid to permit the use of the land for farming (actually, the French thought they had bought the land). There the colonists planted cotton, coffee, castor plants and indigo—which is used in making blue dye—and Tukulor tribesmen were hired to work on the plantations. But the Africans were unruly, quarrelsome and reluctant to work for the white farmers, and Governor Schmaltz decided to shift the experiment to the Oualo region near St. Louis-du-Sénégal.

In the Oualo, however, the colonists were harassed by raiding Moors from north of the river and suffered greatly from the unhealthy climate and many diseases. To some extent, too, they were handicapped by the opposition of long-time residents of St. Louis and Gorée, mostly small dealers in gum arabic and other African wild produce, who disliked farming and felt that it had no future in the country. In addition, they met with the same labor difficulties as at Bakel, for the Africans of the Oualo were also disinclined to work as hired farm laborers. The plantations produced less and less, and finally, in 1836, the series of unlucky agricultural colonies came to an end.

After the failure of Louis XVIII's farm-colony venture and later similar projects, a small-scale trade in gums was carried on. However, Senegal's economy made little progress for many years except for the gradual increase in the export of peanuts. This promising product had been introduced from the New World, probably by Portuguese slave traders in the seventeenth century. Grown for more than a century by the Africans simply for food, peanuts were destined to become Senegal's most valuable export commodity.

Sobered by the loss of so much of their empire and by the meager financial return from their colonies, the people of France were disillusioned with colonial schemes and unwilling to invest in them. As a result, the money and personnel made available by the Paris government to West Africa were very slight. Moreover, the government issued orders that force must not be used to secure peaceful conditions in Africa. Under these limitations, a number of governors who followed Schmaltz in rapid succession were unable to extend French influence into the interior or even to insure the safety of French posts near the coast, and as time went on, conditions became more and more disturbed.

In 1845 a naval officer, L. E. Bouët-Willaumez, was appointed Governor of Senegal. The new governor, who had already won a reputation through his dealings with Guinea Gulf tribes, soon recommended a course of action which he felt was necessary to deal with the problems the French were facing in Senegal. In his opinion colonization would not be successful until peace was forcibly imposed upon the West African regions. He urged, among other things, that the Moors should be compelled to remain north of the Senegal

River instead of being free to cross it to raid and demand tribute from the Negro tribes of the valley; that the government should subdue and break up the Fouta Toro, a feudal-type African state of north Senegal which had been violently resisting French control; and that France should reduce or even discontinue paying the *coutumes* (customary tribute) which for many years had been demanded by the local chiefs. The Paris government, however, took no action on the governor's recommendations.

In 1848 a revolution overthrew King Louis Philippe, who was succeeded by the "Prince-President" Louis Napoleon. One of that revolution's by-products was a decree outlawing slavery in all French possessions. (Slavery had continued to exist in most of the countries where it had become a social institution because the 1815 treaty had abolished only the international trade in slaves.) The effect of the 1848 decree in Senegal was a worsening of the economic situation, which had already started on the down-grade about 1845. Plantation owners lost the regular labor supply which had been furnished by local chiefs in return for fees. The chiefs had been in the habit of condemning violators of tribal laws to long and even indefinite periods of forced labor (which actually was slavery), and then turning these prisoners over to the colonists. Exports, mostly of peanuts, fell drastically between 1845 and 1850, partly because of the increasing hostility of the Moors and the Tukulors, which made both farming and trading difficult, and partly because of the shrinkage of the labor force after 1848.

Thus, by the mid-nineteenth century colonization attempts had failed in Senegal, and the area was in a disturbed state. However, on another front the French were moving ahead. Contacts with the interior and French knowledge of it had been slowly growing. As early as 1819 a French fort was built at Bakel on the Senegal River. In 1821, two others were built, farther west on the river, at Dagana and Richard-Toll. During these years, Frenchmen were exploring the rivers of south and west Senegal—the Gambia, the Bondou and the Senegal itself. And in 1844–45, a small French force was installed at a point on the Falémé River, in the remote eastern reaches of Senegal.

THE GUINEA GULF REGIONS

As for the Guinea Gulf coast (then usually called the *Rivières du Sud* or Rivers of the South because of the many small streams that emptied into the ocean there), little thought was given before 1838 to the French traders in that part of West Africa or to the desirability of extending French influence into the interior. At the request of these traders, the French government sent Captain Bouët-Willaumez (who later, as mentioned above, became Governor of Senegal) to negotiate with local chiefs. He succeeded in making agreements with the African chiefs of Grand Bassam and Assinie, on the shores of Ivory Coast. These agreements, providing for the establishing of French posts, were not acted upon by the Paris government for several years, however, and it was not until 1843 that a French trading post was built at Assinie. About the same time, Grand Bassam was taken over by the French to forestall the English, who were suspected of planning to do the same thing. Within a few years new agreements of friendship and trading rights, confirming previous ones, were reached with other chiefs of coastal tribes, at Sassandra, Lahou and Fresco (Ivory Coast), and in 1853, a post was installed at Dabou, west of Grand Bassam.

On the coast of Dahomey, early in the eighteenth century, France had built a fortified trading post at Ouidah, where Portuguese and English forts already existed. In 1843, the

French administrator at Ouidah traveled up-country to Abomey, capital of the great Fon kingdom, and obtained from King Ghézo the formal recognition of French trading rights at Ouidah. A few years later, Ghézo signed a treaty of friendship and commerce with Bouët-Willaumez.

In the territory of Guinea, troubles broke out in 1839 between French traders and the coastal tribes. When they were not settled by the signing of agreements with the tribal chiefs, military force was used, and in 1849, French rule was extended over that part of the coast.

Thus, by the middle of the nineteenth century, the Senegal and Guinea Gulf coasts, and also the Senegal River valley for several hundred miles inland, were studded with French forts and trading posts. The stage was set for French penetration of the West African hinterland.

Three Great Explorers

The opening up of West Africa by Europeans, which took place roughly from the end of the eighteenth century to the middle of the nineteenth, produced some of the bravest and most colorful exploits of the time. Three names stand out particularly in this exploration: that of Mungo Park, a Scottish doctor; René Caillié, a Frenchman; and Dr. Heinrich Barth, a German.

Mungo Park, who was sponsored by the African Society of London, left the coast of Gambia on his first exploration in 1795, taking with him only an interpreter and an African servant. He crossed the Senegal River at Bakel and continued into the region called Kaarta, lying between the Senegal and Niger rivers in eastern Senegal. In Kaarta—once the site of an old Bambara-tribe kingdom—the Negroes received him hospitably, but he was captured by Moors, who held him prisoner for four months. When he was set free, he resumed his march eastward, but at Ségou on the Niger he was barred by the local chief from going farther and had to return to Gambia in 1797. However, his observations confirmed that the Niger River flowed eastward, and this disproved a widely held theory that the Senegal and Niger rivers were connected. On his second voyage, also from the Gambia coast, which he began in 1805, Park planned to follow the Niger by boat from a point upstream from Bamako to its mouth. This time he made the mistake of setting out with a large and cumbersome expedition which, besides himself and two other Scots, included five boat-builders, a guard of thirty-five British soldiers in full military uniform, and one African guide. This big group was gradually reduced, by death or desertion, until Park had with him only four Europeans when he left Sansanding, some 175 miles east of Bamako. The little troop went on in their boat but vanished without a trace 800 miles beyond Timbuktu in the desolate Niger Bend region in 1806.

René Caillié's amazing visit in 1828 to Timbuktu—above all, his escape from it alive—makes him one of the most notable of the nineteenth-century explorers. Caillié came to Senegal from France in 1816 among the personnel of Colonel Schmaltz (who, the following year, was named Governor of Senegal), and for a time was an officer's servant at St. Louis. In the early nineteenth century the legendary desert city of Timbuktu, with its romantic reputation of trade in gold, slaves, ivory, salt and ostrich plumes, its camel caravans, and its Islamic fanaticism, held a strong fascination for western Europeans. Caillié had long dreamed of entering this forbidden stronghold, and after he reached Senegal, tried to persuade the government to help him make the dangerous trip. But his pleas were repeatedly refused or ignored, and his efforts during ten years to set out for the Soudan without the

Timbuktu in 1828, an engraving made from a drawing by René Caillé. It first appeared in a book which he published in 1830 on his West African adventures. The mosque at the upper left still exists.

government's aid were also frustrated in one way or another. Nevertheless, for several years during that time he studied the Arabic language and the Islamic religion. At last, in April 1827, he was able to join a Dioula caravan bound northward from the Guinea coast. (The Dioulas, it will be remembered, have long been itinerant traders in West Africa.) To go with the caravan Caillié disguised himself as an Egyptian Muslim and claimed to have been taken prisoner by Napoleon's army in Egypt, to have been freed in Senegal, and to be returning to his native country. After many hardships, including illnesses, during travels with various caravans, he passed through the mud-brick gateway of Timbuktu in April 1828— a year after he began his trip in Guinea. Caillié's disguise was so convincing that he was able to remain for two weeks in the holy city, which few white men had ever entered and from which none had hitherto gotten out alive. There he secretly made notes of his observations which he hid in a copy of the Koran. His year-long journey had exhausted all his resources, and leaving Timbuktu penniless with a caravan headed for northern Morocco, he made a painful and dangerous crossing of the Sahara. When he finally reached Tangier, Morocco, he told his almost incredible story to the French consul, who was finally convinced that it was true and helped him to return to France.

Even more remarkable in some ways than the exploits of Park and Caillié were those of the tireless and indestructible German, Dr. Heinrich Barth. Barth, whose expedition was sponsored by the British government, traveled for five years, 1850–55, in north, west and central Africa. This scientist, who was an assiduous note-taker, met and overcame constant obstacles and hardships during his travels. Not the least of these was his uncomfortable clothing—a high-collared military blouse, boots and heavy hat—in which he trudged along in the intense, often humid African heat. From Tripoli on the Mediterranean, by way of Agadès in the south Sahara, he moved through the Hausa country of what is now northern Nigeria. Striking out eastward, he passed through northern Cameroun's plains and mountains to reach the eastern region of the present Chad Republic in central Africa. Then, heading westward, he came successively to Zinder and Say in what is now the Republic of Niger, crossed the whole of the vast Niger Bend region, and arrived at Macina in west-central Soudan. From Macina he traveled by small boat on the Niger River to Timbuktu, where he spent eight uneasy months under the "protection" of the city's Moroccan chief, a sheik named El Bekkai. After this he returned to Chad, first by way of the Niger River as far as Gao, then overland through the Zinder region. Barth's travels ended where they had begun five years before, at Tripoli on the Mediterranean, which he reached after a long and hazardous trip across the Sahara through northern Chad and the Fezzan region of present-day Libya. After his return to Europe, he wrote the fascinating story of his unprecedented travels, which was published in London a few years later. Barth's account of his expedition is still considered one of the most valuable sources of information regarding central and western Africa as it was in the mid-nineteenth century.

The courage and endurance of such explorers as Park, Caillié and Barth can be better appreciated when it is remembered that until very late in the nineteenth century, no traveler in Africa south of the Sahara could move freely or even safely through the countryside. At every turn he met with obstacles and dangers. There were demands by local chiefs for "gifts" and delays caused by having to negotiate with each tribe, and often with each village, for the right to pass, and to obtain guides, food and pack animals. Forced halts of many days were frequent, and often these halts dragged out to weeks and even months, especially when tribal wars were going on. Guides deserted. Added to these grave handicaps were the inability to obtain medicines and the almost total lack of any civilized comforts except a few that could be provided for at the start of the expedition. The white explorers of that period, who made so many interesting and useful discoveries and revealed so much about West Africa to the Western world, therefore fully deserved the honors and fame that usually awaited them when they returned to Europe. Their exploits struck Europeans of the nineteenth century as all the more glamorous because of the tremendous interest in Africa that had been aroused by the tales of seventeenth and eighteenth century traders, explorers and missionaries. The strange customs of the tribes and the wealth that Africa reputedly held—according to the accounts of those early travelers—had set fire to men's imaginations, and any new stories about them were thrilling distractions as exploits in the conquest of space are to us today.

Colonial Expansion: West Africa Occupied and Partitioned

In the middle of the nineteenth century the position of Prince Louis-Napoleon of France, who had been elected President of the short-lived Second Republic in 1848, was greatly strengthened by the *coup d'état* of 1851. A new Minister of Colonies obtained Louis-Napoleon's approval in November 1852 to rebuild the neglected fort at Podor on the Senegal River and to send troops into the Senegal Valley. This was done in 1854, but in the opinion of Senegal's impatient French traders, Protet, the new governor appointed in 1850, did not push this action hard enough. These traders had begun to see how much they might profit by the pacification of Senegal, and they put pressure on Paris to replace Protet. They urged the appointment of a young engineer, an officer who since his arrival in Senegal in 1852 had attracted attention by his forceful personality, his study of the country and his military exploits at Dabou, Bakel and Podor. This army colonel—later, general—whose name was Louis Faidherbe, was destined to become famous as the greatest single architect of France's empire in West Africa.

In November 1854 Louis-Napoleon recalled Protet and appointed Faidherbe as Senegal's governor. This marked an historic turning point in the relations between France and

West Africa. French activity there until the mid-nineteenth century has been described as "Pacification without conquest, development without occupation of territory." With the appointment of the new governor, that cautious attitude was abandoned in favor of Faidherbe's bold approach. According to some of his critics, his "forward policy" amounted to the alternatives of "peace or powder" (that is, gunpowder).

FAIDHERBE AND THE "FORWARD POLICY"

Faidherbe's two periods of service as Governor of Senegal covered about ten years in all—from 1854 to 1861 and from 1863 to 1865. Early during his governorship the lines of strategy for French penetration of West Africa were decided. For a time it had been debated as to whether France should attempt to pacify and colonize the interior by sending expeditions northward from bases along the Guinea Gulf coast. This tactic lost out not only because of the enormous difficulty of crossing the tropical-forest zone of the lower coast, but more especially because Faidherbe took decisive steps toward carrying out his own plan to advance eastward from St. Louis through the Senegal River valley and the vast Soudan region to Lake Chad. He even dreamed of a French African empire that would stretch over the thousands of miles from the Atlantic to the Red Sea, but for various reasons French control never extended farther east than Chad territory—now the Republic of Chad—which borders on the former Anglo-Egyptian Sudan.

Faidherbe's important task was to establish French rule firmly in West Africa, to bring peace to the country and free it of brutal raiders, and to create the basis for its future development culturally as well as politically and economically. The new governor's manner toward Europeans was cold and distant, and he insisted so strongly upon respect for authority that many people considered him autocratic. But Faidherbe—who had learned Arabic and Wolof—loved Africa and its peoples, and did his best to increase his knowledge of them, understand them and help them. At the same time he was determined that the Africans should benefit by France's "civilizing mission" as well as by the peaceful conditions that would result from the suppression of tribal warfare and raids.

Thanks to his wide interests and his energy, Faidherbe's activities produced long-lasting results in many fields. He was responsible for the founding of schools and newspapers, the development of St. Louis into a city, the building of roads and bridges, the organizing of river shipping and the introduction of new crops. Because of his support and encouragement of peanut-growing, Senegal's exports of peanuts doubled within a few years after he became governor. In 1854 he suggested that a railway be built between Dakar and St. Louis-du-Sénégal, and he also pointed out the value of a rail link between the last navigable point on the Senegal River and the first one on the Niger. Although a quarter-century passed before these projects were actually begun, the Dakar-St. Louis line was completed in 1885. The Kayes-Koulikoro railway, after many delays, began operating in 1904.

Shortly after Faidherbe took charge of the Senegal colony, plans were drawn for a fort at Dakar intended to bring the balky Lebou tribe into line. When the fort was finished in 1859, Gorée's military commander compelled the Lebous to give up their annual demand for *coutumes* in exchange for a lump-sum payment. The French flag was then run up on Dakar fort, and the French occupation of Senegal really began.

In the mid-nineteenth century, communications between West Africa and France were very slow. There was no telegraph or cable line, and letters took weeks to arrive by sea.

Since Faidherbe was a strong-willed administrator, keenly conscious of the importance of his mission and of the pressure of events, he usually acted without waiting for the approval of the Minister of Colonies in Paris. In doing so, however, he took into account the fact that he had the Minister's support for his plan to advance into the Soudan.

As soon as he became governor, Faidherbe had to contend with various African enemies of the French, including the Moors of the Trarza and Brakna tribes of southern Mauritania, and the turbulent Tukulor Negroes of the Fouta Toro region of northern Senegal. All of them persistently interfered with French trade along the river and frequently made attacks on the administrative posts that had been built to protect the traders. In addition, an even more threatening adversary appeared in 1855—El Hadj Omar, the Tukulor conqueror whose career has been described in Chapter IV.

Faidherbe's first military moves were aimed at protecting the gum trade along the Senegal River and quelling the Moorish tribes which were raiding and oppressing the Negro peasants who lived along the south banks of the river. Most of these Negroes belonged to the Wolof tribe. The Trarza and Brakna Moors had gained control over the Oualo region which lies inland from St. Louis, and were treating the Wolofs like a vassal people. A four-year campaign by French troops, which began in 1854 with the capture of the Trarzas' capital town, ended with the defeat of this Moorish tribe and the signing of a treaty with the Emir (chief) of the Trarzas. By this treaty it was agreed that the Oualo would thenceforth be ruled by France, and from that time on there were no more raids or demands by the Moors against the Negroes of the region.

As for El Hadj Omar, five years of military action were necessary to subdue him after his declaration of a holy war in 1855 against the whites. When he was defeated in 1860, he withdrew with his fanatical followers to the regions east of the Senegal and Bafing rivers. There he set up an "empire" which under the rule of his son gave the French a great deal of trouble a generation later.

At the time of Faidherbe's appointment, Gorée and its dependencies (Cap Vert and the French establishments south of it along the African coast as far as Sierra Leone) had been separated from Senegal and placed under the command of the chief of the French naval station at Gorée. This was intended to lighten Faidherbe's administrative burdens while he devoted himself to the pacification of the Senegal River valley. By 1859 that task had been largely completed, and Gorée and the coastal posts were again made a part of Senegal and placed under Faidherbe's control. Such an administrative change was essential if Faidherbe was to succeed in consolidating French authority in the coastal regions of the colony and in putting an end to the disorders and raids that were widespread there and were hindering the development of peanut cultivation in the south Senegal area called the Casamance. Once these regions were brought under control, it was planned to pacify the Cayor, lying between them and the Senegal River.

Military operations in the Casamance and the Cayor were carried out according to plan, and by 1861 Faidherbe considered that he could return to private life in France. Senegal received a new governor, but hostilities flared up again in the Cayor country, and in 1863 Faidherbe was re-appointed governor. For two years he directed operations in the Cayor, but the tribes fought so stubbornly that when Faidherbe finally retired in 1865, resistance to the French had not yet been overcome. It was not until 1869 that the tyrannical Wolof rulers of the Cayor (called Damels), whose drunken warriors brutalized the rest of the Wolof population and even sold

An early nineteenth century king of Cayor surrounded by minor chiefs.

them as slaves to the Tukulors, were defeated and forced to make peace. The Cayor region was then annexed to Senegal and divided into seven administrative districts called cantons. These were placed in charge of African chiefs selected by the governor.

Faidherbe's successor as Governor of Senegal (1865–69) was Colonel Pinet-Laprade, who had commanded the campaign in the Cayor and who in early 1865 had distinguished himself in operations in the "Rivières du Sud." To Pinet-Laprade belongs the credit for the development of Dakar from a small African village of thatched huts to a European-style town, and for the creation of its port. Although he took over Faidherbe's task of pacification, including the campaign in the Cayor, military ventures in Africa received little encouragement from the French government during the late 1860's. By that time, the government had neither money nor troops to spare for Africa. Large French forces had been sent to Cochin-China (now South Vietnam) in southeast Asia, first to protect missionaries and later to conquer the whole of Vietnam. In addition, France was engaged in the war with Prussia which ended disastrously in 1870.

SLOWDOWN

For ten years after the Franco-Prussian War, French policy in Africa was timid and hesitant because of the losses which France had suffered in Europe. Money and manpower were needed to rebuild the home country and could not be spared to extend the French occupation in Africa. It was difficult, in fact, to keep order in the territories already under French rule there. A new holy war was started in the Cayor in 1870 by a Tukulor *marabout* named Mahmadou Cheikhou, and it went on until 1875, when he was killed and his warriors defeated. In Ivory Coast the French garrisons were withdrawn from Dabou, Grand Bassam and Assinie, and French interests in those posts were put in charge of a merchant named Verdier. No progress was made in Dahomey, where the king of Porto Novo plotted against the French with British agents from Nigeria and with Dahomeyans of the court of Abomey.

SOUDAN CAMPAIGNS

During the decade of the 1870's, two African adversaries of the French were consolidating their dominions in western Soudan. One of these was Ahmadou, the son of the conqueror El Hadj Omar, who—as mentioned above—had been defeated by Faidherbe's troops in 1860 and forced to withdraw from Senegal to Soudan. There El Hadj Omar had set up a big Tukulor "empire" that stretched from upper Guinea to the Timbuktu region. After his death in 1864, he was succeeded as "king" of Ségou (a town on the Niger River) by his son Ahmadou. In order to hold power over the conquered areas, Ahmadou carried on continual wars of extermination. He and his warriors inevitably collided with another ambitious Soudanese conqueror, the Malinké *marabout* named Samory, who was the second of France's two African adversaries. The hostility between these two African despots made it possible for the French to deal with them separately and eventually to defeat them in turn.

Defeating El Hadj Omar took many years. In 1879 the French government became interested in building a railway between the Senegal and Niger rivers in western Soudan. This was the rail line whose construction had been urged by Faidherbe 25 years earlier. However, before such a railway could be built and operated, it was necessary to pacify the country between Medina (on the Senegal River not far east of the present Senegal-Mali Republic border) and Bamako, some 300 miles farther southeast. A military post was installed in 1881 at Kita, 130 miles west of Bamako. Then for 12 years the French had to contend with Ahmadou and his Tukulor warriors, using armed force after persuasion had failed. At first it was thought that Ahmadou might be won over by peaceable gestures, and he was presented with gifts. Finally in 1887 after several years of persistent agitation against the French, Ahmadou was persuaded to sign a peace treaty, but in spite of this he went on preaching resistance. Consequently an offensive was launched against him early in 1889, and by 1893 he was defeated and El Hadj Omar's Tukulor "empire" disappeared from the African scene.

Samory was a much more formidable adversary than Ahmadou. For 16 years, from 1882 to 1898, his warriors gave battle to the French. This *marabout* was far more

effective as a military leader than as a religious chief. Chapter
IV tells of the appalling devastation that he inflicted on the
western Soudan and its peoples. As the French troops advanced, they passed through destroyed villages emptied of all
their inhabitants. In order to pay for rifles obtained from
traders in Sierra Leone and Gold Coast, Samory is said to have
sold as slaves all the inhabitants of conquered villages who
had escaped massacre.

Early in 1883 Bamako was reached by French army col-
umns, and a campaign was begun from that town against
Samory. After a series of defeats, he signed treaties with the
French in 1887 and 1889, giving them control over stretches
of the south bank of the Niger. Both treaties were soon vio-
lated, however, when he found that the French would not
lend him troops to extend his conquests on the north bank of
the river. Military operations against him were resumed in
1891, but were suspended from 1893 until 1898—a period
during which the Paris government experienced a wave of
pacifism as a result of French army reverses in Tonkin (now
North Vietnam) and Dahomey. Samory made the most of this
by intensifying his raids, massacres and slave-taking. However, when warriors under the command of one of his sons
wiped out a British detachment near the Gold Coast border,
the British sent troops to catch him. This British foray into
Ivory Coast alarmed the French government, which decided
that to protect its interests there it must try to forestall Britain
and put an end to Samory's career. By late September of
1898, a vigorous French offensive resulted in the capture of
the *marabout* and the surrender of the warriors.

Meanwhile, French pacification of the Sikasso region in
southwestern Soudan, the Niger Bend area and the Mossi
country had been going forward. By 1893 the Soudan colony
—a vast region nearly twice the size of France and including

not only the present Mali Republic but also lands that now form part of Guinea, Ivory Coast and Dahomey—was considered pacified. The Niger Bend towns of Timbuktu, Niafounké and Goundam, however, which were defended by Tuareg warriors, were not captured by French troops until 1894. For years thereafter the Tuareg were thorns in the side of the French, for they continued to swoop in from the desert and raid the Negro peasants of the Niger Bend, up to the very gates of Timbuktu. To deal with the Tuareg, the French had to become nomads themselves, and it was in 1898 that the first camel-mounted troop detachments (called *méharistes*) were formed and sent into the desert in pursuit of the raiders. The *méhariste* patrols became regular elements of the French army and for many years carried out the task of repressing lawlessness in the French Sahara.

The Soudan was organized administratively in 1893 under a governor, but because of the difficulty of governing such a huge colony, radical changes were made late in 1899. The Soudan colony was reduced to no more than the Niger Bend, which was divided into military territories with headquarters at Timbuktu and Bobo-Dioulasso (the latter of which is now the Upper Volta Republic's second-most-important town). The rest of the colony was divided between Senegal, Guinea and Ivory Coast. During the 20 years that followed, the Soudan lands were redistributed administratively several times, until in 1920 large areas were reunited as the colony of French Soudan.

THE BERLIN CONFERENCE AND ITS AFTERMATH

In the early 1880's new international rivalries had been touched off in Africa by Belgian activities in the Congo. King Leopold II aimed to create an "independent" African state that would take in the whole Congo River basin, which covers a vast area of western equatorial Africa. The state would be run by a private association, the International Association of the Congo, in which several European powers were represented but which King Leopold of the Belgians hoped to dominate. This project aroused suspicion and jealousy on the part of some European governments, including Britain and Portugal, which attempted to block it. Finally, in November 1884, a conference of all the European countries was called at Berlin. Its object was to iron out the question of recognizing a Congo state and also the principles that were to govern the occupation and partition of Africa by the European countries which already had territorial possessions on the continent.

During the conference, the Congo area become the Congo Free State and received international recognition. Then, on February 26, 1885, the Act of Berlin was signed by all the countries represented at the conference, among which were 13 European nations including Russia and Turkey, and also the United States. (The United States Senate, however, never ratified the treaty.) Among many other provisions, the Berlin Act guaranteed freedom of trade in the Congo River basin and freedom of navigation on the Congo and Niger rivers. It also called for greater efforts to suppress slavery and the slave trade, and stipulated that religion, scientific work and exploration must be protected. French rights in the region of the upper Niger River were recognized. Most significant of all, so far as the future of Africa was concerned, was the treaty's clause providing that any country which might take over lands on the African coast, and in practice this meant far inland, must notify the other powers which signed the Berlin Act, "in order to enable them, if need be, to make good any claims of their own." Only claims supported by solid occupation would be recognized under this clause.

Thus as a result of the Berlin Act, European nations which were already in the process of creating African colonial empires engaged in a feverish race to occupy or at least dominate new areas. Military and diplomatic missions were rushed by the European powers into the interior of West as well as Central Africa to make treaties with local rulers and to set up military and trading posts, and there were frequent clashes.

The history of this scramble for African territory, which in West Africa involved chiefly France, Great Britain and Germany, is too complicated for inclusion in this book. In brief, however, the effect of the Act of Berlin was to greatly speed up the conquest and partition of Africa south of the Sahara, so that by the end of the nineteenth century there was no region of that vast area, except Liberia, that was not ruled—at least on paper—by Europeans.

IVORY COAST AND GUINEA

The first French mission prompted by the territorial-claims clause of the Act of Berlin was sent north in the winter of 1888 from Grand Bassam in Ivory Coast. In January 1889, at Kong in the northern part of what was to become the Ivory Coast colony, it met another French expedition which had come from Bamako in Soudán by way of the Mossi country. This first link between Ivory Coast and Soudan was followed up by further exploration, marked by clashes with Samory's warriors and with hostile tribes in the forest zone. The colony of Ivory Coast was created in March 1893, and Colonel Binger—who had led the above-mentioned expedition from Grand Bassam—was named its first governor. For some years, however, it scarcely existed except on paper because of the disturbed state of the country. This was due partly to the ravages of Samory, who was trying to set up a new empire in northern Ivory Coast after his expulsion from Soudan.

Guinea also was suffering from disorders at that time, especially in the Fouta Djallon region where two branches of the ruling family of the Foula tribe were struggling against each other for dominance. Military expeditions during the late 1880's succeeded in establishing French influence so firmly in upper Guinea that in August 1889 the British in adjoining Sierra Leone formally recognized the French protectorate over Guinea and signed a treaty defining the boundary between the two areas. Meanwhile, the Foula chiefs of the Fouta Djallon did their best to fend off the French occupation, but were finally subdued, and their successors—appointed by the French—signed a treaty in 1897 accepting the French protectorate over the country.

CONSOLIDATION OF FRENCH RULE IN DAHOMEY, UPPER VOLTA AND NIGER

In Dahomey, during the late 1880's and early 1890's, the French were encountering determined opposition by the fierce and powerful kings at Abomey. King Gléglé ordered the French to abandon Cotonou and Porto Novo, and their trading posts in those coastal towns were raided by his warriors. A French official sent to Abomey in 1889 to negotiate with the king was rebuffed. When Gléglé died at the end of that year and was succeeded by Béhanzin, hostilities broke out between the French and the Abomey kingdom. Although the new king signed a treaty in October 1890 recognizing French rights over Porto Novo and Cotonou, he soon renewed his attacks, and a war broke out which lasted until January 1894. Béhanzin was captured and his brother Ago li-Agbo was placed on the throne of Abomey under a French protectorate; the coastal regions were annexed and put under the adminis-

The throne of King Ghézo, who ruled in Abomey from 1818 to 1858. It is set on the skulls of captured enemy chiefs.

tration of Cotonou. For some years during the 1890's a race went on between English, German and French military missions to occupy central and northern Dahomey so as to be able to assert effective claims to these regions. Thanks to rapid military moves and to treaties with local chiefs, the French successfully checkmated the Germans and the British, and by 1898 both Germany and Great Britain had signed treaties with France by which they acknowledged French rights there.

The last decade of the nineteenth century saw the gradual establishment of a French protectorate over the Mossi states of what is now the Republic of Upper Volta. This was accomplished against the opposition of the Nabas (chiefs) of the Mossi tribe, especially the Moro Naba at Ouagadougou, who often has been referred to as the "Emperor of the Mossi." In 1896 French troops occupied his capital, from which he had fled. A new Moro Naba was then placed on the throne, and he consented in January 1897 to the setting up of a French protectorate over the kingdom. For a number of years thereafter the Mossi kingdoms were under indirect administration by the Government-General of West Africa as part of the old colony called "Upper Senegal and Niger." It was not until 1919 that the colony of Upper Volta came into existence.

French control over the vast region later known as the Niger colony was slow in being established, both because of the character of the country and the hostility of the Tuareg nomads, and because of conflicting British claims asserted by the Royal Niger Company. By a treaty of June 14, 1898, however, some of the British claims were dropped. Three French military missions were then sent—from Algeria, the Congo and Senegal—to carry out the task of occupying the country between the Niger River and Lake Chad. The missions from Algeria and Senegal proved to be disastrous for not only did they meet with resistance from the desert tribes along the oasis routes, but the brutal commander of the Senegal column killed the officer sent to replace him and was then killed by his own men. The expedition from Algeria, under the command of Colonel F. J. A. Lamy, suffered great losses of pack animals in crossing the Sahara but was rescued at Agadès when the Zinder post sent camels for them.

The three missions finally joined forces near Lake Chad in April 1899 and immediately attacked the army of a notorious slave-trader named Rabah. This adventurer from the Egyptian Sudan, a Negro-Arab half-breed, had been trying to carve out an "empire" for himself in the Bornou region southwest of the lake. Rabah was killed and his followers fled, but the brave French commander of the Algeria mission, Lamy, also lost his life in the battle. However, the link between the Niger River and Lake Chad, which had been part of Faidherbe's grand plan a half-century earlier, had become a reality. The regions then called the Middle Niger were placed under military government as part of French West Africa, and negotiations were begun with Britain to fix the boundary between them and British Nigeria.

NOMAD RESISTANCE IN MAURITANIA

Mauritania, whose forbidding desert wastes contained, then as now, a sparse population made up of intractable Moorish nomads and some Negroes living along the north banks of the Senegal River, almost totally escaped French control until the early twentieth century.

As mentioned above, the Trarza and Brakna tribes of southwestern Mauritania had been defeated by Faidherbe in 1858 and promised to remain thereafter north of the Senegal River. Nevertheless, these and other nomad tribes continued to roam freely through all the huge Mauritanian part of the Sahara and were a constant threat to adjoining Senegal and Soudan. Regardless of the 1858 treaty, they continued to cross the river from time to time and to raid the herds of the Peuls and Wolofs, after which they melted away into the desert and escaped punishment.

In 1898 the French government sent a well-known Islamic specialist named Xavier Coppolani to the Hodh region of southeastern Mauritania, where by skillful diplomacy he persuaded the Moorish tribes of that area to accept French rule. During the next five years he went on similar missions farther west, where he had some success with the still-turbulent

Trarza tribe. Meeting with some resistance from the Brakna Moors, however, Coppolani had to be given military support. When he was killed in 1905 during a surprise attack by Moorish warriors at Tidjikja, an oasis of south-central Mauritania, the French began an energetic campaign during which they occupied all the oases of the Adrar region. Because the oases were vital to the nomads, the tribes of the Adrar had no choice but to bow to French control, and by the end of 1909 they had surrendered.

Farther north, the great nomad tribes, protected by their knowledge of the desert, continued to raid into the Adrar and to massacre isolated French detachments, and these tribes managed for many years to evade control. Nevertheless, in 1920 Mauritania became a colony and a part of the French West African federation.

Creation of the French West African Government

As the nineteenth century neared its end, the French occupation of West Africa had become so extensive that the Senegal government could no longer administer effectively the far-flung colonies which spread deep into the sahel and sudanese zones and along the Guinea Gulf. At first these colonies had entirely independent administrations with financial as well as governmental autonomy, and were responsible only to the Minister of Colonies at Paris. But because of the need to follow a uniform policy and to coordinate the military operations which were still essential, it was decided to create an over-all government which at a higher level would supervise the administration of the colonies of Senegal, Guinea, Ivory Coast and Soudan.

By a decree of June 16, 1895, the French government established what was called the Government-General of West Africa. The Governor-General, a civilian, was also Governor of Senegal, and his headquarters were at St. Louis-du-Sénégal. His powers, however, were very limited. The colonies supposedly under his control not only had their own governors but kept their administrative and financial autonomy. Moreover, for many years large desert areas—as in northern Niger and in Mauritania—continued to be governed by French army officers as military regions. As for Dahomey, where the resistance of the Abomey kings had been overcome only a short time before, this colony was entirely exempt from the Governor-General's supervision.

The weaknesses of the Government-General's administration were so apparent that later decrees were issued with the aim of strengthening its control over the colonies. On October 17, 1899, the Soudan colony, as mentioned above, was split up and most of it was attached to the neighboring colonies of Senegal, Guinea and Ivory Coast. By the same decree, Dahomey was attached to the group of colonies under the Government-General's control. This timid step toward more effective over-all administration was followed by more positive ones, the outstanding being a decree of October 18, 1904, which gave much wider powers to a centralized government for French West Africa, with a Governor-General, a separate budget, and considerable control over the colonial (later, territorial) administrations. Thus the federation of French West Africa came into being, and with minor changes from time to time it continued to exist, as described in the following chapter, until 1959.

Political Institutions

Within the span of a half-century—a brief period in historical time—French West Africa has passed through the successive stages of a remarkable political evolution.

The five huge colonies that made up the federation created in 1904 underwent modifications of boundary and administration so that by 1920 there were eight of them. They remained colonies until after World War II, ruled by remote control from Paris and with almost no local representation in government.

The Second World War brought many hardships to the colonies but also marked a crucial turning point in their relationship with France. A new spirit of postwar liberalism began to characterize this relationship even before the war ended. It pervaded the resolutions adopted at a conference of Free French officials early in 1944, at Brazzaville in French Equatorial Africa.

Within a few years after the war, however, even the liberalism of the Brazzaville resolutions fell short of the radical changes that progressively took place in the colonies—which by 1956 had become "overseas territories." That year saw the real beginnings of self-government with the passage by the French Parliament of the so-called *loi-cadre* (framework law). This law provided for universal adult suffrage in the African territories and for the election of government councils where, for the first time, the federation's Africans had a voice in the management of local affairs.

From 1956 until 1960, the march of events was quickened by such developments in Africa as the Algerian revolt and the independence of Ghana and Togo, and in France by the collapse of the Fourth Republic. Within a few months after de Gaulle came to power on June 1, 1958, a new Constitution creating the Fifth French Republic and the Franco-African Community was adopted. Under its provisions, seven of the French West African territories became member Republics of the Community. Only Guinea refused to join it and broke away from France. Before the end of 1960 all of these Republics had achieved independence, and by mid-1961 all but Senegal had withdrawn from the Community.

It is worth noting—and greatly to the credit of France—that the transition of the French West African lands from colonial status to nationhood took place peaceably and by negotiation. With the exception of Guinea from 1958 until 1962, and of Mali for a shorter period, the relations between France and its former possessions south of the Sahara continued to be marked by mutual tolerance and cooperation.

The Federation: 1904–1939

When the French West African federation took shape in the last years of the nineteenth century and the beginning of the twentieth, France became the world's second-greatest colonial realm of modern times, outranked only by the British empire.

The Government-General of the federation was situated at Dakar. Under the 1904 decree setting up the federation, authority for the administration of the French colonies in West Africa was highly centralized in the hands of the Governor-General. Centralization of authority also dictated the relations of the French administration with the local population. Except in Senegal, no Africans other than a relatively few chiefs had any power. As their name indicates, the advisory councils at different levels of government could offer advice to the French official who presided at their sessions, but they had no legislative power.

The Governor-General was the only official in the federation entitled to communicate with the Minister of Colonies concerning federation affairs. Although in theory he had to obtain the Minister's approval for most of his official acts, in practice he frequently acted on his own initiative because communications between West Africa and Paris were still almost as slow as in the time of Faidherbe a half-century earlier. Moreover, the Governor-General held considerable *de facto* power in regard to putting decrees into force in the federation: he was able to postpone their application for extensive periods by simply not publishing them and was also able to modify them to suit local conditions. During that period, all legislation affecting the colonies was in the form of Presidential decrees, which were drafted by the Minister of Colonies but which did not take effect in West Africa until published locally by the Governor-General.

The center of the modern city of Dakar, former capital of the French West African federation and now capital of Senegal. At the upper right is the Administration Building.

To a large extent, the slowness in communications enabled —and in fact, forced—the colonial governors to act on their own, also, in many situations where they were supposed to wait for a decision on some administrative question to reach them from the Governor-General. Moreover, the existence of separate colonial budgets—distinct from the federal budget— made possible some independent action on the part of the governors of the colonies.

As for the local administrators in outlying regions, they likewise were often faced with the necessity of deciding urgent questions on their own initiative. In most cases, these administrators were stationed far away from the colonial capitals, in remote villages of the bush that could be reached only by days or weeks of slow travel through difficult country without roads, or by *pirogues* (log canoes) that had to thread their way precariously along waterways broken by rapids, strewn with rocks and sand-bars, or infested by crocodiles.

Aside from the geographical and other factors which, as indicated above, tended to interfere with the administrative centralization so dear to the Paris bureaucrats, there was persistent effort at various government levels to gain greater autonomy. Whenever possible, the Governor-General himself sought greater independence from the remote control of the Minister of Colonies at Paris, and the colonial governors often tried to weaken the grip of the Government-General on administrative activities in their respective colonies. At a still lower level of colonial government, many of the local French administrators similarly carried on a long if cautious struggle for more freedom of action.

Although administrative contacts were hampered by the isolation of almost all the colonial posts, and administrative relationships were not so centralized in practice as in theory, there was at least one unifying element in the French West African governmental structure. This was the existence of a federal budget which supported such public services as agriculture, health, education, road-building and railway construction and operation in the poorer colonies as well as the richer ones. The federation's budget depended mostly on revenues from import and export duties and income from the railways, and these revenues also served as financial backing for loans needed to carry out projects of public interest in various colonies.

THE FEDERAL ADMINISTRATIVE STRUCTURE

When it was first created, the federation consisted of five colonies—Senegal, Guinea, Ivory Coast, Dahomey, and Upper

Senegal-Niger. (The last-mentioned colony included vast areas stretching all the way from the eastern Senegal River valley to Lake Chad.) In the course of the following 16 years, however, some changes were made in the names and areas of the colonies. As a result of these changes, French West Africa after 1920 comprised eight colonies, which subsequent to World War II—from 1946 until 1958—were called overseas territories. Their names were Senegal, Guinea, Ivory Coast, Dahomey, Niger, Upper Volta, Mauritania and Soudan. Although the Upper Volta colony disappeared for a time after 1932 when it was divided up among Soudan, Niger and Ivory Coast, it was reborn as a territory in 1947, to the great joy of the Mossi tribe centered around Ouagadougou, its capital.

The administrative framework of French West Africa resembled a pyramid. At its apex was the Governor-General, who was assisted by high-ranking French officials and an advisory council composed of French citizens and African subjects, all appointed by him. Below the Governor-General and responsible to him were the governors of the eight colonies, each of whom also had a staff of French civil servants and a hand-picked advisory council with French and African members.

Within each colony, the largest units were called *cercles*. (The word *cercle,* translated as "circle," bears no relation to the shape of the units it applied to.) They were administered by French officials called *commandants de cercle.* The *cercles* were composed of subdivisions, also headed by French administrators. The subdivisions in turn were divided into cantons comprising groups of villages. Cantons and villages were in the charge of African chiefs, as described below. Thus the chain of authority went up from the pyramid's base—represented by the 48,000 or so villages—through the

cantons, numbering about 2,200, through the 100-odd *cercles,*
and through the colonial capital, to the Government-General
at the top. In setting up these administrative areas, tribal
distribution was generally disregarded so as to discourage any
moves toward tribal separatism and thus make it easier to
govern the African population.

Unlike the canton chiefs, the great majority of whom were
appointed by the administration, the village chiefs were
elected according to old tribal custom. At one and the same
time they represented the French administration and their
fellow-villagers, for whom they were spokesmen to the
French authorities. Canton chiefs were paid a meager salary,
but village chiefs received only a small rebate on the taxes
they collected. Both the canton and village chiefs had numerous and heavy duties, among which were maintaining order
and respect for the law, keeping tax rolls and collecting
taxes, and seeing to it that roads were repaired and that food
granaries were stocked. Since the income of all the African
chiefs was negligible in comparison with their responsibilities, and since it was physically impossible for their French
superiors to control many of their activities, a large percentage
of these chiefs, especially canton chiefs, abused their powers
and became very unpopular.

To assist the African chiefs and also to counterbalance
them, the French administration appointed councils of so-
called Notables, usually Africans who were prominent and
elderly members of their communities. But like almost all the
other advisory councils in French West Africa, those of the
Notables had no authority, met irregularly, and usually agreed
to virtually any proposals made to them by the French
administrators.

Only in Senegal were certain councils given real powers.
Senegal's Colonial Council, some of whose members were

government appointees, also included elected Africans and Frenchmen. The most important of this council's powers was the partial control which it had over Senegal's budget. On the municipal level, in Senegal, the four towns of Dakar, St. Louis, Rufisque and Gorée had councils with the same type of membership and powers as those of the Colonial Council. Moreover, the Africans born in those towns were French citizens, unlike Africans born elsewhere in the Federation, who were simply French subjects. Even more unusual was the fact that Senegal was the only West African colony empowered to send a deputy to the French Parliament. In 1914, for the first time, an African was elected to that office, which he held until his death in 1934.

Senegal's privileged status and comparatively democratic institutions were the result of historical accident, as described below. They were not extended to other colonies until after World War II, partly because of the French Government's displeasure at the strong criticism of its policies that was often voiced by members of Senegal's councils, and in part because of the Africans' reluctance to meet the conditions required of them to gain French citizenship. One of these requirements was a knowledge of the French language, but the worst stumbling-block was that they would have to renounce various African social customs, especially in regard to marriage and inheritance. Although as citizens they would not be subject to the *indigénat* system—explained below—and forced labor, it was clear that they would be given no political power in return for abandoning traditions and customs that were important to them. Consequently, only slightly more than 2,000 Africans in the federation, aside from those in Senegal who automatically held citizenship, became French citizens during the 30-year period in which the citizenship law was in effect.

French Policy Toward Africans

In dealing with the West African population, French policy suffered from certain contradictions which arose out of the different philosophies of government that prevailed in Paris at various periods. These philosophies fluctuated between two extremes. One of them was marked by liberalism, a guiding principle of the revolution of 1789 as well as of the reforms set in motion by the 1848 revolution in France. The other was dominated by the paternalistic colonialism and authoritarian government initiated under the Second Empire after 1854. For nearly a century Franco-African relations were dominated by an authoritarian system of rule.

As far back as 1833, during an era of liberalism, French law granted full political and civil rights to every freeborn individual in the colonies, as well as to freed slaves. (At that period, of course, so far as West Africa was concerned the law applied only to the coastal establishments of Senegal, because French control did not extend beyond these.) Thus the Africans of St. Louis and Gorée, and later those of Rufisque and Dakar, became French citizens, and their communes (townships) were granted the same status as those of France itself. A few years later, as mentioned above, the citizens of Senegal were given the right to elect a deputy to the French Parliament. Although this right was abrogated under the Second Empire (1854–70), it was restored in 1870.

When Faidherbe, with his knowledge of African customs and traditions, took office as Senegal's governor in 1854, he came to the conclusion that the African citizens of the Senegal communes were not sufficiently evolved in a political sense to be properly subject to the French code of civil law. They were therefore granted a special status under which those who were

Muslims were made subject to Koranic law, and those who were animists, to African customary law. Nevertheless, all of them retained their French citizenship.

THE TRADITIONAL ELITE

During the second half of the nineteenth century, when the French were gradually consolidating their control and administration of the West African regions, they made a number of treaties with tribal rulers, who were usually known as "paramount chiefs." As mentioned in Chapter V, these treaties often provided for recognition of a French protectorate over the region ruled by the chief. In this way, a system of indirect rule was practiced, for the chiefs were allowed to keep their titles and most of their traditional powers, and the French agreed to pay them a small salary and not to disturb existing African social institutions. In return, the chiefs simply promised not to oppose the French occupation, and to facilitate French trading activities.

Before many years had passed, however, the French found that some of the paramount chiefs were incompetent, others were more or less antagonistic, and all were inclined to abuse their powers. Moreover, as French control became more far-flung and firmly installed, the old African political groupings on a tribal basis mostly disappeared and were replaced by territorial divisions. Many of the great tribal rulers—such paramount chiefs as the Damels and Bours in Senegal and the Almamys in Soudan—lost their authority one by one or were simply not replaced.

By 1937, two years before World War II began, there remained only about 50 of the several hundred paramount chiefs who, a few decades earlier, had been powerful rulers in French West Africa. In most areas, only the lesser chiefs (usually the village chiefs) remained, and they were deprived

Tribal chiefs of the Abomey region of Dahomey. Their gold-embroidered caps, parasols and staffs are badges of office, indicating their rank.

of all but their religious prestige. They lost the regular revenues to which they had been entitled by custom, and in place of them they were given small rebates from the taxes they were required to collect. With few exceptions, the chiefs who remained, whether of high or low rank, were reduced to the status of agents of the French government who collected taxes, recruited laborers and soldiers, and settled minor civil disputes.

In fact, even at the time the federation was formed in 1904, indirect rule had already been replaced by direct French rule almost everywhere in French West Africa. Only in a few places had traditional rulers been kept in office because their cooperation was considered indispensable or because it was more economical to retain them. Moreover, a new category of appointed African functionaries, who had no traditional authority, was created as part of the federation's administrative system. These were the canton chiefs, referred to in the following section.

FORMATION OF A NEW ELITE

French colonialism in West Africa—as in other parts of the former French empire—was strongly marked by a sort of cultural evangelism, described by the French themselves as a "civilizing mission." This attitude was based on a conviction of the superiority of French culture, combined with the belief that natives of other countries, no matter how different from Frenchmen in racial and cultural background, could be absorbed, through training, education and social acceptance, into the French cultural pattern. The civilizing mission of France was expected to produce from a small group of privileged intellectuals an upper crust of African elite. In this process the traditional chiefs were by-passed and the rural peasantry were mostly ignored.

The school system was the chief instrument in producing an African elite. Emphasis was placed on the teaching of French, so that by being imbued with the French literary and scientific heritage, the African would become able—it was hoped—to think like a Frenchman. In a number of cases, this did in fact take place. At first it was chiefly from among the sons of ruling families that the government selected youths for instruction in the French language and in administrative and legal techniques. They were expected to become the future leaders of rural West Africa and also to fill subordinate positions in the professions, such as medicine and teaching, and in commerce. The traditional chiefs, however, especially Muslim ones, were suspicious of the French schools, and in many instances palmed off their young slaves instead of sending their sons. Because of this, a considerable number of commoners gained a rudimentary education, whereas the aristocratic families remained tradition-bound and out of touch with the modern world.

The economic privileges accorded to the educated group included partial or total exemption from the fiscal, military and labor obligations that rested heavily upon the population as a whole. Later, as the schools produced greater numbers of Africans more or less educated along French lines, some who were outstanding entered the elite category. The fringe of this privileged class also included certain Africans who had rendered special service to France, such as army veterans, many of whom were fiercely loyal and therefore could be counted on as a pro-French element of the population.

Along with the assimilation accomplished through education, there was a degree of social assimilation such as Africans in pre-war British African colonies never experienced. No color bar existed in French Black Africa, and a cult of equality developed among the Africans, whose ideal—until after World War II—was to be completely accepted as French. Socially, African schoolchildren, soldiers and clerks lived on terms of virtual equality with their French counterparts.

On the other hand, Africans were entrusted by the French with responsible posts only in the cultural sphere, and their participation in the business of government remained almost solely on an advisory basis—with the exception of Senegal's council, its parliamentary deputies and its mayors. Even so, the special privileges that were granted the French-educated elite led to growing friction between that group and the traditional elite. The latter, which included the traditional chiefs and their immediate entourages, having been deprived of all but the shadow of their former power, were jealous of the rise of a new elite class which enjoyed the favor of the

The canton chief of Labé, Guinea, with his principal wife and the local schoolteacher. Both chief and schoolteacher are members of the "new" elite class. They belong to the Foula (Peul) tribe.

French administration and which frequently evaded customary tribal authority. For their part, the French-educated elite considered the traditional chiefs to be hidebound by custom and ignorance and to be a hindrance to African progress.

Friction between the old and the new elites—already evident before World War II—was to grow much sharper during the 1950's; and after independence was gained, the

African administrations of several of the new states simply abolished the traditional chiefdoms. Guinea took this step even before it became independent in early October 1958.

JUSTICE AND COURTS OF LAW

As already mentioned, African custom and French law differ widely. The Africans regard custom as the embodiment of the will of their ancestors, binding on all the clan under the principle of collective responsibility. It is handed down by oral tradition and interpreted by the tribal or family chief, to whom his people owe filial submission. Despite seeming contradictions, African custom has a fundamental unity, based in part on animist religious belief. Its application, however, reflects a traditional social inequality. Punishment for a certain offense is heavier for an individual of low class or caste than for one of higher rank. French law, by contrast, is secular in inspiration and stresses the responsibility of the individual and the equality of all persons before the law.

During the greater part of the federation's existence—until after World War II—these differences were mirrored in its judicial system. Courts applying the French penal and civil codes dealt with cases involving citizens, who then totaled fewer than 40,000 Africans and Europeans in West Africa. These courts also handled the rare cases in which non-citizen litigants chose to accept their jurisdiction.

Besides the above-mentioned courts, there were tribunals judging African *"protégés"*—later called subjects—which applied African customary law in both penal and civil cases. Inevitably most cases were handled by these courts, which were presided over by a French administrator flanked by two African "assessors" chosen from among the *notables* of the region for their special knowledge of local custom. The *commandant de cercle* was often referred to as the father of his

African "subjects," and when he sat in judgment in the customary court he performed duties formerly reserved to the head of a family or clan. Nevertheless he did not, of course, possess the religious and traditional authority of the latter.

Thus, aside from the few courts applying French law, judicial functions were in the hands of the executive branch of the administration, whose powers in the customary courts were supplemented by the *indigénat* system. The *indigénat* was a native-status legal "code" that enabled administrators to impose certain penalties arbitrarily upon Africans who were not citizens, for offenses punishable under law. For example, a French administrator could impose a fine or a jail sentence of a number of days on an African for some minor offense, without a formal trial. There was no right of appeal from his decision. The dispensing of justice in these native courts, as they were then called, therefore reflected the non-separation of powers as between the executive and the judiciary. By contrast, in France itself the principle of separation of the executive and judiciary powers was strictly observed, and this principle was followed also in the judicial system of the four Senegal communes.

MILITARY SERVICE

For many years, African soldiers—at first volunteers, and later, both volunteers and conscripts (draftees)—fought under the French flag in various parts of the French empire. During the Franco-Prussian War of 1870 and the two World Wars, they served in France itself.

Men from warlike Senegalese tribes, especially the Wolofs, took part in the French conquest of West Africa during the nineteenth century, and some served in such far-away places as Mexico and Madagascar. These were volunteers, and it was not until 1904, the same year in which the federation was founded, that a decree was issued providing for conscription of Africans if there were not enough volunteers to fill the West African quota.

In 1912, conscription was begun on a large scale in West Africa. This was expected to produce a large African army that could be used both in Africa and elsewhere. However, as a result of criticism of the conscription decree by some members of the French Parliament, including Senegal's deputy, the government applied the decree with such moderation that until World War I only about 8,000 to 10,000 Africans were conscripted each year.

When that war broke out in August 1914, conscription and also the recruiting of volunteers were stepped up sharply, and within two years, more than 80,000 West African soldiers were serving under the tricolor in Europe. Nearly half of them were Senegalese and Soudanese. By no means all of these Africans, however, were actually performing military duties. Many were assigned to labor battalions and to factories producing war material. Then, early in 1918, conscription was again greatly increased, to include all able-bodied men between the ages of 18 and 35. To reconcile the Africans to this move, conscripts were granted certain privileges, such as exemption from the *indigénat* and from taxation, payment of allowances to their families and preferment for ex-soldiers in some government jobs.

During the inter-war period of 1919–39, the African subjects in West Africa (and also Equatorial Africa) were liable to conscription for three-year periods. This did not apply, however, to Senegalese citizens, those born in the four communes, who were liable only to the same eighteen-month term of military service as were Frenchmen in France during those years. Although West Africa was then expected to furnish about 23,000 conscripts a year, so many of its men were physically unfit that during the inter-war period no more than about 10,000 were accepted for the army annually, out of a population which then totaled close to fifteen million.

As has been mentioned, the African soldier was given certain privileges, and in addition he enjoyed other advantages. He gained an elementary knowledge of the French language, learned a few skills, and saw something of the world beyond the narrow confines of his village. Most Africans who had served in the French army became deeply devoted to their commanders, whose relation to them resembled that of a father or a chief. By extension, African veterans developed a loyalty to France which often proved a valuable asset to the administration in later years.

Yet the benefits and privileges accorded the African soldier were more than offset by serious disadvantages. Military service meant the removal of young and able-bodied men from Africa, to the detriment of agriculture and the African birth rate. Many never returned, for some were killed in battle, some were unable to survive diseases or Europe's cold winters, and a few settled down in France. Those who came back were often restless, dissatisfied, and more or less alienated from the ways of African customary society, whose conservative members in turn tended to regard them with disfavor and suspicion as having been contaminated by their European experience.

The Federation on the Eve of World War II

On broad lines, the political situation in French West Africa in 1939 may be summarized as follows:

1. Its administration was in the hands of a hierarchy of French career officials, was in theory highly centralized and was marked by authoritarianism.

2. Africans did not participate in political life aside from the citizens of Senegal's communes and the handful of French-naturalized Africans in the rest of the federation. The great majority of Africans were subjects, not citizens, of France. Politically as well as culturally, the ideal of the federation's Africans—especially town-dwellers—was to attain full equality with the French. There was little or no independence sentiment.

3. In carrying out their "civilizing mission," the French had produced an elite group of "black Frenchmen," many of whom were socially and culturally assimilated to the whites. This new educated group and the traditional ruling class were mutually antipathetic and suspicious.

4. The judicial system was divided into two categories applying different codes of law—European and native. The vast majority of the population were under the jurisdiction of the native courts and also were subject to the procedure of arbitrary punishment known as the *indigénat*.

5. Certain features of French rule, such as the *indigénat*, forced labor and the head tax, weighed heavily upon the Africans and were increasingly resented by them.

6. Military conscription had become an institution, and many Africans were serving in the French army and in labor battalions in Europe and North Africa. African veterans enjoyed certain privileges and formed a sort of minor elite. As a group, they were notably loyal to France and to their French officers.

The World War II Interlude (1939–45)

Except for an unsuccessful Allied attack against Dakar in September 1940, French West Africa was untouched by military action during World War II. Its economy, however, as pointed out in Chapter VII, was greatly affected by the war.

Until the end of 1942, the federation's Governor-General, Pierre Boisson, remained loyal to the Vichy regime headed by Marshal Philippe Pétain, which was governing France in collaboration with the German military-occupation authorities. In French West Africa, Vichy's tenets—patterned on the master-race dogmas of the Nazis—led to increased racial discrimination and the reinforcement of the arbitrary nature of the *indigénat*. They also resulted in the elimination of the few existing political and labor organizations and to repression of any movements or individuals favoring General de Gaulle, who early in the war had assumed leadership of the Free French government-in-exile, based in London. Official French radio broadcasts by the Vichy regime from June 1940 to December 1942 showed that its grip on French West Africa was weakening. Its appeals for discipline and for increased production alternated with frantic pleas for patriotic cooperation in making the federation a military bastion against the encroachments of Allied forces from the adjoining British African colonies.

Intensification of the most oppressive aspects of colonialism, together with the adherence of neighboring French Equatorial Africa to the Free French cause early in 1940, had important repercussions on French West Africa. For both political and economic reasons, it was clearly in the interest of the federation's Africans to support the Free French, and they did so also because of the harsh repressions of the Vichy regime. Some of their paramount chiefs, especially in the eastern regions, refused to accept the 1940 Franco-German armistice. Many of the *tirailleurs* (African infantrymen) did likewise, and a considerable number of them escaped into Cameroun and French Equatorial Africa to join the resistance movement there. The Moro Naba, chief of the Mossi tribe of the Upper Volta, aroused the wrath of the Vichy-appointed administrators because he exhorted his people to resist the armistice. Before dying by his own hand, he made his heir promise not to assume power as chief "until the true French come back." Africans at all levels of society showed remarkable loyalty to France in its hour of defeat, and many of them were persecuted for their Gaullist sympathies.

When Governor-General Boisson decided in December 1942—after the American invasion of North Africa—to throw in his lot with the Free French, it was discovered that he had never permitted the Germans to fortify Dakar. From that time on, French West Africa faded from the war picture except in the effort which the Free French required it to make in supplying the Allies with natural rubber, oils and other materials.

Although the political and racial oppression practiced by the pro-Vichy French officials in Africa largely ended when they disappeared from the scene, the federation continued to suffer greatly in economic respects from January 1943 until the end of the war in 1945. As a result of the social and economic hardships it had borne during the war years, the African population was eager for the reforms heralded by the Brazzaville conference of 1944.

The Territories' Political Evolution
(1945–60)

The defeat of France and the alignment of many outstanding French Black Africans with the Free French had at least two results of far-reaching importance for French West Africa. One was the rapid development of political maturity among the local population, especially the urban elite group. The other was the realization by the Gaullist government-in-exile that, when the war ended, the relationship between France and its African colonies had to be altered in many fundamental respects.

THE BRAZZAVILLE CONFERENCE, JANUARY–FEBRUARY 1944

In late January and early February 1944, more than a year before the end of World War II, a number of influential Free French politicians and high-ranking colonial officials held a series of meetings in Brazzaville, capital of French Equatorial Africa. This conference adopted various resolutions concerning future policy in France's colonial empire.

Its political recommendations were cautious, despite the fact that they represented a sharp break with much that was typical of the colonial past. Within a few years after the war ended, they proved inadequate to deal with the rapid evolution of French Black African political life. Although the conference declared itself in favor of partial decentralization of the West African administration, it nevertheless advocated the continuance of some form of federal organization that would preserve unity. It proposed that there be much greater participation by Africans in the conduct of the colonies' public affairs, but flatly ruled out the possibility of any form of self-government for the colonies, even in the distant future. It recommended, in fact, that the ties that bound the African colonies to France be strengthened through larger African representation in the post-war French parliamentary bodies. The colonies, it decided, should also elect representatives (deputies) to the constituent assembly which, after the end of the war, would be called together in Paris to draw up a new constitution for liberated France and its overseas empire.

In contrast to the caution of the Brazzaville Conference's political resolutions, its proposals concerning social and economic questions were much more forward-looking. Legislated primarily in the early months of 1946, they blazed the trail for a number of the most striking changes of the post-war period, which profoundly altered many ways of life in French West Africa.

THE CONSTITUTION OF 1946

During the year that followed the liberation of France in May 1945 from the German occupation and the puppet government of Marshal Pétain, a wave of reform feeling swept the country. To a large extent this was a spontaneous revulsion against the harshness of Fascist rule. In part it was promoted by the French Communist party, which had played a large role in French Resistance activity during the war and had emerged as one of the three strong political parties of the early post-war period. In late 1945 and the first few months of 1946, this reform trend greatly affected Franco-African relations and France's policy in its African possessions, both politically and economically. It was at this time that the French public and politicians began to speak of "territories" instead of "colonies" and of a "French Union" instead of a "French Empire."

Elections to the first constituent assembly—which was to draw up the new constitution for France's Fourth Republic and also to act as a provisional legislative assembly—were held in October and November 1945. As recommended by the Brazzaville Conference, French West Africa participated in these elections. The federation had been allotted ten seats in the assembly, five to be filled by the so-called first college of electors and five by the second college. This dual-college electoral system was to be a bone of contention for a number of years, because it insured disproportionate representation of French citizens (mostly white) in legislative bodies. The first college was made up of French individuals living in the territories and of a tiny minority of naturalized Africans, and the second college consisted wholly of French subjects—that is, the mass of Africans. (Except in Senegal, the dual-college system was the rule in French Black African elections until 1956, even though citizenship was granted to former "subjects" under a law passed by the constituent assembly in May 1946. After that law took effect the following month, the first college was made up of Frenchmen and of Africans who had become naturalized French citizens, and the second college included the remainder of the population insofar as they met the requirements of the franchise. The latter were also French citizens but had a special status which is described below (see page 188).

Most of the African deputies elected to the constituent assembly from French West Africa were men who, though newcomers to politics, later became leaders and in some cases presidents of certain West African republics after 1958. Among the latter were Léopold S. Senghor of Senegal and Félix Houphouët-Boigny of Ivory Coast.

The constitution drafted by the first constituent assembly was rejected by the French people in a referendum of May 1946. During the summer of that year, the second constituent assembly drafted a compromise text, which was accepted in a referendum held the following October. One significant respect in which the second constitution differed from the first was that it failed to include a clause allowing the former colonies to decide what their relationship to France should be. This clause was omitted because France, between the two referendums, underwent a conservative reaction that quenched much of the post-war enthusiasm for liberal reforms.

THE FRENCH UNION

Under the terms of the constitution of the Fourth Republic, France and its various overseas possessions formally received the name of the French Union. The colonies of French West Africa—like those of French Equatorial Africa—were re-baptized "overseas territories" and were to be integral parts of the French Republic, with elected representation in its Parliament. The French Republic, together with its overseas territories (and overseas departments such as Algeria, the French Antilles, and Réunion Island), was to form one part of the French Union. In addition, the Union was to include so-called "associated territories" (the United Nations trust territories of Togo and Cameroun) and "associated states" (certain countries of North Africa and Indochina).

THE POST-WAR REFORMS

The political reforms of the early post-war period, which had such far-reaching effects in France's overseas territories, were the result of pressure from three groups in France and French Africa.

One of these was made up of French liberals of various party persuasions who, in the flush of post-war enthusiasm, made common cause with the French Communist party. As already mentioned, that party emerged as a powerful political force in France at the end of the war because of its activity in the Resistance during the German occupation.

Another group that pushed for reform consisted of African students in France, leaders of trade unions in Africa, and the Communist Study Groups which had already been formed in

Léopold Sédar Senghor, President of Senegal. Besides being one of Africa's foremost political thinkers, he is a poet whose work is highly regarded, both in France and in Africa.

some French African territories before the end of the war.

A third and important pressure group included the Africans elected to the 1946 constituent assemblies. Besides Léopold Senghor and Félix Houphouët-Boigny, referred to above, this group included such influential post-war political figures as Lamine Gueye of Senegal, S. M. Apithy of Dahomey, and Mamadou Konaté and Fily Dabo Sissoko of Soudan.

Most of the political reforms which had their origin in the

resolutions of the Brazzaville Conference were embodied in laws passed by the first constituent assembly during the early months of 1946, before the conservative reaction in France drained the force of the post-war wave of liberal idealism. The reforms accomplished during that short period marked both a great advance over the pre-1939 era and a return to the liberal concepts of the 1789 revolution. In March and April 1946, the following reforms were legislated by the assembly:

1. The grant of "republican liberties"—the right of association and of meeting, which legalized the development of political parties and labor unions in French Black Africa.
2. Abolition of forced labor and of the *indigénat*.
3. Suppression of the jurisdiction of native courts in penal cases, which from then on were to be tried under the French penal code.

Early in May 1946, the assembly passed one of the most important of the reform measures. This was the so-called "first Lamine Gueye law," which conferred French citizenship on all inhabitants of the overseas territories, while allowing them to retain their personal—that is, customary—civil status. This meant, for example, that the practice of polygamy (really polygyny, see page 55), illegal in France, continued to be legal in the overseas territories. The law, which became effective on June 1, 1946, was embodied in the constitution of the Fourth Republic as Article 80.

Far-reaching changes were made also in the administrative and legislative structure of the overseas territories. Decentralization was the order of the day, although its effects were not widely felt and a few months later the trend was again toward centralization. A federal assembly called the Grand Council was set up at Dakar to deal with matters affecting the eight territories as a whole, but each territory was given an assembly, or council-general as it was first called. These assemblies were elected under the dual-college system and were empowered to vote on territorial budgets and taxes as well as other questions of territorial concern. The Grand Council's 40 members (five from each territory) were to be elected by the territorial assemblies from among their own membership.

A step taken by the first constituent assembly which was of enormous importance to the future of French Black Africa was the creation of an economic-development organization that had been decided upon by the Brazzaville Conference. On April 30, 1946, the assembly passed a law setting up the Investment Fund for Economic and Social Development (in its French abbreviation, which for the sake of brevity will be used in this book: F.I.D.E.S.). The task of this organization was to prepare long-range plans for the development of the overseas territories and to supervise the use of French public funds allotted for their fulfilment. Although F.I.D.E.S. was basically non-political in nature, it was designed to supplement the political as well as social and economic reforms launched at the same time. Further details concerning the operations of F.I.D.E.S. are given in Chapter VII.

THE SLOWDOWN OF REFORMS: 1946–56

During the summer of 1946, as mentioned above, the post-war wave of French enthusiasm for reforms in the African territories and in their relations with France began to subside in the face of a conservative reaction.

One of the early signs of this was the defeat of the first draft constitution in the May 7 referendum. Soon conservative politicians in France joined forces with influential French commercial interests in Black Africa in trying to reduce the impact of the reforms that had been put on the books in March and April. The dual electoral college already mentioned, which gave the white population disproportionately high representation, was imposed in all elections except in Senegal. The powers of the newly created territorial assemblies and federal Grand Council of French West Africa were restricted almost entirely to financial matters such as the budget. And because of fears that the "republican liberties" which had been granted to Africans might encourage the rise of independence sentiment, especially in a federated territorial structure, the conservatives favored administrative decentralization of the French West and Equatorial African federations. They were opposed, however, to any weakening of French control.

This resurgent conservatism slowed down the tempo of further reforms to a very slow pace. During the 1946–56 decade, there were only three important reforms that affected Black Africa.

One of these was the so-called "second Lamine Gueye law" of 1950, which, like the citizenship law of 1946, was named for its sponsor, the Senegalese Socialist deputy Lamine Gueye. This law was designed to assure equal treatment for Africans as to pay and working conditions in the civil service.

In December 1952 the French Parliament adopted another law aimed at improving the condition of workers in Africa, the Overseas Labor Code. Passed mainly as a result of pressure by labor leaders, both French and African, it granted African wage-earners equal status with French workers in regard to minimum wages, family allowances, length of the working day, collective bargaining and paid vacations.

The third reform measure of the 1946–56 period was the municipal law of November 1955. This piece of legislation, which represented the first move to install local-government institutions throughout French Black Africa, provided for the creation in French West Africa of twenty-nine municipal governments (communes) with local mayors and councils chosen by a combined roll of all the electors concerned—the "single electoral college" so much desired by Africans.

The three laws just described were important stepping-stones on the path to complete equality of Africans and Frenchmen, which was the highest political goal of the Africans in the overseas territories during the post-war decade. The reforms they accomplished, however, were so few in number, so slow in arriving, and so haltingly put into force that the Africans gradually began to lose heart and to turn to very different objectives.

THE GROWTH OF POLITICAL PARTIES

Before World War II, Senegal was the only French West African colony to have a political party, and this party was merely a branch of the French Socialist party. The 1946 reforms instituted elections throughout the federation and encouraged the formation and growth of parties. Since the Socialists were the first in the field, they won almost all the elections held that year for the French Parliament and the territorial assemblies. But the Socialists remained too closely tied to the mother party in France, and soon they were defeated by the candidates put up by the Federation's first genuinely African political organizations—the Rassemblement Démocratique Africain (R.D.A.), or African Democratic Rally, and the Indépendants d'Outre-Mer (I.O.M.), or Overseas Independents.

The R.D.A. Of these, the first and more important was the R.D.A., which was founded in October 1946 by an African doctor from the Ivory Coast, Félix Houphouët-Boigny. Its aim was to give legislative support to African aspirations for more political power, which were threatened by the French conservative reaction. In getting his movement under way, Houphouët felt the need of aid from more experienced politicians. He found an ally—the French Communist party, which was eager to make use of the newborn African movement to further its own ends. Despite its opportunism, however, the French Communist party rendered a great service to the R.D.A. in its formative years by teaching its leaders how to organize a political party and conduct effective propaganda campaigns. Using the Communist party as a model, the R.D.A. developed a strong structure which was framed on a pyramid of authority. The chain of command extended down from a "politburo" (executive committee) at the pyramid's apex, through regional groups, to village cells at the base. Its propaganda consisted of simple slogans, easily understood by the mass of the population. The slogans also had revolutionary overtones that appealed to the young educated townspeople, who wanted to throw off the authority of the French administration and the traditional chiefs. It was not surprising, therefore, that membership in the R.D.A. grew by leaps and bounds. Branches were organized and flourished in all the territories except Senegal, where the Socialists were already entrenched, and Mauritania, where the traditional chiefs were still powerful.

In fact, the success of the R.D.A. was so rapid and widespread that the French administration, the Christian missionaries and the African chiefs all became alarmed. In some territories they joined forces to encourage the formation of parties opposed to the R.D.A., and they used their influence to bring about the defeat of R.D.A. candidates in elections. Almost all the parties so formed were small and weak for their programs were negative rather than positive, and they were held together simply by the loyalty which a few people felt for a particular leader or region.

The I.O.M. The only effective opposition to the R.D.A. was provided by the second French African political organization mentioned above—the Overseas Independents (I.O.M.). It was formed at Paris in 1947 by a group of French West African deputies headed by the Senegalese poet and statesman, Léopold S. Senghor. Shortly before, he had broken away from the Socialists led by Lamine Gueye and had founded in Senegal the Bloc Démocratique Sénégalais (B.D.S.), or Senegalese Democratic Bloc. This was one of the few strong territorial parties that was not linked to the R.D.A. Senghor disapproved of the R.D.A.'s revolutionary doctrines and its alliance with the French Communist party, though not of its goals. He therefore organized the I.O.M. as a group of moderate African deputies and senators who could bring enough pressure to bear in the French Parliament to obtain the passage of laws that would further African progress. The new group's policy met with the approval of the French government, and with the administration's help in Africa the I.O.M. won more seats than the R.D.A. in the National Assembly elections of June 1951.

EVOLUTION OF THE PARTIES

One of the chief reasons for the R.D.A.'s defeat in 1951 was the dramatic reversal of Houphouët-Boigny's policy the year before. Early in 1949, clashes had taken place between the French administration and the R.D.A. in Ivory Coast. The French authorities believed that the local branch of the R.D.A. was plotting to take over the country, and they did not hesitate to use stringent methods to forestall any such attempt. Many local leaders of the R.D.A. were jailed, and its membership declined. At about the same time, the influence of the French Communist party in the Paris Parliament had waned. Both these developments made Houphouët realize that his alliance with the French Communists and his use of their revolutionary tactics had become more of a liability than an asset to his movement. He therefore decided to sever his ties with them and did so late in 1950.

There were two main results of this reversal of policy by Houphouët. The first was that he began to try to collaborate with the French government. At the outset the French were suspicious of his motives and again worked to defeat the R.D.A. in the 1951 elections. Within a few years, however, they became convinced of the Ivory Coast leader's sincerity and welcomed his cooperation. The second result of Houphouët's change of front was that a few territorial branches and leaders of the R.D.A. refused to abandon the revolutionary Marxism of the party's first years and were expelled. Most R.D.A. members, however, followed Houphouët's lead. In fact, by the time the next legislative elections were held, in January 1956, the R.D.A. had completely changed its character. It had become a bulwark of conservatism, whereas the I.O.M., moderate at the start, had moved in the meantime towards a more radical position.

Just at the time when the R.D.A. was rejecting doctrinaire political theories and operating according to the political realities of the moment, the I.O.M., under Senghor's intellectual leadership, was formulating a political doctrine. This doctrine summed up African demands that the local assemblies be given a share of executive power in their respective territories, and that the French Republic (which included the overseas territories) be transformed into a federation of autonomous states. In the light of later developments in West Africa, this was not a radical program, but it was considered so at the time. It was too daring and too abstract to be widely approved or understood by the I.O.M. membership, and Senghor lacked the party machinery needed to engineer its acceptance. Indeed, where the I.O.M. was strong the R.D.A. was weak, and vice versa. The I.O.M. was simply a loose alliance of moderate African politicians who were fairly effective in the French Parliament but poorly organized in Africa. On the other hand, although the R.D.A. had become weak in political theory, its organizational strength in Africa was such that it not only survived Houphouët's drastic change of policy but actually grew in power.

While the I.O.M. members were busy in Paris helping to push through the French Parliament the reform legislation of 1950, 1952, and 1955 mentioned above, the R.D.A. leaders were successfully mending their political fences in Africa. The 1956 elections confirmed the come-back of the R.D.A., showed the decline in I.O.M. strength, and virtually eliminated the Socialists as a major political force in French West Africa. In almost every territory the R.D.A. either won a decisive victory or bettered its previous position. It was clear that the R.D.A. had again become the dominant party in French Black Africa, and therefore logical that its leader, Houphouët, should be appointed a minister in France's new government.

This was the most liberal government which France had had since 1946, and its Minister of Overseas France, Gaston Defferre, aided the legislative drive for reforms in the African territories. The principles of these reforms were embodied in the one general "framework law" (*loi-cadre*), and they reflected the ideas of Houphouët, who had helped to draft it.

Trend towards Autonomy and Unity

The passage of the *loi-cadre* by the French Parliament on June 23, 1956, marked a turning-point in the history of

French Black Africa. By its terms, both the dual electoral college and the two federal governments-general (of French West and French Equatorial Africa) were abolished. In order to maintain coordination at the federal level, the government-general in each of the former federations was replaced by a High Commissioner, representing the French government, and an elected Grand Council, which was to concern itself only with a limited category of matters of common interest to the territories. At the same time, universal adult suffrage was introduced, and most important of all, Africans could elect a government council in each territory that would share in the executive power with the French administrations there.

Although this reform fell short of granting full self-government to the Africans, it cleared the way to much greater autonomy and was warmly welcomed by them. Only a few leaders, including Senghor, dared to risk unpopularity by pointing out certain weaknesses in the *loi-cadre*. In Senghor's view, its most serious defect was the "balkanization," or splitting up, of West Africa that would result from eliminating the federal administration and the common services that it had performed on a federation-wide basis. He did not see how such poor territories could afford to have eight separate administrations to handle such matters as health, transport and education, which had previously been the responsibility of the Government-General. An even worse feature, he felt, was the divisions that this autonomous development would cause among the West Africans, for thenceforth they would have in common only their ties with France. He therefore proposed the formation of what he called a primary federation. This federation would preserve the practical advantages of the old Government-General but would differ basically from it in being a voluntary grouping entered into by the Africans for their mutual benefit.

Houphouët, on the other hand, for very practical reasons was opposed to any revival of the federal set-up. Under the old system, the surplus revenues of Ivory Coast, the richest country in French West Africa, had been turned over to the poorer territories, but an autonomous regime would mean that his people could use all of their income for their own territory's development.

Because the disadvantages of the *loi-cadre* that would result for the poor territories were not immediately apparent, and as most French Africans could see only its political benefits, Senghor's warnings went unheeded for some time. It was only in 1957, after the law had been put to the practical test which disclosed its drawbacks, that Senghor's proposal for a primary federation began to win considerable support in French West Africa.

By the end of 1956, the trend towards African unity had been accelerated by other events both in Africa and in France. As a result of pressure in the United Nations, French Togo— a trust territory—had already been conceded in August 1955 a much larger degree of self-government than France's overseas territories had won up to that time. The French protectorates of Morocco and Tunisia had been granted their independence in 1956, and the British-ruled Gold Coast was moving rapidly towards the sovereignty it attained under the name of "Ghana" in March 1957. French West Africans did not yet talk of independence, but there was clearly a tendency to close ranks, and they gradually disengaged themselves from French institutions and controls.

In January 1957, most of the French West African labor unions joined together to form their own autonomous organization, the Union Générale de Travailleurs d'Afrique Noire (U.G.T.A.N.), or General Union of Black African Workers, which will be referred to again in Chapter VII. The same month, the African Socialists—who until that time had belonged to a scattering of territorial organizations—founded the Mouvement Socialiste Africain (M.S.A.), or African Socialist Movement. In January 1957, also, Senghor organized a new interterritorial party called the Convention Africaine, which he hoped would be composed of parties united on a territorial basis. Senghor's ideal of political unity was not acceptable, however, to the various territorial-party leaders, and his Convention Africaine was a failure. In any event, Houphouët would still have been able to block such a move in the territories where the R.D.A. was in control.

Yet by early 1958, the trend towards unity had gained such momentum that Houphouët lost control of his party, and the R.D.A. split apart. Some territorial branches remained loyal to him, but the Parti Démocratique de Guinée (P.D.G.), or Guinea Democratic Party, led by Sékou Touré, and the Union Soudanaise (U.S.), or Soudanese Union, under Modibo Keita, left Houphouët and joined the growing ranks of Senghor's federalists. Together they formed the Parti du Regroupement Africain (P.R.A.), or African Regrouping Party, in the spring of 1958, and its members began to demand not simply African unity but independence from France as well.

THE NEW CONSTITUTION AND THE REFERENDUM: 1958

At about the same time that the P.R.A. was being organized at Dakar, important events were taking place in France. They culminated with the return to power of the former Free French leader, Charles de Gaulle, in June 1958, after more than a decade of retirement. Almost as soon as he became Premier he announced that France would have another constitution, which would be submitted to a popular referendum the following September.

During that summer, the government prepared the draft of a constitution providing for a Franco-African Community, which would take the form of a federal republic. France would still be the head of the Community, but its other members would no longer be overseas territories but autonomous states.

To explain the issues involved in the September referendum and to take the Africans' political temperature, so to speak, de Gaulle made a tour of French Black Africa late in August 1958. What he learned from that trip, short as it was, led to a change of relationships within the Community and profoundly altered the course of events in French West Africa. The Africans argued so strongly for recognition of their right to independence that de Gaulle told them it could be attained by any territory whose population cast a negative vote in the referendum. Even if a territory should vote in September to join the Community, he said, it could leave the Community later if it so desired. At the same time, however, he gave the Africans a warning that made his offer of independence seem less tempting: If a territory voted "no" in the referendum, it would receive no further aid from France.

The terms that de Gaulle offered to French Black Africans were prompted in part by the aspirations they expressed to him during his journey and in part by the changed attitude of many Frenchmen towards the overseas territories. Many had become so discouraged by the disastrous Indochina war and by the long-drawn-out and costly conflict in Algeria that they were eager to rid themselves of responsibility for the rest of the overseas dependencies. For 12 years France had been pouring great sums of money into Black Africa, but these seemed only drops in the bucket compared with the Africans' enormous needs. French conservatives, especially, believed that it would be better to use public funds at home, and that it was time for France to pull out of Africa altogether. This group felt sure that, despite de Gaulle's promise of continued French financial aid to territories that joined the Community, independent sentiment among the Africans would cause some territories to vote against it. Consequently, in the summer of 1958 a large segment of French public opinion, both liberal and conservative, supported General de Gaulle's offer to the Africans. The final draft of the constitution, embodying de Gaulle's most recent concessions, was agreed upon on September 4, after the General's return from Africa.

Contrary to the French conservatives' expectation that many Africans would choose independence in preference to continued French financial support, most leaders of French Black Africa saw clearly that the continuance of economic aid from France was vitally necessary to their countries. Moreover, because de Gaulle's prestige was very high among them, they put faith in his promise that territories which joined the Community would be free to leave it later. Under their urging, the African electors of all the French West African territories except Guinea voted overwhelmingly, on September 28, 1958, in favor of the Constitution of the Fifth French Republic.

Guinea's breakaway. For several reasons, Guinea voted almost unanimously (95 per cent) to reject the Constitution, and with it, membership in the Community. The least important of these reasons—though it was much played up in press dispatches—was the clash between the young P.D.G. leader, Sékou Touré, and General de Gaulle during the latter's African tour. A more fundamental cause lay in the background, personality and training of Sékou Touré. His maternal grandfather was the fierce opponent of France, Samory, whose career has been described in Chapter V. Unlike other French West African leaders, Touré had not been exposed to French higher education. Moreover, he had been trained in African Communist "study groups" as a trade-union organizer of strongly Marxist leanings. Thanks to his anti-French heritage from Samory, his fervent nationalist feelings and his Marxist indoctrination, Sékou Touré firmly believed that Guinea must become an independent country under wholly African control. So far as Guinea's economic future was concerned, the fact that the country possessed huge deposits of bauxite and iron convinced Touré that it could make its way without French aid.

Politically, Touré was in such a strong position that he could be reasonably sure the Guineans would follow his lead without question. He controlled the country's labor unions and was the undisputed leader of the most tightly organized political party in all French West Africa. As head of Guinea's government council, he had already removed the traditional chiefs from their positions of authority. His dynamic and colorful personality cast a spell over the mass of the population, and when he asked them to vote "no" to the Community they did so without hesitation. Their vote for complete independence meant the severance of political ties with France and also the immediate end of French aid in all forms.

After Guinea became independent, it very soon found itself isolated politically and in a bad situation financially. Such immediate help as it was able to obtain came from only two sources. One was Ghana, whose leader, Kwame Nkrumah, had ambitions to create and dominate an all-African, or Pan-African, movement that would include all the countries of the Dark Continent. Seeing in Sékou Touré a leader with ideas like his own, and in Guinea the first prospective partner in his Pan-African movement, he loaned a large sum of money to the hard-pressed Guineans and persuaded Touré to form a union with Ghana in November 1958.

The second source of the aid received by Guinea at that crucial time consisted of the Communist countries of Eastern Europe. By means of loans and trade agreements, and by sending technicians to replace the French who had left the country abruptly in large numbers, the Soviet Union and its satellites gained their first foothold in sub-Saharan Africa. They made the most of their opportunities there, and for the next three years it seemed that Guinea might gravitate towards the Communist bloc.

Regardless of the risks to its independence that it ran in accepting help from such countries as Ghana and the U.S.S.R., the fact that Guinea—whose leader had dared to say "no" to de Gaulle—was able to survive as a sovereign state made a great impression on many French West Africans. This was particularly so among the younger generation, which was extremely nationalistic and had Marxist leanings. In short, the example of Guinea and Ghana served as a powerful stimulus to independence sentiment among their neighbors.

The Mali Federation

So far as the African territories were concerned, the 1958 referendum on France's new constitution was expected to decide only their future relations with France. The referendum did not touch on the other burning issue of the period in French Africa—that of unity—which General de Gaulle left up to the Africans themselves to settle. This issue again came to the fore as soon as all the French West African territories except Guinea had voted to join the Community as autonomous republics.

Senghor was still in the forefront of the drive for African unity, but he now had at his side an even more ardent advocate of it—Modibo Keita, Premier of Soudan. At a series of meetings late in 1958 and early in 1959, the two leaders planned a new grouping of French West African states, to be called the Mali Federation. It was originally expected that the Federation would include also Dahomey and Upper Volta. However, those two states withdrew from the group before it was formally set up on April 4, 1959, so that its only members were Senegal and Soudan.

General de Gaulle did not welcome the formation of the Mali Federation, for at that time he was organizing the Franco-African Community as a Paris-dominated structure, and he saw no need for any inter-African federation. In another quarter, the new federation met with determined opposition from Houphouët-Boigny, who was occupied with laying the foundations of a rival inter-African group of states, the Council of the Entente.

Undaunted, Senghor and Modibo went ahead steadily with the task of making their reduced federation a going concern. By the end of 1959 they had persuaded de Gaulle not only to consent to independence for the Mali Federation but also to permit it to remain a member of the Community and to continue receiving French aid. De Gaulle saw that unless he granted independence to the Mali Federation with good grace, its leaders probably would opt for independence and at the same time leave the Community. To be sure, such a move by de Gaulle would almost certainly alienate Houphouët, who had been France's firmest friend among West Africa's leaders. Nevertheless, the French President took this risk, and on June 20, 1960, the Mali Federation proclaimed its independence as a member of the Community.

De Gaulle's sweeping concession to the federation was the first step in the dissolution of the Community, which by mid-1961 was only a shadow of its former self. As will be seen in Chapter VIII, relations between France and the independent states that emerged from the old French West African federation have been based since that time upon bilateral treaties and agreements. It is possible that if the concession made to the Mali Federation in 1960 had been accorded to all the African territories in September 1958, Guinea might have voted to become a member of the Community, which would therefore have had a longer life. But a year's time and a profound change in the political atmosphere of West Africa, largely because of developments in Guinea and Ghana, had been required in order to produce the circumstances under which the concession was made.

No sooner had the leaders of the Mali Federation reached their main goal than they had a serious dispute. It quickly became evident that Senghor and Modibo held conflicting views as to how the federation should develop and even as to how it should be organized. Senghor wanted a loose union that would permit Senegal—by far the richer of the two partners—to use most of its revenues to promote its economic growth. He also wanted to maintain a multi-party political system, to create a government of the parliamentary type and to preserve close ties with France. Modibo, on the other hand, sought a tight political union with Senegal, a government that would be controlled by a single party (preferably his own), and a pooling of the two countries' resources. As a Muslim, he opposed the candidacy of Senghor, a Catholic, for the office of president of the predominantly Muslim federation. As a Marxist, he insisted on strict state controls over a planned economy. And as a Soudanese, he was disdainful of the "Frenchified," undisciplined and bourgeois Senegalese.

The disagreement between the two leaders came to a head on the night of August 19, 1960, when Modibo and his followers made an unsuccessful attempt to take over the federation government and seize control of Dakar, its capital.

Reacting vigorously, the Senegalese arrested and deported Modibo and his principal aides, then proclaimed that the federation was dissolved and that Senegal was an independent nation. The Soudanese were furious with Senegal for this action and with France for soon recognizing Senegal's independence. They closed the frontier with Senegal, announced that they would leave the Community, and proclaimed that Soudan would thenceforth be known as the sovereign Republic of Mali. The Mali Republic became a severely disciplined one-party state, nationalistic and Marxist in its economic policy. Soon it moved towards a partnership with the Ghana-Guinea Union which, as mentioned above, had been formed in November 1958. Though it later created its own currency, Mali remained in the franc zone and continued to receive economic aid from France.

THE COUNCIL OF THE ENTENTE

First the formation and then the collapse of the Mali Federation had widespread repercussions throughout the countries of former French West Africa. As already indicated, its appearance on the political scene had intensified Houphouët's efforts towards putting together a rival bloc, the Council of the Entente. The latter, however, differed fundamentally from the Mali Federation.

The Council of the Entente, formed May 29, 1959, comprised the four contiguous states of Ivory Coast, Dahomey, Upper Volta and Niger, whose leaders did not seek a close political union but aimed at cooperation in economic and cultural matters for their mutual benefit. The two landlocked countries, Upper Volta and Niger, needed the trade facilities afforded by the seaports and railroads of Ivory Coast and Dahomey, and all but Ivory Coast were so poor that they had to have financial help from outside even to balance their operating budgets. Hamani Diori (then Premier of Niger) and Maurice Yaméogo (then Premier of Upper Volta) were close collaborators and friends of Houphouët-Boigny, because they had all been members of the orthodox R.D.A. This could not be said of Premier Hubert Maga of Dahomey, who at one time had belonged to the I.O.M. The Dahomeyans, however, were poor and were afraid of being swallowed up by their huge and powerful neighbor, Nigeria, so they felt that it was to their advantage to join the Council of the Entente.

Money was the most tempting bait that Houphouët had to offer other African countries as an inducement to join the Entente. In deference to his partners' pride he called it a "solidarity fund." The fact that Houphouët was now willing to subsidize his African "poor relations" indicated how far he had gone in adapting himself to the new political climate in West Africa. For a long time he had held out against a primary federation, mainly because he felt that all of Ivory Coast's revenues should be used at home. Once he realized, however, that in trying to stem the tide of African unity he had lost his leadership position in West Africa, he changed his course as completely as he had done in 1950. As it turned out, the economy of Ivory Coast, far from stagnating because of handouts through the solidarity fund, flourished as never before. Houphouët's country rapidly became the wealthiest in French-speaking Black Africa. By persuading France to grant independence to all the Entente and inducing them to withdraw from the Community, Houphouët regained much of the political prestige that he had previously enjoyed.

When the Entente was organized, many people thought it would never get off the ground. Then its early collapse was predicted when disagreements arose among its members. One such case was a quarrel between Ivory Coast and Upper Volta over their respective shares of customs duties, which caused the latter country to move closer to Ghana. In 1961, when the Union Africaine et Malgache (U.A.M.), or Afro-Malagasy Union, was created, it again seemed that the Entente might be doomed (see pages 250–252). Yet the Entente has not only survived but even grown stronger, as was demonstrated in early 1963, when the murder of Togo's President Sylvanus Olympio caused the Entente members to pledge aid to each other against any threat of subversion. The very modesty of its aims, the flexibility of its organization and above all the recognition by its members of their interdependence—all these characteristics have enabled the Entente to thrive while some better-known African alliances such as the Mali Federation, the Ghana-Guinea-Mali Union and the Casablanca and Monrovia blocs (described in Chapter VIII) have either broken up abruptly or faded away.

Political Characteristics of the New States

By the end of 1960, all the territories of former French West Africa had become independent nations. By mid-1961, only Senegal—of all the former F.W.A. territories—was still a member of the Franco-African community. Although the new nations have thus taken different paths in their relations with France, they have developed according to an almost identical pattern. This is so because all of them have the same basic social structure, have experienced the rule of the same colonial government and must deal with the same problems in trying to reach the same objectives.

Now the countries of French West Africa are all politically independent republics, but they have not yet become truly united nations, nor have they developed their economies to the point where they can get along without outside aid. They face common handicaps in creating national unity and in

President Modibo Keita of Mali receives the symbolic key of the city of Abidjan from President Félix Houphouët-Boigny of Ivory Coast, during a visit in 1962.

modernizing their economies. These handicaps are the artificial political frontiers which they have inherited from the colonial period; the persistence of tribal and regional loyalties; the uneven distribution, illiteracy and undernourishment of their populations; and the backwardness of their agriculture and animal husbandry.

All of them believe that to overcome these difficulties and to attain their goals of internal unity and national development, they must have a single-party system of government. This political phenomenon, which is common to the French-speaking West African nations, will be examined in more detail below.

First, however, it might be useful to turn to the summary of the principal administrative and political institutions of the eight states found in Appendix I on page 316 ff. Further details regarding the inter-African organizations and alliances mentioned, such as the Casablanca and Monrovia Groups— both now disbanded—and the Afro-Malagasy Union, will be found in Chapter VIII. All the eight states are members of the United Nations and its specialized agencies, as well as other organizations, such as the World Bank. All except Guinea are associated with the European Economic Community, usually called the "Common Market"; this relationship is described in Chapter VII.

SINGLE-PARTY RULE

In the French-speaking states of West Africa, the single party has become predominant by eliminating organized political opposition, either through force or through persuasion. Then, by altering the country's constitution with the consent of the population, it has gained. control of the machinery of government. To do these things effectively, each such party has had to develop an organization so strong and widespread that it takes in all elements of the population. It has also had to work out a program or policy that embodies the people's aspirations and to find a leader who can arouse popular enthusiasm and command loyal support.

Naturally, not every one of French West Africa's single parties has been equally successful in all three of these efforts. Some of them, like the parties of Guinea, Mali, Senegal and Ivory Coast, have been under the leadership of men whose personalities have great popular appeal and who have inherited the authority attached to traditional chiefs. Others, such as the parties of Dahomey, Niger, Upper Volta and Mauritania, are headed by less glamorous individuals who by means of shrewd political moves have simply outmaneuvered their rivals. A few parties, including the Guinea Democratic Party, the Soudanese Union and the Senegalese Progressives' Union, have had not only popular leaders but programs based on ideas that appeal to the intellectual elite. However, the majority of the single parties in former French West Africa have programs based not on any abstract principles but simply on the attainment of practical objectives.

Nevertheless, even though dynamic leadership and an idealistic program are very helpful when a party is being formed and is acquiring control of the government, its retention of power depends more on the thoroughness of its organization. In this respect, as already indicated, the R.D.A.'s organization has served as the model for all of former French West Africa's single parties. By following its example, they have been able to gain control of their countries' political life, and in most cases to maintain that control.

THE SINGLE PARTY VS. THE TRADITIONAL CHIEFS

In many areas, the authority which tradition has conferred on the chiefs is still an obstacle to the realization of the single party's aim of complete control of the population. Even though their influence is on the wane everywhere and was never great in the coastal zones of Ivory Coast and Guinea, some chiefs are still powerful in the Saharan borderlands of Mauritania, Mali, Niger and Upper Volta. Their position was also strong among the Peul of the Fouta Djallon mountains until December 1957, when the Guinea Democratic Party, at one fell blow, removed the chiefs there from their

Delegates to a regional political conference of the Guinea Democratic party at Mamou, Guinea. Their identification papers are being checked at the door.

posts of authority. This example was followed in Mali by the Soudanese Union, although not so abruptly.

The Guinea Democratic Party and the Soudanese Union—being the two most tightly organized and radical parties in former French West Africa—were eager and able to take such a decisive step. The weaker single parties of Mauritania, Niger and Upper Volta, however, have been too dependent on the political support of the chiefs, as well as on their role as an element of social stability, to risk such drastic measures. They have preferred to let the chieftaincy die a natural death by not appointing any new chiefs and by transforming the younger ones into agents of the central government.

All of the single parties under discussion here have employed another tactic both to undermine the chieftaincy and to extend their control over the countryside. By creating new administrative units and local-government institutions, such as elected regional and municipal councils, they have won both more popularity and more control. This step has seemed, on the surface, to give the people a larger role in the management of their own affairs and to help them free themselves from the arbitrary exactions of the chiefs. To a certain extent this is true. Nevertheless it is the single party, speaking for the government, that names the new heads of the administrative units and that also sends its own agents into the regions and townships to see that the party's directives are carried out. Under this system there are parallel chains of command —one comprising the civil servants and the other the party's agents—which extend down from the central executive committee (sometimes called the "politburo") to the village council. In this way, what is nominally a decentralization of the administration becomes in practice a means of reinforcing the party's organizational control. At its worst, the new set-up serves as a strait-jacket to suppress any possible opposition.

Its good feature, however, is that it offers a two-way channel of communication between the party's politburo and the humblest villager.

FEATURES OF THE WEST AFRICAN SINGLE PARTY

Despite the fact that all the newly independent countries of French Black Africa are in some ways police states run by oligarchies, their leaders also usually take pains to "respect" legal forms and democratic principles. Their constitutions—and all of the countries of former F.W.A. except Guinea have had at least two constitutions since 1958—are clearly modeled on that of the Fifth French Republic. They have been progressively adapted, however, to their African setting.

As in France, the power of the executive has been steadily increased at the expense of the legislative and judicial branches, and there no longer exists in any of the French-speaking West African countries the system of checks and balances which Americans consider the essential safeguard of a democracy. The single-party leader has now become also the Prime Minister and President of his country. Under the new constitutions, he is elected directly by the people (whom he can also consult on specific issues by means of a referendum) and is no longer responsible to the elected assembly. The people, who are ill-informed and have the habit of obedience, are so thoroughly regimented and indoctrinated by the party's militants that they invariably acquiesce in or even warmly support the leadership of their Premier-President. Only the party's executive committee—on which special-interest groups such as youth, labor and women's movements are represented—exercises any effective control over him. As for the frequent reshuffling of cabinets in French-speaking African states, this often merely reflects shifts in the balance of power among the various party leaders.

Just as the single-party leaders have shown their concern for preserving Western forms by changing the constitution to give legal justification to their ever-growing power, so they have been equally insistent that their governments are not autocracies but democracies—African-style. All the leaders frankly say, however, that they will not permit the existence of an organized opposition to their regimes. Such an opposition, they claim, would only waste time and energy that would be better spent in building the nation according to the program their party has drawn up.

Inevitably, the single party—try as it will—has not succeeded in eliminating all opposition to its rule. Its opponents are individuals or groups who either disagree on principle with the party's policy or, as is more often the case, want power for themselves. Inasmuch as the single party has set itself up as the creator and symbol of national unity, it denounces all those who persistently oppose it as "traitors to the nation."

Inside the party framework, and there alone, it tolerates 'and even encourages discussion of its policies. Once the leader and the politburo have determined a course of action, however, the obedience of the party members to their decisions is demanded. Those who refuse to confine their criticism to the accepted channels, and those who make any move that seems aimed at overthrowing the government by force, are dealt with summarily. They are jailed or exiled as fomentors of a "plot," which the government announces with fanfare as a pretext for assuming more power. Even in remarkably stable Ivory Coast, for example, three cabinet ministers were jailed in January 1963 on charges of trying to overthrow the government.

It should not be thought, however, that such arbitrary and extreme tactics are every-day occurrences in French-speaking

African countries. Most issues are usually dealt with by the time-honored African procedure of palavers (group discussions) and compromise. Under these truly African regimes, the single party is perhaps the only practical mechanism through which national unity can be created and the national economy can be modernized. Time is of the essence, for conflicting local loyalties are still strong and external pressures aimed at altering national boundaries are growing.

More harmful to these countries' future development than the party's monopoly of power is the way in which some party leaders are making use of it. It is true that all of the new African governments have drawn up national-development plans aimed at raising the living standards of the population. In practice, however, many of the leaders are less concerned with promoting the people's welfare than with lining their own pockets and owning expensive houses and automobiles. At this stage, French-speaking Africa's resources are not developed to the point where even its leaders should squander the money of their countries on showy Western luxuries.

The extravagance and corruption that are so evident in some African countries today will, if they persist, have two unfortunate consequences. One is that the already considerable gap between the masses and the elite will grow still wider. The other is that if the leaders of those countries close their eyes to such practices among their followers and allow themselves status symbols such as huge presidential palaces instead of concentrating on productive enterprises needed for the economic growth of their nations, they will become even more dependent than they already are on financial support from foreign sources. Almost inevitably such a course will endanger not only their freedom of action but also their sovereignty.

Biographies of the Heads of State

The leaders of the French-speaking nations of West Africa vary widely in their backgrounds, as can be seen from these short biographical sketches.

Sourou Migan Apithy, President of Dahomey. Apithy, born April 8, 1913, at Porto Novo, Dahomey, is a member of the Goun tribe. He is a Catholic and attended the mission school in Porto Novo. His higher education was gained in Bordeaux and Paris, where he received a diploma in political science. While in France he also qualified as an accountant. His political career began in 1945–46 when he was elected to represent Dahomey and Togo in the Constituent Assemblies convened at Paris to draft a new French Constitution. From 1946–59 he served in the Dahomey territorial assembly and as deputy from Dahomey in the French National Assembly, and in 1956 he was elected Mayor of Porto Novo. After two years as Premier of Dahomey, from May 1957 to May 1959, he was chosen Vice-President in December 1960. He was elected President on January 17, 1964, after the coup d'état of October 1963.

Hamani Diori, President of Niger. Born in June 1916 at Soudouré, Niger, he was educated at Niamey, Porto Novo and Dakar, where he attended the famous William Ponty School. Diori's parents were Muslims, and he regards himself as a true Muslim, but a "modern" one. In the late 1930's he taught in Niamey and in 1938–39 in Paris, where he was professor of the Hausa language at the National School of Overseas France. After World War II, in 1946, he was elected Niger's deputy to the French National Assembly. In the late 1940's he was active in territorial politics, and ever since has been the leader of the Niger branch of the R.D.A.

Diori was not reelected to the National Assembly in 1951 and resumed teaching. He again became Niger's deputy at Paris in 1956, was named Premier of Niger in December 1958 and was elected President in October 1960.

Félix Houphouët-Boigny, President of Ivory Coast. One of the most renowned of former French West Africa's statesmen, Houphouët-Boigny was born October 18, 1905, at Yamoussoukro, Ivory Coast. Son of a Baoulé chief, he is a Christian. After his early schooling at Bingerville, he studied at the Dakar Medical School, where he received a diploma as African Doctor in 1925. From 1925 to 1940 he practiced medicine in Ivory Coast and was a canton chief. He became interested in politics, and during World War II founded the first political party in Ivory Coast. Although he was instrumental in forming the left-wing R.D.A. (African Democratic Rally) in 1946, he broke that party's connection with the French Communist party in 1950. He was a prominent member of French West Africa's Grand Council from 1947 to 1959, as well as deputy in the French National Assembly from 1945 to 1959. Among his many high posts have been that of Minister of State in the French government, 1956–57; Minister of Health in Paris, 1958–59; and Premier of Ivory Coast, 1959–60. He was elected President in August 1960. Houphouët-Boigny is a wealthy cocoa planter with large landholdings.

Modibo Keita, President of Mali. A Muslim of the Bambara tribe, Keita was born May 4, 1915, at Bamako, Soudan. After attending local schools, he was graduated from Dakar's William Ponty School as a teacher. He was elected Mayor of Bamako in 1956 and was a member of the Grand Council of F.W.A. in 1957–58. Among his numerous elective posts, he served in the French Union Assembly, 1953–56; as deputy in the French National Assembly, 1956–59; and as

Secretary of State to the French Premier, 1957–58. He was elected President of the Mali Federation in 1959, and when the federation was dissolved, became President of the Mali Republic in September 1960.

Mokhtar Ould Daddah, President of Mauritania. Ould Daddah was born December 27, 1924, at Boutilimit, Mauritania, of a maraboutic family of the Ould Biri tribe. His education began at the higher Islamic institution of Boutilimit and was continued at the School for Chiefs' Sons in St. Louis-du-Sénégal. In 1948 he went to Paris where he won his *baccalauréat,* a law degree, and a diploma from the School of Living Oriental Languages. After returning to Mauritania, he became vice-president of the first territorial Government Council in 1957. In July 1958 he was elected President of the Islamic Republic of Mauritania. Although dependent for political support on the traditional chiefs, he is trying to modernize his country.

Léopold Sédar Senghor, President of Senegal. One of the most famous and gifted of African leaders, Senghor was born at Joal on the Senegal coast in October 1906. He is a member of the Sérère tribe and a Catholic. After primary schooling at a Catholic mission near his home, he attended the *lycée* first in Dakar and then in Paris. His studies at the University of Paris were rewarded with the highest academic honors thus far accorded an African. He remained in France, teaching the French language and French literature in Tours and Paris, until the outbreak of World War II. During the early months of the war he fought with the Colonial Infantry in France and was taken prisoner by the Germans in June 1940. He organized resistance groups in their prisoner-of-war camps, and, after his release because of ill health, joined the French Resistance. Although after the war he continued teaching and writing he became active also in political life, founded several important political parties and held many official posts in Senegal and in the French government in Paris. In April 1959 he was elected president of the Mali Federal Assembly, and in September 1960, President of Senegal. He has published a number of collections of poems, highly praised by French critics, and a political essay on African socialism.

Sékou Touré, President of Guinea. The most controversial leader of French-speaking West Africa was born in January 1922 at Faranah, Guinea, of a Susu father and Malinké mother. After attending Koranic school and a French primary school, he did secondary-school study by correspondence. In 1940 he became a clerk with a French trading company and in 1941 a P.T.T. (Posts and Telegraph) employee. His labor-union activity began in 1945, and he became so influential as a labor leader that in 1956 he was elected president of the General Confederation of Workers of Black Africa (C.G.T.A.). In 1946 he participated in founding the R.D.A., and in 1952 he became secretary-general of its territorial branch, the Guinea Democratic Party (P.D.G.). He was elected Mayor of Conakry in November 1956. Other elective offices included that of deputy for Guinea in the French National Assembly (1956), Grand Councillor of F.W.A. (1957), and vice-president of the Guinea Government Council (1957). Shortly after the country voted for independence in the September 1958 referendum he became President of Guinea, in October 1958. Touré's hold over the Guinean masses has been ascribed to his eloquence, dynamism, strongly Marxist sense of organization and African patriotism.

Maurice Yaméogo, President of Upper Volta. A Catholic of the Mossi tribe, Yaméogo was born at Koudougou, Upper Volta, on December 31, 1921. After attending primary school there, he went to a Catholic mission secondary school and then entered the civil service. He became a member of the territorial assembly in 1946, at the early age of 25, and a member of the French West Africa Grand Council in 1948. From 1954 until 1957, his civil-service career was interrupted by participation in politics and by labor-union activity with the C.F.T.C. (French Confederation of Christian Workers). In 1957 he was named Agriculture Minister of Upper Volta and in 1958, Minister of Interior. Later in 1958 he became Premier. He was elected President of Upper Volta in December 1959.

Economic Institutions

French-speaking West Africa has evolved far more rapidly in political respects than in economic ones. Although the countries that composed the former federation have won political independence, their economic situation has not yet basically changed from what it was in the 1950's.

After World War II, an important transformation took place as the result of the investment in French West Africa, for the first time, of enormous amounts of French public funds. This was in accordance with a plan designed to modernize what had been a typically colonial economy. The plan proved successful in developing means of communication, urban centers and scientific research, but it did not change the basic pattern of the federation's foreign trade. Moreover,

French West Africa became even more dependent on French aid for such development of its economy as did take place.

Since the French-speaking West African nations became independent, there have been signs of a significant change in their economic orientation. This has taken the form of state-controlled economic systems and diversification of sources of foreign aid. The reorientation can be traced to the determination of the individual states to gain economic independence through national planning, but at the same time to maintain their uncommitted position in relation to the world's great-power blocs.

Inevitably, natural resources and geographical location have a great influence on economic development, but they are not the only factors in it. Although all the inland West African nations are poor, so are Guinea and Dahomey, both of which are on the coast. The countries with the largest manpower resources are Mali, Upper Volta and Dahomey, yet all of them are impoverished, and their surplus population must emigrate to survive. Although Mauritania, Guinea and to a lesser extent Senegal have the richest mineral deposits, those countries cannot compare in prosperity with Ivory Coast, which has few known reserves of minerals and depends mainly on income from such exports as coffee, cocoa and bananas, whose prices have steadily fallen in an over-supplied world market. Senegal—of all the eight nations the most industrialized, the most politically advanced and the one nearest to the European market—might seem to occupy a very favored position, but its national budget shows larger deficits each year, and its industries have been working nowhere near capacity.

To a greater extent than other factors, French policy during the colonial and post-war periods created the background of today's problems and policies in French-speaking West Africa. That policy had both constructive and restrictive features. On the credit side it provided a federal administration under which all the territories benefited by a common currency, a unified tariff and freedom from internal tariff barriers, a system of road and rail communications and improved health and working conditions. These benefits, however, were seriously offset by the trading policy known as the Colonial Pact, by French trading monopolies, by crop specialization for export while food production was neglected, and by overstaffed, costly administrations at both the federal and territorial levels.

As indicated in the following pages, the economy of French-speaking West Africa has begun to evolve, but the course of that evolution in each country depends to a great extent on such unpredictable elements as inter-African cooperation and conflicts, the success or failure of national planning and the relations of the new states with the rest of the world.

The Colonial Era

On the whole, the economy of French West Africa before World War II followed the classical colonial pattern. Its exports consisted almost entirely of agricultural, animal and forest products and its imports of manufactured articles. The mother country, France, was by far the biggest market as well as the most important supplier of its West African colonies. This complementary and noncompetitive form of exchange of goods was euphemistically called the Colonial Pact, even though it involved no element of agreement on the part of the colonies. The interests of the latter were clearly subordinated to those of the colonial power, and trade between them was almost a closed circuit from which other countries were largely shut out either as purchasers or suppliers.

The economic philosophy of the Colonial Pact rested on two broad principles. First, the colonies were expected to be self-supporting and to receive no financial aid from France except in an emergency. Second, economic exchanges between the colonies and France took place under a system known as imperial preference. This meant that, through preferential import and export duties and quotas, French commercial interests were assured a favored—and in fact monopolistic—position in the colonies. It also meant that the kind, the quantity and the price of the colonies' export commodities, as well as their imports, were controlled by France. There was little private French capital investment in the colonies, and most of it went into commercial enterprises, especially monopolistic import-export companies, which could be counted on to bring quick profits to French investors.

During the several decades of the federation's existence, centralization was the dominant theme in its economic life as well as in its administration. There were no customs or other artificial barriers between the eight colonies, which were treated as parts of a whole; there was a common currency and tariff regime; and the life of the federation was centered on Dakar, the capital. Most of the railroads that were built ran inland from the coast across colonial boundaries to producing regions, but no farther. And the budgets of the poor colonies, especially Niger, Upper Volta and Mauritania, were kept in balance by subsidies from the Government-General's revenues, most of which came from the more prosperous coastal colonies.

Partly because of the way the Colonial Pact operated, and in part for other reasons, the colonial period was one of regional specialization in French Black Africa. Although to a great extent this specialization resulted from the stress laid by the French government and commercial interests on the production and export to France of materials needed by industry there, climate and soils also played an important role, as did problems of both internal and external transportation.

Interior colonies such as Soudan and Upper Volta, which had the highest density of population but poor soils, little rain and inadequate communications internally and with the port towns, were for the most part restricted to growing food for their own inhabitants, gathering wild products and herding. By contrast, the coastal colonies, with only 10 per cent of the federation's total population, were the source of almost all the valuable export crops. From Senegal, the principal export was peanuts; from Guinea, bananas; from Ivory Coast, coffee and later cocoa; and from Dahomey, palm oil.

Such economic development as occurred in French West Africa before World War II—aside from the Niger Project, mentioned below—was financed by the federation's own meager resources, with only slight aid in the form of loans from the government in Paris. Thus no real effort was made to industrialize French West Africa or to modernize its tradition-bound economy. Economic planning in the post-war sense did not exist, except for a program prepared by the Popular Front government of Premier Léon Blum in 1936, which was never actually launched.

In the economic field, the Government-General's pre-war efforts included a long-drawn-out campaign against famine in the poor interior colonies. This involved stocking of food reserves through the agency of the government-sponsored Native Provident Societies (Sociétés Indigènes de Prévoyance, or S.I.P.). Almost the only government-backed venture of the pre-war period which was aimed at regional economic development was the Niger Project, started in 1932 in western Soudan. That costly project, which originally was expected to open up a vast area to irrigated cotton and rice cultivation, is described below. Other moves by the French to spur the economy consisted of carrying out works of public utility—chiefly means of communication such as roads, railroads, the port of Dakar, and river navigation—and encouraging the production of export crops in the coastal areas.

The Rural Economy

French West Africa's economy has for centuries been chiefly a rural one. The great majority of the population are African peasants occupied in cultivating export or subsistence crops, in herding and in fishing. Unlike Algeria or Morocco, it has not had a white-settler problem at any period. There have never been more than a few European planters in the rural regions, mostly in Ivory Coast and Guinea.

The predominance of agriculture in French-speaking West Africa has been somewhat modified since World War II because of the drift of young peasants to the towns. This has increased since 1960 because of the efforts of the new African regimes to attain self-sufficiency in their countries through diversification and the creation of consumer-goods industries. Despite these trends, however, agriculture is still the most important sector of the West African economy.

Traditionally, the West African peasant has used primitive methods—shifting cultivation, the burning over of grasslands and clumsy hand implements. The dry season, with its ever-present threat of famine, brings prolonged periods of idleness

At Kindia, Guinea, bananas are packed for export in plastic bags.

and has often been the cause of large-scale migration of labor.

Animal husbandry also suffers from archaic traditional methods and customs. The huge herds of cattle that graze in the sudanese zone receive little care and, because they are kept as visible signs of wealth rather than used for farming, fertilizer or food, are of only slight usefulness. Problems of processing, refrigerating and transporting meat—and even more, of finding buyers for it among a poor population which still lives largely under a system of barter and has little money —have been difficult to solve. Sheep and goats, like cattle, are for the most part jealously guarded as mobile capital, especially by the nomadic tribes. As for chickens, ducks and other fowl, which have to fend for themselves, they can scarcely be said to count as an appreciable food or trade commodity.

Another occupation which is of potential economic importance, but which has been much neglected, is that of fishing. Great resources of fish, much needed as a source of protein, exist in the seas along the coasts, but except in a few places and on a small scale, they remain largely unutilized. Although considerable quantities of fish are taken from rivers and ponds, they are mostly consumed locally, only a small percentage being dried or smoked so that they can be shipped over greater distances.

Forestry does not play an important part in the West African economy as a whole. Only Ivory Coast has forests of valuable trees sufficiently extensive to warrant lumbering operations for export, and even these were depleted over the years by reckless cutting with little or no attempt at reforestation.

Agriculture in West Africa—and this applies to the former British territories as well as to the former French ones—has had to contend with both physical and psychological handicaps. Physical handicaps include widespread soil erosion, swarms of locusts and birds, the great distance of the producing areas from both domestic and foreign markets and the dispersion of the populations over enormous areas. Psychological handicaps include an uneconomic attitude toward livestock and the persistence of antiquated methods of cultivation.

Until comparatively recent years these agricultural problems were not seriously tackled on a wide front. Before 1939, however, the French did begin two experiments in rural West Africa. These were the federation-wide Native Provident Societies (or S.I.P.) and the Niger Project in Soudan. Not until after World War II was another large-scale project launched, that at Richard-Toll on the Senegal River.

THE NIGER PROJECT

The Niger Project, an ambitious development scheme officially called the *Office du Niger,* was begun in 1932 after some years of preliminary studies and work. The original plan was to develop a huge inland-delta region of the Niger River in Soudan, chiefly for irrigated cotton cultivation and secondarily for rice-growing. The project's goal, which was never attained, was eventually to bring under cultivation nearly 1.25 million acres of cotton fields and almost as large an extent of rice fields. To work these vast areas, the plan called for ultimately assembling a labor force of 800,000 Africans, mostly recruited from other territories and settled as colonists.

The Niger Project—on which many millions of dollars were spent by the French during the course of a quarter-century—has made a definite contribution to former French West Africa's economy, although on a lesser scale and in different ways than those first envisaged. By 1949 rice-growing had become more important in the project than cotton cultivation, and changes had been made in the system of allocating land to the African colonists. Thanks to the credits provided by F.I.D.E.S.—the French financing organization described below—modern equipment was bought and farming in the project area was becoming more mechanized. In 1952 the project showed a small profit for the first time in its 20 years of existence, and its colonists earned a cash income estimated at ten times that of the average Soudanese peasant family.

Since independence, the Niger Project, despite continued difficulties and unprofitable operation, has been taken over by the Mali Republic.

THE RICHARD-TOLL PROJECT

Another costly regional-development scheme, also nationalized since independence (in this case, by Senegal), is the project begun by the French government in 1946 at Richard-Toll in northwestern Senegal, where there is a large inland delta of the Senegal River. Its aim was to contribute substantially to Senegal's domestic production of food and thus to reduce the need to import foodstuffs. Mechanized cultivation of irrigated rice fields at Richard-Toll was part of a much larger project to develop the whole of the Senegal River valley.

By 1957, after much money had been spent on the project and problems such as destruction of crops by swarms of birds had been largely overcome, the total project area of about 14,000 acres had been brought under cultivation. However, Richard-Toll's contribution to Senegal's food supply has been relatively small. The project probably will play only a minor role in the new plans for joint development of the Senegal Valley which were agreed upon in July 1962 by Senegal, Mauritania, Mali and Guinea (see page 254).

Transportation

Inadequate means of communication and transportation have long been, and still are, among the most formidable barriers to the economic development of French-speaking West Africa (see Appendix II).

RAILROADS

In the late nineteenth and early twentieth centuries, the French government thought that the isolation and economic stagnation of the inland sudanese zone could be remedied by creating a network of rail lines that would converge at the Niger River. Only the Dakar-Niger and Conakry-Niger railroads, however, have been built as far as that river.

Construction of the railroads, mostly by army engineers using forced labor, was carried on by fits and starts over a period of nearly 60 years, from 1880 to the eve of World War II. Most of the railroad construction, however, was done during the first three decades of this century.

The total length of the four existing rail systems—Dakar-Niger, Abidjan-Niger, Conakry-Niger, and Benin-Niger—is 2,423 miles, the greater part of which is single-track. Some idea of the small extent of these rail facilities may be had by comparing the figure just given with the 25,000 miles of lines in France itself, whose area is only one-eighth that of the former federation.

ROADS

French West Africa's roads were developed later than its railroads, and were planned either to carry traffic beyond the inland termini of the railroads or to connect various sections of the rail system.

By 1939 the eight colonies possessed altogether about

43,750 miles of roads, many of which were little better than tracks (called by the French, "pistes"). Of these, only 15,000 miles were usable by motor vehicles throughout the year, for they had to be closed to such traffic during the rainy seasons. The whole federation had only 450 miles of hard-surfaced roads, and a sizeable percentage of these was accounted for by paved streets in the principal towns.

Between 1945 and 1960, however, the road system was improved, and more than 1,000 miles of roads are now paved. These do not form a continuous network, but consist of city streets and relatively short sections of road in the eight countries, usually connecting ports with upcountry centers where commodities are assembled for export. One of the longest continuous paved roads in West Africa is the coastal highway which runs from Accra, in Ghana, across Togo and Dahomey to Lagos in southwestern Nigeria.

The improvement of road facilities, together with the fact that further extension of the railroads seems unlikely, has led to a great increase in the number of cars and trucks, especially the latter. Competition between trucks and railways is intense. Because of their wider range and lower costs of operation, reflected in cheaper rates, trucks now transport large amounts of the freight that formerly moved by rail. Many of the trucking companies have been African-owned since before independence.

Airline Services

Airplanes played a very minor part in the transportation of freight and passengers in French West Africa until after World War II, but by 1954 there were 120 well-equipped

Track-maintenance men work on the Cotonou-Parakou railway in Dahomey.

landing fields throughout the federation. These were used regularly by commercial planes, mostly DC-3's, and the air network totaled about 11,000 miles.

Until recently, most of the air traffic between France and the countries of former French West Africa, as well as within that area, was handled by the French-owned airlines, Air France and U.A.T. (Union Aéromaritime des Transports). In March 1961, however, an important new company, Air Afrique, was formed with the official backing of the newly created Afro-Malagasy Union. Air Afrique, besides its operations within former French West Africa, provides jet-plane service to and from France. In the autumn of 1963, Air France began turning over some of its internal African routes to Air Afrique.

Because of the vast geographic extent of French-speaking West Africa, its distance from Europe and the inadequacy of its surface communications, the development of air transport has brought about many changes in ways of life there. The usefulness of air transport in that area, however, has been hampered by high rates, which to a large extent reflect the high cost of maintaining planes and airfield installations and of fueling. New airlines which have been formed by most of the national governments are now coming into the picture, and if they are well subsidized and efficiently run, they may eventually be able to offer lower rates on internal services.

PORTS

During the early years of the French colonial regime, West Africa's seaports played a vitally important role in European penetration of the interior. Later they became key elements in the growth of trade and agriculture in the colonies.

Besides Dakar, West Africa's greatest port, and its close competitor, Abidjan, French-speaking West Africa's seaports include Conakry in Guinea, Grand Bassam in Ivory Coast, and Cotonou in Dahomey. Three of these—Dakar, Abidjan and Conakry—have natural harbors, but the others possess only long piers extending some hundreds of feet into the ocean, beyond the great sandbar, where ships must drop anchor in the open sea and be loaded and unloaded by means of small boats. At Cotonou, an artificial deep-water port which has been under construction for several years was to be completed in 1964. Some lesser ports also handle some of the seaborne trade, but very little, lacking sheltered harbors.

Senegal has two important river ports—Kaolack and Ziguinchor—through which a large part of the country's peanut crop is handled.

INLAND WATERWAYS

Except for the Senegal and the Niger, all the rivers of French-speaking West Africa are more or less encumbered with rapids and sandbanks, and all are torrential in the rainy season. One characteristic common to them all, including the two principal waterways just mentioned, is the wide difference in the volume of their water during the dry and the rainy months. At certain seasons they normally overflow their banks, and in low-lying regions they flood great areas, forming interior deltas and wide-spread marshes.

Light native craft are able to ply shallow lagoons and minor rivers, but for boats of larger size and draft, inland navigation is limited to portions of the Senegal and Niger rivers and to the coastal lagoons of Ivory Coast and Dahomey.

Labor

From early colonial times until after World War II, forced labor was widespread in French West Africa and was a generally accepted method of getting work done, especially in undertakings of public interest such as roads, railroads and port improvement.

There were three main categories of forced labor. The principal one (called the *corvée,* or prestation labor) involved the work on public projects that Africans had to perform without pay, under the provisions of a law which required that each able-bodied male must contribute a certain number of days of such work each year. Another was that done by military conscripts, many of whom were taken into the army not for military service but for work on public projects. For example, between 1927 and 1938, some 15,000 laborers of military status worked on the Niger Project and on railroad construction. The third type of forced labor was that performed by prisoners, on whom jail sentences often had been imposed for trivial civil offenses.

Even before World War II the government had begun to realize that prestation labor was uneconomic, produced mediocre results, caused much hardship and resentment among the Africans, and reduced the federation's agricultural output. Increasingly, as time went on, the authorities permitted Africans to make cash payments instead of performing prestation labor. (The Africans, it should be noted, were often unable to take advantage of this because they had so little money.) As mentioned in Chapter V, however, forced labor was widely used in French West Africa during World War II, first by the Vichy regime and later by the Free French (page 180).

The attitude of the 1944 Brazzaville Conference towards the question of forced labor was somewhat ambiguous, but in launching the post-war reforms the Constituent Assemblies that met in Paris took a positive stand. On April 11, 1946, the first of these two assemblies unanimously adopted a law to abolish such labor throughout French Black Africa. This was followed in 1947 by reforms in regard to the use of penal labor, and in 1950 by a law banning work by military conscripts on public-development projects. By that time, the only pre-war form of forced labor that remained was that of the servitudes sanctioned by African custom. Domestic serfdom persisted in certain regions, especially among the nomads, and even in recent years there have been occasional reports that French West African Muslims have sold such servants as slaves in Saudi Arabia.

Migratory Workers

Another aspect of French West Africa's pre-World War II labor picture which to some extent still exists today involved migratory workers. For many years, at the start of the long dry season in Soudan and Upper Volta, there was a mass migration of young and able-bodied men from those regions to the coffee and cocoa plantations of Ivory Coast and Gold Coast (Ghana) and the forest concessions of Ivory Coast. As of 1956, there were some 320,000 northern laborers working for wages in Ivory Coast and thousands more in Gold Coast, some of whom were permanent settlers. Today, however, partly because of changed economic conditions and partly because of the nationalistic tendencies of the new West African states, these migrant workers from the eastern sudanese zone are less numerous than they were during the 1950's.

Another type of migratory labor was represented by the so-called *navétanes*—men from western Soudan who went to Senegal and the Gambia to work as share-croppers on the big peanut farms.

"Human Investment"

Since independence, the sudanese-zone governments have

discouraged migrations because they want to utilize their manpower for carrying out national development plans. Moreover, all of the new French-speaking West African states are continuing the efforts begun by the French administration during the 1950's to build up a skilled labor force.

In doing so, most of them have resorted to a practice which they euphemistically call "human investment." This term is used to describe the work done by young Africans on various public projects, as a result of urging by political party leaders. Officially it is claimed that such work is performed spontaneously and enthusiastically in the name of patriotism, but the International Labor Organization has criticized it as a disguised form of forced labor.

ORGANIZED LABOR

Before World War II, labor organizations were almost nonexistent in French West Africa, for its laborers were too dispersed and illiterate to organize, and the French administration opposed unions there. They were in fact illegal until France's Popular Front government issued a decree in March 1937 authorizing their formation in the federation among workers other than those having French civil status. In that year the first labor organizations, which were Socialist-sponsored, were formed among African government workers and white-collar employees in Dakar and Bamako.

During the war, these embryonic unions were abolished by the federation's pro-Vichy regime, and it was not until the Free French government-in-exile drafted overseas-labor legislation in 1944 that the principle of African labor organization was again given an official blessing. However, because of the conservative reaction that followed the reforms of early 1946, the law known as the Overseas Labor Code was not actually adopted by the French Parliament until November 1952. This very liberal law, which many employers in French Africa opposed and often attempted to circumvent, guaranteed to all French Black African wage earners the right to belong to unions, equal pay for equal work, a guaranteed minimum wage, a 40-hour week, family allowances and a number of other benefits.

Labor organizations that developed in French West Africa after World War II were for some years linked with one or another of the big French labor federations—the Communist-dominated General Confederation of Labor (C.G.T.), the Catholic-sponsored French Confederation of Christian Workers (C.F.T.C.) and the Socialist-oriented Workmen's Force (F.O.). By 1949 the C.G.T. locals in the federation, to which a very large percentage of the organized workers belonged, had been "captured" by radical political parties, which through them used strikes to promote political objectives. In 1953 the unions successfully used the strike weapon to force strict application of the 1952 labor code by the government and private employers.

During late 1956 and early 1957, French West Africa's labor movement underwent some basic changes. The local branches of the three French labor federations mentioned above broke away from them, and after considerable maneuvering, three autonomous African federations were formed. Of these, the most important was the General Union of Workers of Black Africa (U.G.T.A.N.), formed at a labor conference in Cotonou in January 1957. U.G.T.A.N.'s attempt at that time to unite under its leadership the whole organized labor movement in French West Africa was resisted by a number of unions because of the aggressive radicalism of some of its promoters. This radical tendency was confirmed when, two years later, its headquarters were established at Conakry. There, under the guidance of Sékou Touré, the labor leader who later became Guinea's president, the U.G.T.A.N. embarked on a distinctly Marxist program.

Through its branches in other French West African countries, which by that time were already politically autonomous, the U.G.T.A.N. carried on campaigns to overthrow conservative governments, particularly those of Senegal and Ivory Coast. To counter these moves, the governments first gave support to the territorial U.G.T.A.N. branches and then broke the links of those branches with the Conakry headquarters. Their next step was to abolish the branches and to attempt to replace them with single national labor movements controlled by the single political party. Some countries, however, especially Senegal and Upper Volta, have not been very successful in establishing single-party political control of their national labor movements.

It is interesting to note the change that has occurred in the attitude of West African nationalists toward the labor movement in former French West Africa. Before independence the nationalist parties used labor organizations as a weapon against the French administration, but since the governing power has passed to the nationalists they have tried to eliminate any opposition tendencies among labor groups and to establish political control over them.

CIVIL SERVANTS

The most difficult unions to control have been those of civil servants, for not only were these unions the oldest and strongest, but their members had been a privileged minority of the population since the early days of the federation. The civil-servants' unions have created thorny problems for the new national governments, whose policy toward them has, therefore, greatly changed.

For nationalistic reasons, all the French-speaking West

African states began, at a very early stage, to "Africanize" their administrations, that is, to replace French officials and technicians by Africans as quickly as possible. This was done by Guinea as early as 1958 and by Mali in 1959, and the other countries were not far behind. Because a large number of the suddenly promoted African civil servants were inadequately trained, were political appointees or turned out to be dishonest, many of them have proved unsatisfactory. As for the older generation of African civil servants—holdovers from the federation regime—the single-party leaders in most of the countries are inclined to mistrust them for two reasons. To begin with, they were trained by the French and under them attained an economic status far above that of the mass of the population. Then, to maintain their privileges, they organized unions which, both before and since independence, almost paralyzed the administrative machinery by staging strikes against the government.

On principle as well as for practical reasons, none of the new African governments can afford to pay their functionaries, who are greatly in the minority, salaries conspicuously out of line with the low income of the mass of the population. Even in relatively prosperous Senegal and Ivory Coast, civil servants have had to accept pay cuts, lose special privileges such as free housing and the use of official automobiles, and comply with the directives of the single party. In their case, as in that of youth movements, the new regimes are learning that the nationalists' allies of the colonial period tend frequently to be uncooperative if not actually hostile.

Economic Effects of World War II

Although, as explained in Chapter VI, World War II touched French West Africa very little militarily, it brought economic repercussions which were keenly felt by all of the African population. For more than five years the federation experienced drastic shortages of consumer goods because of the almost total cessation of imports. These shortages, incidentally, gave rise to a beginning of industrialization in the federation, especially in Senegal. Factories were built to manufacture certain consumer goods, such as soap, that could no longer be obtained from France or other overseas sources. Processing plants, such as peanut-oil mills, were established. The peanut-oil industry continued to prosper, and in fact to expand greatly, after the war, but many other manufacturing enterprises that had been started because of wartime shortages had to cease operating when imports picked up after the return of peace.

A blueprint for the revival and modernization of the French Black African economy had already been produced by the Brazzaville Conference more than a year before the war ended. It inspired many features of post-war French policy in Africa, especially in regard to the long-range development project called the Plan for Modernization and Equipment, which is described below.

Resolutions of the Brazzaville Conference

Among the resolutions adopted at the Brazzaville Conference early in 1944 (see pages 183–184), those relating to economic matters embodied three important concepts. One was a general condemnation of the principles on which the Colonial Pact was based; another strongly favored comprehensive economic planning in the overseas territories, which would deal with both production and distribution; and a third resolution stipulated that African welfare and interests should be protected.

Many features of the legislation affecting the overseas terri-tories which was enacted by the first Constituent Assembly in the early months of 1946 were inspired by the liberal spirit of the Brazzaville conferees. Even though the Colonial Pact later proved to be far from dead, and African welfare did not receive as much consideration as the Brazzaville resolu-tions required, the post-war reforms brought about profound changes in West African life within a few years. Of these reforms, one of the most sweeping was the development of the African economy in accordance with the ambitious Plan for Modernization and Equipment.

Plan for Modernization and Equipment

In conformity with a law of April 30, 1946, directly inspired by one of the resolutions adopted at Brazzaville two years earlier, French government economists and technicians drew up a long-range program called the Plan for Modernization and Equipment, also known as the Monnet Plan. The overseas portion of this plan, as it was originally conceived, had as its objective the modernization of the economy of the African territories while at the same time safeguarding the welfare of the African population. It prepared the ground for massive investment of French public funds in overseas territories. This was the first time that a commitment on such a scale had been made by France.

Among the organizations created to carry out the Plan in Black Africa, the two principal ones were the Investment Fund for Economic and Social Development (whose French name is abbreviated as F.I.D.E.S.) and the Central Fund-management Office of Overseas France (C.C.O.M.). F.I.D.E.S. was to be financed by subsidies from France and by contributions from the territories themselves. C.C.O.M. was to handle the F.I.D.E.S. accounts and to grant long-term loans at low interest rates.

Thanks to the Plan and the huge sums spent in connection with it, French West Africa's economy underwent a great expansion during the years of the Plan's operation, from 1946 until 1960, when the former territories became sovereign nations. (Since 1960, as described below, activities similar to those of the Plan have been continued in West Africa by new organizations based on Franco-African cooperation.) Broadly speaking, its outstanding accomplishment was to increase greatly the production of export crops and the facilities for processing and shipping them. At the same time, a guaranteed market for several important export crops, such as coffee and vegetable oils, was assured in France, at prices higher than those prevailing in the world market. Roads and railroads were improved, much new mechanical equipment was brought in, ports such as Dakar and Abidjan were enlarged and modernized, and the principal towns began to grow rapidly because of the federation's heightened commercial activity and of urban improvement. A few industries, especially mining, were encouraged and given financial support, but other industrial development that might furnish competition with industries in France was frowned upon.

Although striking economic advances were brought about in the federation by the Plan, serious flaws began to appear as time went on. Some of these grew out of changes that took place in the scale and the financial scope of the Plan, which resulted in a virtual return to the practices of the Colonial Pact. Because of pressure from French conservatives, the dominant motive of the Plan's activities soon became the integration of the economy of the overseas territories with that of France, and the welfare of the Africans became a minor consideration.

An aluminum-ore treating plant on the island of Kassa at Conakry, Guinea. The island consists almost entirely of this ore.

The emphasis on export crops led to over-production of certain commodities, especially vegetable oils, coffee, and bananas, which could not be entirely disposed of in the French market and were hard to sell elsewhere. For the same reason, food crops were neglected. Senegal, for example, by concentrating on peanut-growing became ever more dependent on imported foods such as rice from Indochina and millet from neighboring Soudan. Then, too, imported manufactured goods from France, at high prices, held a privileged position in the federation, mainly because of French controls over the use of foreign exchange which prevented the spending of hard currency (dollars and pounds sterling) to obtain such goods from cheaper foreign sources, especially the United States and the British Commonwealth. This, of course, caused a rise in the cost of living in the territories. Furthermore, the decline of food production, along with the drift of young

Africans to the towns, was accompanied by increasing unemployment, juvenile delinquency, and crime.

AFRICAN DISCONTENT WITH F.I.D.E.S.

The situation just described aroused both African and French discontent, for different reasons. The Africans, who freely voiced their criticisms in the territorial assemblies, were disgruntled because of the decline in the amounts granted by F.I.D.E.S. each year, and also because the Paris directorate of that organization decided what projects it would finance, often disregarding the advice of the assemblies. The Africans desired not only to have more control over the projects financed by F.I.D.E.S. but also to give them a different orientation. They also wanted more stress on industrialization, an end to the French monopoly of the export-import trade and of transport facilities, and greater production of consumer goods in Africa to meet the needs of the domestic market. They complained, too, that agricultural methods were still archaic and that labor was still untrained, unstable and seasonal. Finally, the Africans alleged that such improvements as the Plan had accomplished were beneficial mainly to French merchants and industrialists, and that the living standards of Africans were no higher than they had been in the inter-war period of 1919–39. Partly as a result of the assemblies' criticism and partly because of a change in the attitude of the French public toward the economic and political situation in Africa, the government, from about 1952 on, made greater efforts to increase local production of food crops and consumer goods for Africans.

FRENCH CRITICISM OF F.I.D.E.S.

By the mid-1950's, many French taxpayers were becoming increasingly restive in view of the heavy financial and tax burden resulting from long-term massive investment of public funds in the overseas territories. Proportionately—that is, on a per capita basis—the French were doing more for their African dependencies than were the people of any other Western power with colonial responsibilities. So far as the average Frenchman could see, his tax burden would continue indefinitely without any appreciable returns to the French treasury or permanent benefits to the Africans. Funds granted by F.I.D.E.S. could be used only for construction purposes, and the territories were supposed to finance the upkeep of completed projects. But it soon became apparent that the territories simply did not have the resources to do so. As a result, France had to provide the funds not only to install French West Africa's equipment but also to maintain and operate it.

Even the maximum investments made by France seemed no more than a drop in the bucket of Africa's gigantic needs, and were evidently not increasing African well-being or earning African gratitude. The French were distressed by reports that funds were being wasted on projects such as Abidjan's papermill and Richard-Toll's mechanized rice culture, which were technical successes but economic failures. In any case, some Africans were now demanding independence, and many French people began to complain that such funds would be better used in modernizing their own country's antiquated economy. They objected strongly to the building of ultra-modern hospitals and schools in Africa when many towns in France had inadequate ones. A large segment of the French population came to feel that France either should pull out of Africa entirely or find ways of sharing the burden of development of the overseas territories with other Western powers. This change in French public opinion was partly responsible for France's insistence that its African dependencies be associated with the European Economic Community.

Common Market Membership

As a condition of signing the Treaty of Rome which created the European Economic Community (E.E.C.) in 1957, France's representatives insisted that the French overseas territories should be admitted as associate members. The five other European countries which were joining the E.E.C. agreed to this reluctantly. West Germany and Holland, especially, had no interest in investing money in French West Africa, with which they had little trade, and they resented the pressure exerted on them to shoulder part of the development burden there. The French West Africans, for their part, were annoyed by France's failure to consult them regarding their views as to Common Market associate membership. In addition, they feared that their association with the E.E.C. would not benefit them but would simply revive the Colonial Pact on a wider scale, thus forcing them to produce raw materials needed not only by France but also by the rest of the E.E.C.'s industries, and to serve as captive markets for Europe's manufactured goods. Only gradually were these suspicions overcome by the realization that the advantages of association with the Common Market would outweigh its drawbacks, and that the African countries had the option of withdrawing from it at the end of 1962.

General de Gaulle's return to power as Premier of France in mid-1958 was followed by both political independence for the French West African countries in 1960 and an increase in French economic aid to its former African dependencies. To win the Africans' acceptance of their relationship with the E.E.C., France now promised not to reduce the scale of French investments in Africa. This reassurance was coupled with other concrete advantages which association with the Common Market afforded to West Africa's imports and exports. France's traditional near-monopoly of their foreign trade would be relaxed, and other countries would begin to have more of a share in it. The French-speaking West African countries no longer had to buy most of their imports in the high-priced French market but could place orders in the cheaper West European markets, where their exports would receive preferential treatment. They also benefited in the matter of aid because of their Common Market associations, for most of the $520 million which France's five European partners agreed to invest in the dependencies of Common Market countries over a five-year period was allotted to the French African territories.

It is therefore not surprising that when the time came to renew their associate membership in the Common Market, all the now-independent states of French West Africa except Guinea were eager to continue their association with it. By hard collective bargaining, they were able to win even better terms of membership than they had enjoyed before.

Developments Since Independence

Since 1960, when the French-speaking West African countries became politically independent, three aspects of the evolution of their economies have been conspicuous. One is a strong trend towards inter-African economic and technical cooperation. Another is their continued great dependence upon foreign aid, especially from France. And the third is the preparation of national economic plans that presuppose tight state control.

The new states are keenly aware of their economic and financial weakness as individual nations. Their frontiers are artificial ones inherited from the colonial period, but their fervent nationalism rules out, at least for the present, any change in political boundaries, many of which cut across natural economic regions. They have been impressed by the failure of premature political "unions" such as the Mali Federation and the Ghana-Guinea-Mali Union. Moreover, some recent campaigns for pan-African political unity, such as the one led by Kwame Nkrumah of Ghana, have been regarded with suspicion by various African countries which fear that these moves are tactical ones aimed at gaining personal power. All far-sighted African leaders have recognized the necessity for cooperation between African nations in the technical and economic fields.

Although in some instances such efforts have been quite fruitful, the Customs Union of West African States, for example, launched in June 1959 has gone on the rocks, for both political and economic reasons. In forming that union, the leaders of all the French-speaking West African countries except Guinea—which at that time were autonomous but not yet independent—planned to allow free circulation of goods between them without payment of any customs duty or tax. With the break-up of the Mali Federation in August 1960, the Mali Republic closed its frontier with Senegal and set up a customs regime regulating commercial exchanges with the other West African states.

By the end of 1962, numerous trade barriers had been raised at the frontiers of the Union's member states, in some cases to protect their young industries. It was evident that the Customs Union of West African States was a failure, even though the agreement under which it had been created had not been formally abrogated.

COUNCIL OF THE ENTENTE

The first organization aimed at promoting economic cooperation between the French-speaking West African countries came into existence more than a year before independence had been attained by its four members. This was the Council of the Entente, formed in May 1959 by Ivory Coast, Dahomey, Upper Volta and Niger. The Entente—which because of its success later served as the model for the Afro-Malagasy Union, discussed below—was initially a non-political grouping of countries having common economic, social and technical interests. After a time, however, the Entente's activities inevitably took on a political coloration (see page 270).

Among its first moves were the establishment of a customs union and the creation of a so-called "solidarity fund" to which each of the four countries contributed 10 per cent of its revenues. These revenues were divided annually between them in inverse proportion to the amount contributed by each. Ports and railroads were put under joint management of the countries concerned, road transport was coordinated and common action was undertaken in fighting epidemics.

In 1961 and 1962, the Council of the Entente underwent certain crises, but survived them. In February 1961 Ivory Coast's financial dominance of the Entente caused a dispute between that country and Upper Volta, with the result that Upper Volta's President Maurice Yaméogo re-established customs barriers on the frontier between the two countries. A few months later, in June 1961, he signed some important economic agreements with Ghana, including one eliminating the customs regime between the two countries. The following year, Yaméogo boycotted the meeting at Cotonou at which, in conformity with the agreement for rotation of the presidency of the Entente, he was to turn over that office to Hubert Maga of Dahomey. These flare-ups have not, thus far, fundamentally harmed the Council of the Entente, and it is still a going concern. However, a more serious threat to its existence arose during 1963, when on two occasions Dahomey and Niger clashed over seemingly unrelated issues. These disputes, and others involving the Entente, are described in Chapter VIII.

O.A.M.C.E.

Inspired by the success of the Council of the Entente, another and larger organization of French-speaking African countries, which Madagascar also joined, came into existence in 1961. This was the Afro-Malagasy Union (U.A.M., in its four Equatorial African states and Madagascar, included Cameroun, Togo and the former Belgian trust territory of Rwanda, which became independent in July 1961. In French-speaking West Africa, its members were Ivory Coast, Dahomey, Upper Volta, Senegal, Mauritania and Niger. The aims of the U.A.M. were both economic and political in nature; a discussion of its political aspects will be found in Chapter VIII.

Economic collaboration between the members of the U.A.M. was the concern of the Afro-Malagasy Organization of Economic Cooperation (O.A.M.C.E.), founded by the 12 original member states in 1961. (At the same time, these states established the Air Afrique airline.) Besides a governing council, which met irregularly, it had a number of technical committees concerned with such matters as economic and social development, finance and currency, and scientific and technical research. Through the O.A.M.C.E., the U.A.M.'s member states hoped eventually to create a common civil service, a merchant marine and a unified tariff regime. The general aim of the organization was to coordinate action on economic problems, and some thought was given to its role in integrating the U.A.M. in an eventual African Common Market.

In 1962 the O.A.M.C.E. presented a solid front in that year's negotiations for continuance of French Black African association with the European Economic Community.

As described in Chapter VIII, the U.A.M.C.E. (Afro-Malagasy Union of Economic Collaboration)—which replaced the U.A.M. (Afro-Malagasy Union) in March 1964, is expected to play a role almost identical with that of the O.A.M.C.E.

Regional Collaboration

Since the French-speaking West African countries became independent, there has been regional collaboration in economic and technical fields between some of these countries and also between some of them and neighboring English-speaking African states.

One of the most important agencies of cooperation between French-speaking nations of West Africa—and one that is also closely bound up with financial and commercial relations with France and the franc zone—is the West African Monetary Union. When the Monetary Union was formed in May 1962, after long negotiations between France and the seven states other than Guinea, two features vital to the economic life of those states were agreed upon. The first was the adoption of a common currency—the C.F.A. (*Communauté Financière Africaine*) franc. Like its predecessor of the 1945–60 period, also referred to as the C.F.A. (*"Colonies Françaises d'Afrique"*) franc, the new unit of currency is worth two old French francs, or somewhat less than half a U.S. cent.

The second important feature of the agreement was that the stability of the C.F.A. franc was to be guaranteed by the French Treasury. At the same time a bank was established, called the Central Bank of the West African States, which issues the C.F.A. franc currency and has general control of credit. Although the Mali Republic withdrew from the Monetary Union in July 1962 and created its own currency, it remained within the franc zone.

The existence of the C.F.A. franc has greatly facilitated and encouraged commercial and financial relations between the six cooperating states.

Regional economic development on a cooperative basis is of growing interest to the West African nations. An outstanding example of this is to be seen in the plans for development of the Senegal River and its basin which have been under study jointly by Senegal, Mali, Mauritania and Guinea since July 1962. This big project, on which preliminary research has already been done by United Nations and Soviet experts, includes the building of several dams and hydroelectric plants, the displacing of the Dakar-Niger railroad line and the dredging of channels for navigation. Because the enormous cost of these operations will far exceed the capacities of the four countries' national budgets, it will be necessary for them to seek foreign financial aid. In June 1963, President Léopold Senghor of Senegal proposed that cooperation on the Senegal River project should be the basis for a closer regional economic group.

The French-speaking states of West Africa are also joining forces to continue the work begun in the 1950's by French technical and scientific organizations in, for example, the anti-locust campaigns and the struggle against endemic diseases such as sleeping sickness.

COOPERATION BETWEEN ENGLISH AND FRENCH-SPEAKING WEST AFRICA

In developing closer economic relations between English-

and French-speaking West African countries, which both areas generally desire, one of the main obstacles is that the English-speaking nations belong to a group of states using the pound sterling as their basic currency—the so-called sterling bloc—while the French-speaking nations, except for Guinea, are tied to the franc zone. Nevertheless, several projects have been launched, with varying success. In the economic sector these include customs unions between Upper Volta and Ghana (set up in June 1961) and Dahomey and Nigeria (in August 1962). Typical of cooperation in the technical realm are the arrangements between Senegal and its close neighbor, Gambia, the small British-controlled enclave which became autonomous on October 4, 1963. Since 1961, when a Senegalese-Gambian inter-ministerial committee was formed, the two countries have worked together in certain matters such as the maintenance of communications. It is expected that they will eventually come together in a political federation.

Another example of broad technical collaboration is the action by eight West African governments, discussed at a conference in Niamey, Niger, in February 1963, to modernize the juridical status of the Niger River and to undertake the economic development of the river throughout its length. The first step taken at the Niamey meeting was to nullify the clauses of the 1885 treaty of Berlin which concerned the Niger. A draft agreement was prepared, providing for freedom of navigation on the river and for establishing an international river commission at Niamey to supervise joint development of the Niger's resources, including fishing, irrigation works, power and navigation. The agreement was signed in October 1963 by nine countries—Niger, Mali, Upper Volta, Guinea, Ivory Coast, Dahomey, Cameroun, Chad and Nigeria.

Still another area of collaboration between French and

English-speaking African governments concerns an export commodity. An instance of this is the agreement reached between Senegal and Nigeria in May 1962 to coordinate their policies in the marketing of peanuts. These two countries, which are Africa's largest exporters of peanuts, have formed an African Council on Peanuts, which may be joined by Niger, a much smaller but nevertheless important, producer.

Foreign Aid

As indicated earlier in this chapter, all of the French-speaking West African countries are more or less dependent on foreign aid to supplement their resources, balance their budgets, and promote the development and modernization of their economies. For many years before these countries became sovereign states in 1960, they received financial and technical aid almost exclusively from France. Since then, although French aid has continued on a large scale (except to Guinea) frequently in the form of outright grants, other foreign countries have come into the picture as sources of loans and technical assistance. In addition another important source of aid to former French West Africa—again excepting Guinea, which has no ties with it—is the Common Market, as described above.

As for foreign aid from individual Western countries and certain Communist-bloc states, such aid is usually closely involved with foreign policy. For this reason, a more detailed discussion of foreign aid to the French-speaking West African states will be found in Chapter VIII.

National Economic-Development Plans

Without exception, the governments of the new states of French-speaking West Africa have embarked on comprehensive national plans for economic development. These all have been drawn up with the aid of foreign experts. As already mentioned, technical assistance has been received by these states from various sources: from the Communist bloc (though not exclusively) in the case of Guinea and Mali and to some extent Senegal; from France, the other Common Market countries, the United Nations and the United States in the case of Senegal and the five other West African nations.

The first countries to draw up plans and begin to carry them out were Guinea and Mali. In both cases, because of the views of their leaders, these plans strongly reflected Marxist doctrines. Senegal's plan, adopted in March 1961 and launched the following July, was also based on an ideology, in this case "African socialism," as it is called by President Léopold Senghor. Senegal's is the only plan, among those adopted, for which the ground was prepared by long preliminary studies carried out by trained personnel over a period of two years. Slowest to draw up national plans have been the four Entente countries (Ivory Coast, Dahomey, Upper Volta and Niger), and their plans neither reflect any particular ideology nor embrace the whole national economy.

All of these development plans, which cover varying periods of time ranging from two to five years, have certain basic features in common. Reverting to an important principle laid down at the Brazzaville Conference of 1944, they stress the human element. Their objective is not only African material progress and welfare, but also their spiritual development. As to methods and goals, planners have tried to make these truly African and to avoid imitating any foreign plans, whether Western or Communist. Furthermore, efforts have been made to avoid useless, wasteful or harmful competition between national plans—for example, in the building of hydroelectric installations. Instead, the governments are trying to coordinate their plans so as to develop complementary projects on a regional basis.

Other characteristics which the plans have in common are those dealing with agriculture, trade and industrialization. In agriculture, all the plans aim fundamentally to modernize farming methods and peasant living conditions—to replace the hoe and the brush fire by tractors and fertilizers, to liberate the African peasant from his bondage to monoculture, and in short, to bring him into the twentieth century. At the same time, the African nations hope to obtain better and more stable prices for their export products in the world market by presenting a united front. The African Council on Peanuts formed by Senegal and Nigeria is an example of this.

With regard to foreign and domestic trade, the most drastic move has been the attempt to break the grip of foreign companies on the importation and exportation of goods. State companies have been granted sweeping monopolies, and cooperatives are being formed to eliminate middlemen. Only in Ivory Coast has the free-enterprise system remained largely untouched, and even there the government is beginning to step in and assert some control over trade.

In the field of local industry, the plans generally aim at relatively small-scale industrialization, mostly in the field of consumer-goods production. The object is to reduce imports and bring down the cost of living. Even so limited an industrialization, however, is expected to improve mass living standards. These, until now, have been benefited very little by the few industries installed since World War II, which were concerned with the processing of some local raw materials, principally peanuts and almost wholly for export, and mining. In Guinea the mining and exporting of iron and bauxite, and in Mauritania the mining and exporting of iron and copper have required such heavy investments that they have had to be financed by international Western capital. Though the national revenues of Guinea and Mauritania have profited by the payment of taxes or duties on exported ores and the industry has provided a few jobs for unskilled local laborers, mining has not been of great benefit to the economy of either country as a whole. Moreover, the revenues derived from the ores, which represent a wasting asset, will inevitably decline as these mineral reserves are depleted.

Chief Economic Problems

Both nature and man are responsible for the most pressing economic problems faced by West Africa's governments.

Although nature has endowed the land with some valuable mineral deposits, most of the region labors under the handicaps of poor soil and adverse climates. Peasant conservatism—a world-wide trait—is intensified in West Africa by an apathy caused largely by the debilitating climate, the violence of natural phenomena, and endemic disease and malnutrition. In addition, because of certain local traditions, rural West Africans are resistant to change in general and to the modernization of agricultural and herding practices in particular. The deep-rooted custom of shifting cultivation and the periodic redistribution of land tend to discourage the individual farmer from making improvements on a plot of earth that he will not cultivate for long. Traditionally, the herder rears animals not for use in plowing or as a source of food or fertilizer, but as a form of unproductive capital that contributes to his social prestige. At best the result is waste, and at worst it furthers the destruction of the region's meager natural resources.

From the colonial regime the French-speaking West

A young weaver of the traditional cotton-cloth strips, which are sewed together to make larger cloths. His workshop is a sidewalk in the old quarter of Bamako, Mali.

Africans have inherited both assets and liabilities. Improved communications and foreign trade have made part of the population more mobile and more accessible to material and spiritual influences from other lands. Better health care and economic techniques have improved production and nutrition to some extent. On the other hand, they have led to a population increase which in some areas is outrunning the means of subsistence and causing an exodus of young peasants to the mushrooming towns. In the most densely populated areas, the young men emigrate regularly during the long dry months when traditional farming comes to a standstill. Some become wage earners in the coastal lands where the labor supply is limited and jobs are relatively plentiful. Many, however, simply remain idle, spending their time in gambling and traveling from one marketplace to another, or drift to the towns, where they live parasitically at the expense of relatives. Under these conditions, much of West Africa's manpower is not utilized, and urban centers are plagued by unsanitary housing and living conditions as well as by increasing crime and juvenile delinquency.

One unfortunate relic of the colonial period consists of the political frontiers of the new states, which cut across natural economic regions as well as across tribal groups. These artificial demarcation lines have hampered the full development of natural resources on a regional basis, and have encouraged smuggling across the frontiers by tribesmen on both sides. Because of the political risks that would be incurred by adjusting their frontiers more rationally, the present independent governments of French-speaking West Africa have decided to maintain them as the lesser of two evils.

Still another, and even more damaging, legacy of the colonial regime has been an over-heavy administrative structure that is far too expensive for the newly independent states to afford, considering their meager revenues. African civil servants are both too numerous and too well-paid by comparison with the vast mass of their rural compatriots. Expenditures for administrative personnel absorb about two-thirds of each nation's revenues, which would be better put to use in developing the country. As already mentioned, the powerful civil-servants' unions have resisted attempts by the national governments to cut down the number and pay of their members, and thus to reduce the widening gap between them and the rural masses. The present governments of French-speaking West Africa would be in a stronger moral position to push their austerity programs if their leaders were not also responsible, as pointed out in Chapter VI, for causing a heavy drain on public funds.

Maintaining a scale of living which reflects that of the former overseas administrators from France, West Africa's civil servants and politicians have not only set a bad example to their compatriots and siphoned off funds to unproductive expenditures, but in doing so, have increased their countries' dependence on foreign aid. Young men tend to seek an education because they hope that it will qualify them for a white-collar job in the government. Farming and manual labor have come to be regarded by many African youths as both demeaning and unremunerative. The praiseworthy effort now being made to give girls more opportunities for schooling and professional careers is having a further detrimental effect on food production, for in many areas of West Africa it is the women who have customarily done most of the farm work. To maintain the fast-growing army of civil servants, politicians and white-collar workers, the new nations have been compelled to solicit ever-greater financial aid.

In 1963, some indications of a more realistic and sober outlook among a few of West Africa's enlightened leaders could be seen. They have begun to realize the dangers inherent in a system that encourages parasitism, favoritism and corruption, and are putting more stress on austerity and on increased economic production. Two of the poorest West African nations, Mauritania and Upper Volta, have even refrained from asking France for subsidies to balance their budgets, which are chronically in the red. A new attitude toward foreign aid is beginning to be adopted by both donor and recipient nations. It reflects the realization that economic and psychological independence must be earned by the people of the recipient country themselves through increasing internal productivity—and that aid must not be used as a permanent crutch and to maintain artificially high living standards for a small, privileged class of semi-educated persons.

French-Speaking West Africa and the World

Within the span of one generation French West Africa has progressed from a status of isolation and dependency to that of eight political sovereignties. Along with this has come sudden involvement in international affairs and a growing consciousness of the "African personality," as well as a dawning awareness of the harsh economic realities that must be faced by poor and underdeveloped countries.

Although political independence was attained by the French-speaking West African states without bloody struggles, and—except in the case of Guinea—was won with the cooperation and economic assistance of France, those states have been experiencing acute growing pains, for many of which a cure has not yet been found. The new countries have explored various avenues of international cooperation, the most promising of which, from a long-range point of view, seem to consist of inter-African organizations. French-speaking West Africa is increasingly inclined to deal with its problems, and those of the continent as a whole, through common action with other African nations, for it has been disappointed in its experiences with the Afro-Asian bloc, with the threatened spread of the East-West cold war to African lands, and even with the United Nations, on which it had pinned high hopes.

The Africans are trying to establish and consolidate their place in what the late President John F. Kennedy so aptly described as a dangerous and untidy world. For a long time they will need both aid and a comprehension of their problems on the part of older nations.

Pre-independence Contacts

During the long years before the French-speaking West African states won their independence, foreign relations—in the strict sense—did not exist. Under the colonial regime it was the French government at Paris that had sole responsibility for them. However, some contacts besides strictly local and territorial ones had existed for centuries, and after World War II they became more frequent and extensive. They included, for example, trade currents between coastal and hinterland areas, and religious contacts, especially between

Muslim regions. The Muslim brotherhoods had members throughout North and West Africa, and their traveling leaders served as links between them. Moreover, the traditional tribal chiefs had subjects whose allegiance to them took no account of colonial frontiers.

After World War II still another, and important, avenue of contacts between French-speaking Africans took shape with the growth of a modern-educated elite. Members of this elite came to know one another in such inter-territorial schools as the William Ponty School at Dakar, in the universities of France, in the Grand Councils of the French West African and Equatorial African federations, and in the Paris Parliament and the French Union Assembly. However, even the Africans who constituted this elite knew very little about their counterparts in the British, Portuguese and Belgian African territories, and until the mid-1950's were preoccupied by the relations of their respective territories with France.

The awakening of French West African interest in other countries and peoples occurred only about 1955. In May of that year the first Afro-Asian conference was held at Bandung, Indonesia, and was attended by 29 government delegations. Almost all of these were from Asian nations as only a few African countries were independent at that time. The long-range effects of the Bandung Conference were significant for Africa because it was at that conference that the so-called Afro-Asian bloc was born. However, as the conference was preoccupied mainly with Asian problems, its immediate impact on Africa was not great. A much more powerful impetus to nationalism in French-speaking Africa, and to the widening of African contacts, was given by the winning of self-government by Togo, which became an autonomous republic in August 1956; by the independence of Ghana in March 1957; and by that of Cameroun in January 1960.

Afro-Asian Bloc

The Afro-Asian bloc is the oldest and most comprehensive grouping of underdeveloped countries which, in one way or another, have felt themselves to be victims of Western imperialism. For some years after it was formed in 1955, this bloc was unified by certain common sentiments and aims— antagonism toward the Western colonial powers, the goal of freeing all colored peoples still under colonial rule, and a policy of neutralism or non-alignment in relation to both the West and the Communist world. These attitudes underwent some modifications in the late 1950's, first as a result of the Anglo-French-Israeli invasion of Suez and second because of internal struggles for power and influence.

The Suez crisis late in October 1956 marked a turning-point in the Afro-Asian attitude toward the West and in the bloc's concept of neutralism. The invasion seemed to prove that old-style imperialism was far from dead and caused an upsurge of anti-Western feeling. With this there came a stronger sense of solidarity among the underdeveloped countries of Africa and Asia, which closed ranks and developed a double standard of international morality. Although they condemned the Suez invasion, they refrained, at almost the same time in 1956, from voicing strong disapproval of the Russian occupation of Hungary. These reactions reflected their feeling that the attack on Suez was aggression against one of their number, whereas the Hungarian debacle did not concern them because it was far away and involved a conflict between white nations. At this period, Afro-Asian neutralism became dynamic and selective. It began to be used as a lever in the struggle for foreign aid, in which Western countries were played off against Communist ones. Nevertheless, Communist aid was preferred, as was clearly shown at the Cairo conference of December 1957, because it came from supposedly disinterested, "anti-colonialist" countries.

Cairo Conference

Early in the 1956–60 period—sometimes called "the period of the clenched fist"—the first Afro-Asian conference to be held in Africa was called together at Cairo in December 1957. Forty-nine countries were represented, compared with the 29 which had sent delegates to the Bandung meeting in 1955. Violently anti-Western in tone, the conference marked the start of the Soviet Union's active campaign to influence sub-Saharan Africa.

But Russia did not run away with the conference. Two other strong personalities entered the arena of African power politics: Egypt's Gamal Abdel Nasser, who sought to use the conference to build up his prestige as an African leader; and Ghana's Kwame Nkrumah, the most vociferous champion of pan-Africanism, who came to Cairo at the head of a large Ghanaian delegation.

Conakry Conference

After the Cairo meeting, 28 months went by before the second full-scale Afro-Asian conference was held on African soil, at Conakry, Guinea, in April 1960. During this period dramatic events had taken place in sub-Saharan Africa, especially in Ghana and Guinea, which reflected the changing political picture in West Africa. Guinea (which, as mentioned in Chapter VI, had chosen total independence from France in September 1958) formed a "union" with Ghana in November 1958. Although this first attempt to unite English and French-speaking African countries did not result in a true political union, the mere announcement of it had a strong psychological impact on Negro Africa. In 1958, too, Ghana convened two important conferences of African countries at Accra—one governmental, the other non-governmental—which were intended to promote Nkrumah's pan-African goals.

At the Conakry conference there was larger representation from African countries than there had been at Cairo, although few of the French-speaking West African states sent delegates. Anti-Western feeling and action still dominated the discussions. However, some weaknesses and rifts in the Afro-Asian bloc began to appear. Most of the Asian countries, for various reasons, were less interested in unity than were the Africans, and the latter showed little concern for Asian problems. Furthermore, moderate Africans were increasingly disengaging themselves from the extremist Asian and African elements who had come to dominate the conference proceedings. Increasingly, the fight for leadership of the bloc was left to the Soviet Union, Communist China and Egypt—the nations that were financing the bloc's continuing operations.

MOSHI CONFERENCE

The third Afro-Asian conference was held at Moshi, Tanganyika, in February 1963. The leadership struggle by this time had become acute. Egypt receded into the background, but the ideological conflict between Russia and Communist China was openly carried on. Communism's internal quarrels dominated the Moshi conference and many Africans resented the extension of the inter-Communist and anti-Western cold war to Africa. This conference weakened the Afro-Asian bloc still further, although the bloc's members continued to maintain a joint stand in the UN on certain "colonial" issues and in seeking larger African representation in the organs of that world body.

By and large, the interests of the bloc's African members were concentrated on African affairs, and their goal generally was African unity. Hence the disintegration of the Afro-Asian bloc became to them of secondary importance, for as early as 1959 they had been increasingly absorbed by the forming of wholly African groupings.

Inter-African Groups

In chronological order, the first two all-African international groups created in West Africa were the Ghana-Guinea Union and the Mali Federation. The leaders of both of these hoped to build close-knit political unions that would serve as the core of larger groupings, but both failed—for many but not all of the same reasons. With the passage of time, it became clear that the leaders of the Union and of the Federation had vastly different ideas as to the way in which their respective groups should evolve, and personal antagonisms aggravated their differences of opinion. Neither group succeeded in drawing to it the other countries whose presence might have helped to offset these personality conflicts and enlarge the group's resources.

Differences in language, institutions, currency and international affiliations prevented the Ghana-Guinea Union from fully materializing. It never progressed beyond the stage of coordinating the two countries' communications systems and their foreign policy on certain issues.

The Mali Federation, on the other hand, even though at the beginning its members had more points in common than did the Ghana-Guinea Union, came to an end dramatically within a year and a half after its formation. When the more militant and Marxist Soudanese leaders found themselves unable to impose on the Senegalese their views in regard to foreign relations and the internal structure of the Federation, they made the unsuccessful effort described in Chapter VI to seize control by force. On the heels of that failure, they broke off all relations with Senegal and did not resume them for nearly three years. This break had very adverse effects upon the economies of both countries. However, neither the Soudanese president, Modibo Keita, nor the President of Senegal, Léopold Senghor, were thereby discouraged in their efforts to promote African unity, and each later joined other groups led by very different partners. Soudan, which became the Mali Republic after its break with Senegal, joined the Ghana-Guinea Union a few months afterwards. Senegal moved closer to the Council of the Entente, and together they promoted the first large grouping of French-speaking Negro African states. This grouping was originally known as the Brazzaville bloc, from the city in which it was founded, or as "the Twelve" ("les Douze"), from the number of states it comprised. These states were Senegal, Mauritania, Ivory Coast, Dahomey, Upper Volta, Niger, Cameroun, Chad, the Central African Republic, Congo (Brazzaville), Gabon and Madagascar. A few months later, when the bloc was formally organized, it took the name of Afro-Malagasy Union (Union Africaine et Malgache, or U.A.M. That union is described below).

GHANA-GUINEA-MALI UNION

Formation of the Brazzaville bloc in early December 1960 acted as a spur to the presidents of Ghana, Guinea and Mali to create an organization opposing it. On almost every foreign-policy issue, as well as on the structure of government and on the kind of African unity to be arrived at, the three leaders held views diametrically opposed to those of the Brazzaville bloc. All three states were dominated by a single, strongly organized party, their economies were largely state-controlled, they were suspicious of a revival of Western imperialism in Africa, and they wanted a tight pan-African political union. Their "union," however, never amounted to more than some coordination of their economic, cultural and diplomatic policies. Within two weeks of its formation all three countries joined a larger grouping of African states with tendencies similar to their own, which came to be called the Casablanca bloc. Their group then largely lost its separate identity.

CASABLANCA BLOC

Early in January 1961, King Mohammed V of Morocco called a conference at Casablanca to consider developments in the ex-Belgian Congo. Only the radical nationalist and extremist states were invited, and the king's invitation was accepted by three sub-Saharan countries—Ghana, Guinea and Mali—and three North African Muslim states—the United Arab Republic, Libya and of course Morocco as the host country. It was also attended by representatives of the Algerian rebels (the F.L.N., or National Liberation Front) and by an observer from one Asian country, Ceylon. Tunisia was not invited because, although it had helped the F.L.N., it had opposed Morocco's territorial claim to Mauritania. The Ceylonese never attended later meetings of this bloc, and Libya not only failed to reappear but eventually joined a rival organization, the Monrovia group.

These defections left the Casablanca bloc with only six members, but even these few were a mixed lot. Not only were they separated geographically, but they belonged to different linguistic and monetary zones and had different types of government. The bloc was made up of Arabs and Negroes, English- and French-speaking Africans, monarchists and republicans. In some respects the Casablanca bloc, on a much more limited scale, resembled the Afro-Asian group. Its members maintained generally good relations with the Communist states and usually voted with them in the UN. All of them denounced neo-colonialism in general and the policy of France and the European Economic Community (Common Market) in Africa in particular. All supported Patrice Lumumba as head of the Congolese (ex-Belgian Congo) government and opposed the U.N.'s handling of the Congo crisis. Moreover, all of them denounced Portuguese colonialism in Africa and *apartheid* (racial segregation) in South Africa, and favored giving material help to liberation movements in those areas as well as in Algeria. In 1961 the Casablanca bloc drew up a charter and formed an embryonic organization comprising an advisory assembly, a permanent secretariat, and three committees for the coordination of political, economic and social affairs. At the same time a joint military command was created. The following year this bloc began formulating plans for an African development bank, customs union and common market.

Despite these wide areas of agreement, however, differences regarding three main points of foreign policy developed, as did personal antagonisms. Although all the bloc's members supported Lumumba in the Congo, Ghana did not concur in its partners' wish to withdraw all their troops serving under the U.N. Congo command. Again, it was Ghana that had undermined support for Moroccan claims to Mauritania by recognizing the independence of Mauritania a few days before the Casablanca conference began. Moreover, Ghana, along with Guinea and Mali, objected to a resolution sponsored by Egypt denouncing Israel as a "bridgehead of Western imperialism" in Africa. Although all three countries —which had received considerable technical aid from Israel—

voted for the Egyptian resolution, they disliked Nasser's tactics in forcing through its passage. Indeed, all of them, as well as the King of Morocco, resented Nasser's domination of the Casablanca conference. For the first time, Nasser was attending an all-African conference, and he clearly showed there his desire to lead Negro as well as Arab Africa.

A month after the conference ended, King Mohammed V died. His death eliminated an Arab leader who was a personal friend of all three heads of the Negro member states of the Casablanca bloc, and they never felt the same confidence in Mohammed's son and successor on the throne, Hassan II. Then the death of Lumumba, the end of the Algerian war, and, above all, the increasing closeness of the French-speaking Negro African states—which became more marked during 1962—did away with many of the elements that had held the bloc together. Its leaders drifted ever farther apart. Sékou Touré and Nkrumah decided at the last moment not to attend the bloc meeting held at Cairo in August 1961, and the next year the bloc's scheduled conferences were repeatedly postponed. The bloc's strength was obviously waning long before it reached the point of formal dissolution, which took place a month after the Organization of African Unity (see page 280) was formed at Addis Ababa, Ethiopia, in May 1963.

Afro-Malagasy Union

While the Casablanca bloc was falling apart, the strength of the "Twelve" of Brazzaville was steadily growing. In many ways the paths of the two groups followed parallel lines, and the Brazzaville bloc was also subject to internal stresses and strains. Both blocs had been formed at conferences called on foreign-policy issues, drew up and signed charters in 1961, and created sub-groups to coordinate their economic, defense and cultural policies. Both aimed, also, to enlarge their respective memberships, although only the Casa-blanca-bloc members were willing to surrender some of their sovereignty to a political pan-African union.

Even before the Brazzaville bloc was formally organized in March 1961 as the Afro-Malagasy Union, there were differences of opinion among its members concerning both specific and general foreign-policy issues. In regard to the former Belgian Congo, President Fulbert Youlou of the ex-French Congo supported the secession of Katanga and its "President," Moïse Tshombé, whereas the others rallied behind the central Congolese government at Léopoldville. After Tunisia, in July 1961, tried to occupy the French naval base at Bizerte by force, all the U.A.M. states except Ivory Coast and Niger voted in favor of Tunisia when that crisis was brought before the U.N. In December 1962, Dahomey refused to attend a round-table conference at Douala, Cameroun, which had been called to deal with a dispute between Gabon and the ex-French Congo, on the ground that the scope of the conference should be widened. Subsequent to the assassination of President Sylvanus Olympio of Togo in January 1963 by disgruntled soldiers, some U.A.M. members favored recognizing the new Togolese regime formed immediately thereafter. Other members, however, would not recognize that government because it had come to power through violence.

On less specific issues, there were also conflicts of opinion and action. Relations of the U.A.M. nations with the Communist countries diverged widely from whole-hearted endorsement of diplomatic and trade ties and the acceptance of aid to outright rejection. As to Red China, Senegal recognized it officially in 1961 and supported its admission to the U.N., but Ivory Coast refused to have any dealings with Peking. None of the U.A.M. states except the Congo (Brazzaville), however—up to the time this is written—has exchanged ambassadors with the Chinese Communist government. The dramatic recognition of the Peking regime by President de Gaulle in February 1964, however, may profoundly affect the attitude of French African leaders toward relations with Red China.

The Soviet Union and its eastern European satellites have been more successful with the U.A.M. states. Senegal's premier and Dahomey's president made official visits to Moscow in 1962 and 1963 respectively, and several other members of the U.A.M. have reached agreements with Iron Curtain countries for trade and cultural exchanges. After the Soviet Union lifted its veto on Mauritania's admission to the U.N. in 1961, relations between Moscow and the U.A.M. governments grew increasingly amicable.

With regard to the Muslim countries of North Africa, the U.A.M. states with predominantly Muslim populations, and especially those that border on the Sahara, have necessarily developed a special policy. Many Muslim Negroes attend the Islamic schools of Tunisia, Morocco and above all, Egypt, and those North African countries have been generous in granting them scholarships and sending teachers to their countries. Nevertheless, Morocco's expansionist ambitions have alienated all the U.A.M. states except, possibly, Senegal, which has tried to reconcile the Moroccans and the Mauritanians. Egypt, too, has supported Moroccan territorial claims which the U.A.M. states oppose, but some of those states have even more serious grievances against the Cairo government. Although, for example, the president of Niger, Hamani Diori, has finally signed an agreement of cooperation with Egypt, he did so reluctantly because of the fact that for some years Nasser has harbored and encouraged Diori's political enemy, Djibo Bakary.

Of all the North African nations, Tunisia is by far the most highly esteemed by the heads of the U.A.M. states. They admire its president, Habib Bourguiba, for his moderate policies and his support of Mauritania. Popular as he is, however, Bourguiba could not win the support of all of the U.A.M. states when it came to the Bizerte issue, mentioned above. Algeria's independence, finally achieved in 1962, now poses problems for the states with nomad populations. Although all of the U.A.M. countries have upheld Algeria's claim to sovereignty, those whose peoples include large nomad tribes are afraid that the restless nomads may secede and join their "white" fellow-Arabs and Berbers to the north. The U.A.M. nations must somehow remain on good terms with their northern neighbors, but the future of the Sahara's population and of its mineral wealth causes them great concern. Moreover, the long-standing hostility of Africa's Negroes towards its Arabs is kept alive by the periodic aggressiveness of the North Africans.

Notwithstanding these divergent attitudes, the U.A.M. remained intact until March 1964 because of its type of organization and leadership and because it had more areas of agreement than of disagreement. All of the U.A.M. countries are largely dependent economically on France, and this bond is strengthened by historical association as well as by present-day friendliness and cooperation. Above all, the end of the Algerian war and the cessation of nuclear-weapons testing in the Sahara by France removed the principal obstacles to good Franco-U.A.M. relations.

It is worth noting, too, that the U.A.M. benefited by far better organization than that of its Casablanca rival. Its sub-groups were more solidly structured, meetings were more carefully prepared, and the conferences of heads of state were more regularly held and better attended. The U.A.M. states prudently rejected a close political union, and opposed any alteration of existing frontiers between them as well as intervention by one state in the internal affairs of another. The stronger member states did not try to steamroller the weaker ones, and three of the latter—Dahomey, Congo and Upper Volta—were made permanent headquarters of the U.A.M.'s sub-groups. Cotonou was the site of its permanent secretariat, Brazzaville of its postal and telecommunications committee, and Ouagadougou of its defense organization. The chairmanship of the U.A.M.'s periodic conferences rotated among the heads of member states, and conferences were held successively in their capitals.

Furthermore, the outstanding leaders of the U.A.M. did not try to throw their weight around. Félix Houphouët-Boigny of Ivory Coast, who was the leader in organizing the Union, has been willing to remain in the background. He realizes that he is at his best in behind-the-scenes diplomacy and let Léopold Senghor of Senegal—a far abler orator— be spokesman for the Union at international gatherings. The U.A.M. was a close-knit organization of sovereign states, whose leaders stressed points of agreement and tried to find mutually acceptable compromises. On issues where such compromises proved difficult to reach, they postponed decisions rather than risk conflict. More homogeneous in every way than the Casabalanca bloc, the U.A.M. succeeded in avoiding most of the pitfalls which led to that bloc's demise: a heterogeneous make-up, unwillingness to compromise and disruptive rivalries among its leaders.

Nevertheless, in March 1964, owing to external and internal pressures, the U.A.M. transformed itself into a regional economic organization called the Afro-Malagasy Union of Economic Cooperation (or U.A.M.C.E.). The background of this reorganization is described below in the section dealing with the Organization of African Unity.

Monrovia Group

The U.A.M. was the only association of states which, as an organization, joined the Monrovia group that was formed in the Liberian capital in May 1961. It was the situation in the ex-Belgian Congo that motivated the Monrovia meeting, just as it had the one held at Casablanca four months before. This gathering's sponsors, among whom were both revolutionary and moderate African leaders, hoped that it would result in a common African stand on the situation in the Congo.

Representatives of 20 African nations, including 15 heads of state, came to Monrovia. Some of the countries represented there—Nigeria, Sierra Leone, Liberia, Togo, Ethiopia and Somalia—had never before taken part in an inter-African conference. The Monrovia meeting and the subsequent one at Lagos showed that there was new interest on the part of English-speaking West and East Africans in bringing about African unity. The delegates at the Monrovia sessions were generally pro-Western, disposed to support U.N. action in the Congo, and insistent upon independence for Algeria and for the Portuguese colonies in Africa. Speakers at the conference showed a moderation that contrasted sharply with the vehemence that had characterized utterances of the Casablanca bloc's spokesmen. Leaders of that bloc were expected to attend the Monrovia meeting, but at the last minute they failed to appear. Early the next year they also abruptly declined to attend the Monrovia group's next meeting at Lagos, Nigeria, in January 1962. On the first occasion, their absence was explained by the refusal of the other participants to adopt the principles laid down at Casablanca in January 1961 as the working basis for the conference's agenda. At Lagos, their nonappearance was reportedly due to the unwillingness of the

Monrovia group—and specifically that of the U.A.M. leaders
—to invite representatives of the Algerian rebel government
to attend.

As a result, the Monrovia group failed to attain one of its
primary objectives—the reconciliation of "revolutionary" and
"reformist" Africa. Indeed, the whole tone and organization
of the Monrovia group resembled those of the U.A.M. Its
keynote was reasonableness, prudence, and moderation. Moreover, the permanent organization which it established was
one of sovereign states cooperating in economic, technical and
social matters and pledged not to interfere in each other's
internal affairs. Like the U.A.M., too, it stressed unity, soft-
pedalled controversial issues, and emphasized cooperative
effort to solve common practical problems. Inevitably this approach displeased some of the states which wanted to air their
grievances against fellow-members and to bring up matters
likely to cause discord, such as African membership in the
European Common Market. A number of the English-speaking states were outspokenly annoyed with the U.A.M. for
blocking an invitation to the Algerians and thus keeping all
of the North African states away.

Consequently, by the time the Lagos conference ended, it
already seemed that this new grouping was unlikely to en-
dure. It suffered another blow at the U.N. in October 1962
when Morocco won a seat in the Security Council, defeating
Nigeria despite the latter's backing by all the Monrovia-group
countries. Then, too, discord arose over the question of recognition of the government that had been set up in Togo after
the assassination of President Olympio in January 1963. A
special meeting of the Monrovia group's foreign ministers
called to settle that issue failed to do so, and this ended the
organization's effective existence. The Monrovia group never
met again, but its hard core—the U.A.M.—survived intact,

thus breaking what had appeared until that time to be an established pattern. The Council of the Entente had been largely submerged in the U.A.M., and the Ghana-Guinea-Mali Union was absorbed by the Casablanca bloc, but now the smaller unit, the U.A.M., outlived the larger grouping of which it had been a part. In fact, the U.A.M. served as a model for the Organization of African Unity, the important inter-African body which came into being at Addis Ababa in May 1963.

ORGANIZATION OF AFRICAN UNITY

The conference which convened in the Ethiopian capital of Addis Ababa late in May 1963 was the largest and most impressive gathering of African states in the continent's history. By that time almost all of the African continent consisted of sovereign states, and only three of them were not represented at Addis Ababa. These were Togo and the Union of South Africa (neither of which was invited) and Morocco, whose king refused to attend because of the presence of Mauritania's president, Mokhtar Ould Daddah. Preparations for this meeting took longer and were more carefully planned than for any of the preceding African conferences, and its many sponsors were determined that it should be a success. Throughout 1962 and early 1963, almost all of the revolutionary and moderate African leaders exchanged visits, the main objective of which was to promote the cause of African unity.

This conference marked the victory of "moderate" Africa, for its members rejected Nkrumah's appeal for a close-knit and militant political union and accepted the charter for an Organization of African Unity (O.A.U.) drafted by the conference's host, Emperor Haile Selassie. The O.A.U.'s charter provided for an assembly, a council, and a committee to settle disputes between members. The assembly was to be composed

*Meeting of African heads of state at Addis-Ababa, Ethiopia,
May 26, 1963. At this conference, the Organization of
African Unity was formed.*

of heads of state and was to meet once a year. The council,
whose members were to be the foreign ministers of member
states, would meet twice a year and be responsible to the
assembly. This council was to prepare the ground for the
assembly meetings and also to coordinate inter-African activities in the fields of health, social and economic affairs, defense
and scientific research. The O.A.U.'s budget, financed by
contributions from member states, was to be managed by a
permanent secretariat, and a special fund was also created to
be used on behalf of liberation movements in still-dependent
African territories.

Although the formation of the O.A.U. was the only practical accomplishment of the Addis Ababa conference, it was a
very important step and was largely attributable to the self-

restraint and spirit of cooperation shown by all of the assembled leaders. Nkrumah did not sulk because his proposal had been rejected; Nasser refrained from making his customary attack on Israel; Houphouët was polite to Nasser; and Senghor publicly embraced Modibo Keita, to signal the reconciliation of Senegal and Mali. As at Monrovia, controversial issues were avoided, and areas of agreement were stressed. Among the latter were the material and moral support of liberation movements in still-colonial territories, condemnation of racial discrimination in South Africa and the United States, and the elimination of barriers between white and Negro Africa and between French- and English-speaking African countries. African demands for the barring of all nuclear-weapons testing and for greater representation in U.N. organs were endorsed, and so were Africa's policy of unity and non-alignment and the principle of an African common market and development fund. Colonialism was strongly condemned, but there were no bitter outbursts against France and Great Britain, and little mention was made of "neo-colonialism."

The "spirit of Addis Ababa," to which many references have since been made, was clearly that of creating and preserving African unity. In the pervasive atmosphere of enthusiasm that characterized this conference, there was an obvious determination to ignore problems that were difficult to solve. One of these was the absence of King Hassan II, which indicated that Morocco had not yet given up its claim to Mauritania. Another was the conflict between Somalia and its neighbors, Ethiopia and Kenya. Still another was that of recognition of the new Togolese government. Moreover, no firm stand was taken in regard to the survival of such associations as the U.A.M. The real test of Africa's new-found unity was to come later, when these unresolved problems became acute. The first such test occurred when the O.A.U. foreign ministers met at Dakar in July 1963.

Fortunately for those statesmen, a few inter-African conflicts had been settled before their Dakar meeting convened. Elections had been held in Togo, and since then, all the O.A.U. states had recognized the new Togolese regime. Senegal and Mali had been formally reconciled, and Morocco had indicated that it would soon join the O.A.U. The debates at Dakar were stormy, unlike the discussions at Addis Ababa, but the O.A.U. foreign ministers managed to deal with a few troublesome questions. They agreed as to which of the nationalist movements in the Portuguese colonies the O.A.U. would support, and chose Addis Ababa as the site of the organization's permanent secretariat. They could not agree, however, as to who would be named secretary-general of the O.A.U. and—more important—as to the fate of the U.A.M.

The members of the U.A.M. itself were undecided as to whether to disband their organization, but the only positive step that they took prior to the Dakar meeting was to discontinue their own separate representation at the U.N. Mauritania, which no longer needed the support of the organization against Morocco, favored dissolution of the U.A.M., but its partners preferred a wait-and-see attitude. It would be unwise, they argued, to abandon an organization that had proved its worth, before the newly created O.A.U. was built up on solid foundations. At Dakar they might have agreed to disband had it not been for Sékou Touré's violent attack against the "resurgence of insolent U.A.M. activities." Other O.A.U. states, notably Nigeria, agreed with Touré that the U.A.M. was not a genuine regional economic association and that its close ties with France made it an obstacle to the attainment of genuine African unity. Nevertheless, the "spirit of Addis Ababa" again prevailed at Dakar, and the foreign ministers compromised by recommending that the U.A.M. be merged gradually with the O.A.U.

Nine months later, in March 1964, a tentative step in this direction was taken by the heads of the U.A.M. states, as mentioned above. In principle, the U.A.M.'s successor, the U.A.M.C.E., is to be concerned solely with economic colloboration on a regional basis, but in fact its future scope has not yet been clearly defined.

Only a few months after the Dakar meeting, the strength of the O.A.U. was put to its first practical test. This centered on the conflict that erupted in October 1963 between Morocco and Algeria over ownership of a portion of the western Sahara. Although this territorial dispute was geographically remote from Negro Africa and involved only two North African countries, it was nevertheless of concern to all the O.A.U. members. It raised not only the problem of the future of the Sahara and of its nomad populations, but also that of altering the frontiers that had been defined by the continent's various colonial regimes in the past. The handling of this dispute by the O.A.U. in February 1964 substantiated the stand taken by all African leaders that African problems should and indeed can be settled exclusively by Africans. However, it is not yet certain that the dispute is settled.

The army mutinies in East Africa early in 1964, which were referred to the O.A.U. by Tanganyika's president, Julius Nyerere, posed a new challenge to the organization's effectiveness, and many other such problems are certain to arise. Sooner or later, the O.A.U. will probably have to deal with such thorny questions as the vulnerable position of African minorities living in African countries where they were not born, and tribal massacres of the kind that took place during 1963–64 in Rwanda.

Relations with Communist Countries

SOVIET UNION AND SATELLITES

The Soviet Union displayed little interest in Africa until after World War II, and for the first years thereafter it let the French Communist party push Communist objectives in French West and Equatorial Africa. The French party organized Communist Study Groups in the main towns of the two federations which were attended by some of the Africans who are now prominent leaders, such as Sékou Touré. It also recruited Marxist teachers for service in African secondary schools. In 1946, well-known French Communists helped to found the R.D.A.—the African political party described in Chapter VI—but they did not encourage its nationalist tendencies. At that time they hoped that the Communist party might take over the French government and with it the French empire, so they firmly discouraged separatist sentiments.

In the late 1940's, Communists sent from France by the party toured Negro Africa, trying to strengthen the territorial branches of the R.D.A. and the local Communist (C.G.T.) labor unions. At that period, too, in French parliamentary bodies, the Communist party echoed the grievances and supported the aspirations expressed there by their R.D.A. members. Nevertheless, some of the African nationalists began to realize that the French Communist party was subordinating their interests to those of the European proletariat. Moreover, after 1947 the power of the party was obviously declining in France. In brief, the party's support—which had been an asset to the R.D.A. in the first postwar years—appeared by 1950 to have become a liability. The belief that this was the case was the chief reason for Houphouët-Boigny's decision in 1950–51 to sever his movement's links with the French Communists and to cooperate with the local French administration in Africa (see pages 193–194).

The French Communist party's failure to retain the loyalty of the R.D.A. probably impelled the Soviet Union to take a more active and direct interest in French West Africa. Since the Russians knew little about Africa, they established research centers in Moscow and Leningrad, which not only produced scholarly work but also trained some Soviet nationals for service in Africa. The knowledge that the Russians gained from such studies, as well as their experience with the R.D.A., caused them to make a reappraisal of the African continent's possibilities.

Taking stock of the situation there, they found that almost no Communist parties existed in French Negro Africa. To be sure, there were the splinter groups of the R.D.A. which had balked at following Houphouët's change of policy, and there were also some well-organized C.G.T. unions. The radical splinter groups had little influence, however, and by 1957 the Communist labor unions were seeking autonomy from the French C.G.T. In the French sub-Saharan territories there was no sizeable proletariat, no class struggle, and the sole Communist party—the Parti Africain de l'Indépendance (African Independence Party)—was composed of only a handful of youthful extremists. Pan-Africanism, not Communism, was arousing popular enthusiasm. To the Russians, the outlook for a frontal assault seemed most unpromising, and as a result they devised a propaganda line centered on two ideas. One of these was that the Soviet Union provided the best example for the Africans to follow in order to win genuine independence. The other was that Africa's most helpful and disinterested friend was the Soviet Union. Only the Communist bloc, the Russians insisted, could provide Africans with the type of aid they needed and, moreover, the assistance offered by the

Western countries was dangerous to accept because political strings were attached to it. These ideas were transmitted to Africa in radio broadcasts and repeated tirelessly to the African youth and labor leaders invited to visit and study in Eastern European countries. They were also publicized at the Afro-Asian conferences.

Moscow and Guinea. As the African countries successively gained political independence, the Russians were able to approach their leaders and peoples more directly, for until then they had been hampered by the controls established by the colonial regimes. The dire economic plight of Guinea after it cut loose from France in 1958 presented the Soviet Union with a golden opportunity. Moreover, Sékou Touré and some members of the P.D.G. (Democratic Party of Guinea) politburo had already undergone Marxist training and in some cases had visited Iron Curtain countries. Guinea, it seemed, might well become a shining example of what Russian aid could do for an underdeveloped African country.

Three days after the Republic of Guinea was proclaimed on October 2, 1958, it was recognized by the Soviet Union, and the satellite countries quickly followed suit. Numerous Communist missions arrived at Conakry, and they were almost the only foreign source of trade and aid at that time for the hard-pressed Guineans. In April 1959, Russia sent one of its ablest diplomats, David Solod, as ambassador to Guinea, and in the autumn of that year, Sékou Touré paid a state visit to Moscow. The peak of Russo-Guinean relations was reached in 1960. By that time, perhaps as many as 700 European Communist technicians were working in Guinea on various projects, including the building of a powerful radio station and a huge printing press, and the improvement of Guinea's railroad and port facilities. About 200 Guinean students were enrolled in Eastern European educational institutions. In

March 1960, Guinea abruptly left the franc zone and created its own currency, reportedly at Communist instigation. By the end of the year, about three-fourths of Guinea's trade consisted of exchanges with the Communist bloc. It is worth noting that almost all of Guinea's exports in 1960—aside from minerals—were absorbed by that bloc in payment for the funds and merchandise which the Communist countries had provided to Guinea under various agreements.

During the last months of 1960 and the early part of 1961, however, Communist penetration of Guinea met with some setbacks. Creation of the Guinean franc and establishment of many state controls over trading encouraged smuggling and produced inflation. Sékou Touré's attempt in 1960 to establish diplomatic relations with both East and West Germany proved to be a serious mistake. The West German government forced him to back down and to restrict his relations with the East Germans to trade. Eastern European technicians were not popular in Guinea because they were socially aloof and few of them spoke French. The Conakry government also saw to it that the Guineans kept their distance by forbidding all foreigners to engage in propaganda activities among the local population.

If the Eastern Europeans were turning out to be less helpful than the Guineans had hoped they would be, neither was Guinea proving wholly satisfactory to the Soviet Union. Although Sékou Touré's two visits to Moscow provided useful propaganda material, the Russians were annoyed by the speeches he made there praising neutralism and the "African personality" and reiterating that "Communism is not the path of Africa or of Guinea." They also frowned on his tolerance in Guinea of individual property ownership and of the Fria company, a large Western-financed alumina-producing enterprise whose activities provided the country with half of its revenue. Nevertheless, they found satisfaction in Touré's refusal to be aligned politically with the West and in his advocacy of revolutionary movements elsewhere in Africa. As a mark of their approval, they awarded Touré the Lenin Peace Prize in May 1961.

At the end of 1961 there came a dramatic change in Soviet-Guinean relations. The Guinean government announced it had proof that the Soviet ambassador in Conakry was involved in a plot to overthrow Sékou Touré, suppress his party and install a Communist regime in Guinea. Ambassador Solod was recalled at Touré's request, and the Guineans were rude to Anastas Mikoyan, one of the top members of the Soviet Cabinet, when he rushed to Conakry to smooth things over. The Russians began to realize that they had overplayed their hand and had underestimated the intensely African patriotism which motivated Sékou Touré's policy. They have continued to provide Guinea with trade and aid, but relations between them and the Guineans have cooled. In April 1962, the Guinean government began making overtures to the Western nations and patching up its quarrel with France. Sékou Touré, however, has no intention of committing Guinea to the Western camp, any more than he has of breaking off relations with the Eastern European countries. His policy has always stressed non-alignment, but now he is trying to establish a better balance between Communist and Western aid.

Moscow and Mali. Mali is second to Guinea among the countries of French-speaking West Africa in which the Communists have made most headway—and for some of the same reasons. A number of the Union Soudanaise leaders have gone through Marxist training, and many of the Malian youth and labor organizers hold decidedly radical views. The Russians lost no time in recognizing the Mali Republic in September 1960, sending missions to its capital, Bamako, and inviting Malians to come to Moscow. President Modibo Keita made a state visit to Russia, where he was granted a sizeable loan, and later he was awarded the Lenin Peace Prize. Soviet technicians have been working in Mali, prospecting for minerals, surveying an extension of the railroad and helping to build a cement factory. Trade and aid agreements have been signed by Mali with the Soviet Union and its satellites.

Thus the same pattern as in Guinea was applied to Mali, but at a slower tempo and without the same enthusiasm on either side. Modibo Keita, well aware of the deterioration of Guinea's economy, did not follow Sékou Touré's example. He has avoided burning his bridges with France and the Common Market, from both of which he continues to receive aid. Naturally this has not been very palatable to the Russians, any more than was the warm reception given by the Malians to Chou En-lai in January 1964.

Three other French-speaking West African states have relations with the Soviet Union and its satellites. After some hesitation, Senegal exchanged ambassadors and trade missions with the Soviet Union, and in June 1962 Mamadou Dia became the first premier of a U.A.M. country to make an official visit to Moscow. There he invited Soviet technicians to help develop Senegal's economy, especially in making a survey of the Senegal River Valley's economic potential. These gestures on the part of Senegal derive from its leaders' philosophy of "African socialism," which leads them to believe that they should accept aid from both the Eastern and Western blocs. It does not mean that the Senegalese have any love for Communist doctrines, for of all the peoples of West Africa they are probably the most bourgeois in their outlook.

As for Dahomey and Niger, they also moved in 1962 to establish contacts with the Soviet Union and other Eastern European countries. Good-will and trade missions have been exchanged between them, and various agreements have been signed, but only in Dahomey has the Eastern bloc installed embassies. Among the U.A.M. countries, the two that have remained the most adamant in avoiding Communist contacts are Ivory Coast and Mauritania.

FAR EASTERN COMMUNIST STATES

Inevitably, Red China was slower than the Soviet Union in getting a foothold in Africa. The Chinese Communists did not consolidate their control of the mainland of China until late in 1949, and the first area in which they expanded was, naturally, Asia. The Bandung conference of May 1955 gave them their first opportunity to make contacts with African leaders, but these contacts were limited because few African countries were represented there. After the Suez crisis of 1956, the Chinese Communists became interested in Nasser and established diplomatic relations with Egypt. They sent delegates to the Afro-Asian conference at Cairo in December 1957, but at that time the Chinese were very much the junior partners of Russia. In 1958 the Chinese began moving out from under the Soviet Union's shadow and working independently in Africa. By 1959 they had become involved in the Algerian war and were giving considerable aid to the F.L.N. rebels.

The year 1960, which saw the dawn of independence in many African countries, gave China—as it had the Soviet Union—greater opportunities to operate in sub-Saharan Africa. Many organizations dealing with that continent's affairs were created in mainland China and also in Africa. In April 1960, a Sino-African Peoples Friendship Association was founded in Peking, and it established branches in some African countries. At about the same time, a Pan-Chinese Federation of Students and Youth was formed, to work with African labor and youth leaders, and it opened a few bookshops in Africa. The most important propaganda media, however, were the New China News Agency and Radio Peking. By 1960 the former had stationed representatives in Africa to supply news and propaganda themes for African consumption. Radio Peking was broadcasting 70 hours a week to Africa in French, English and Portuguese. Communist China sent many missions to African countries and invited hundreds of Africans to visit Peking.

Peking's Methods. As might be expected, Guinea and Mali have been the countries in French-speaking West Africa that have been most receptive to Red China's overtures. Peking was only slightly later than Moscow in recognizing Guinea's independence, but it was not until early 1960 that ambassadors were exchanged. Since then, a few hundred Chinese have been working to improve Guinea's rice production, start a tea plantation, and build a cigarette factory. Despite fantastic rumors suggesting that thousands of Chinese were flooding into Guinea, their number has never equalled that of the Eastern European technicians, nor has Communist China's trade and financial aid, though substantial, come up to that given by the Russians.

Although Red China's activities in Guinea have been on a smaller scale than those of Eastern European countries, the Chinese have not been handicapped—as have the Eastern European Communists—by Guinean suspicions of meddling in the country's internal affairs. Several times, Sékou Touré has expressed admiration not so much for Communist ideology as for the way in which China has dealt with its practical problems. He has praised the Chinese for their frugality and industry—qualities that he would like to see imitated by his own people—and has indicated his belief that China's aid to Africa is genuinely disinterested.

With Mali, Peking has also established diplomatic and

*Communist China's Premier, Chou En-lai, with
President Sékou Touré of Guinea during the former's visit to
Conakry in January 1964.*

trade relations, but the aid it has given the Malians is slight.
It has sent a few technicians and some equipment to Bamako,
and offered a small number of scholarships in Chinese schools
to Malian students. Mali has reciprocated by sending good-
will missions to Peking, breaking off relations with the Chinese Nationalist government in Taipeh, and supporting Red
China's efforts to gain admission to the United Nations.

Peking's relations with other French-speaking Negro African countries are negligible, being mostly confined to scattered
contacts with labor and youth leaders. Senegal, Dahomey and
Ivory Coast have maintained diplomatic relations with the
Nationalist Chinese, and for this and other reasons Peking
has no ambassadors in those countries. Conservative leaders,

such as Houphouët, oppose Chinese Communist contacts both on principle and because of fears that they may lead to Africa's becoming an outlet for China's enormous surplus population. As to Red China's Far Eastern satellites, their relations with Africa are very limited. A few of the French-speaking African leaders who go to Peking also visit North Korea and North Vietnam. Guinea and Mali have diplomatic relations with the Hanoi government, and both of them have a few North Vietnamese technicians.

In the themes of its propaganda directed to Africa, Peking has drastically changed front several times. At the outset, China's "Great Leap Forward" was pictured as a sensational short cut to economic development, but when its failure became obvious in 1959, this line was dropped. Being late-comers on the African scene, the Chinese Communists have not had the time to study Africa as the Soviets have done and therefore have concentrated on a practical approach. They have tried to make Peking a pole of attraction for Africa's future leaders, and have stressed their solidarity and the problems which they have in common with the African peoples. Like the Africans, they say, the Chinese are a colored people who have suffered from Western imperialism. China, too, is a backward country, but is overcoming its under-development by revolutionary methods that the Africans could also profitably use. By the force of their example, the Chinese would be happy to show Africans the way, and China's 650 millions are pictured as standing solidly behind their African comrades.

Initially, both Moscow and Peking encouraged African neutralism as an effective means of undermining Western influence, and stressed the disinterested nature of Communist aid to Africa. By 1962, however, Communist China's propaganda to Africa began to diverge sharply from that of the

Soviet Union and to compete with it. Peking has also had a prime objective which is clearly self-interested—to win African support for Red China's admission to the U.N. In their competition with the Russians to establish the dominant Communist influence in Africa, the Chinese arrived on the scene late enough to profit by Russian experience and Russian mistakes, and they have been more tactful and less aggressive in their dealings with the Africans. Peking realizes that it cannot compete with Russia's material aid to the African countries, much less that of the West, so it must stress a different appeal. This is the "communism of the poor and of the colored peoples" in contrast to the "communism of the rich," as exemplified by the white, European Russians. By our hard work under the party's leadership, the Chinese say, we have mobilized our huge population and pulled China up by its bootstraps, almost wholly on the basis of our own resources. Africa can do the same, if it follows Communist China's example and revolutionary methods. They warn, however, that if the Africans let themselves be tempted by Russia's appeal for peaceful coexistence, they will never emerge from their backward conditions and will again become the victims of the West's "neo-colonialist plots."

African reaction to these propaganda themes is mixed. Most of the French-speaking African leaders feel that it would be both just and realistic to admit Red China to the U.N. Many of them approve of the industrious and frugal way of living of the Chinese who come to work in Africa, and they are proud that a non-white people like the Chinese have become a strong and dynamic nation. Peking's strident call to revolution also appeals to young African firebrands, who are opposed to the conservatism of their elder statesmen and who are impatient to take over power from them. On the other hand, China's revolutionary message alarms those

Africans who, for one thing, are opposed to communism and, for another, fear the "yellow peril." Moreover, the undisguised materialism of the Chinese alienates religious-minded Africans. Even the Africans who are attracted to Communist ideology have little desire to tighten their belts and work as hard as the Chinese do. To them, independence has been the goal because they believed it would enable them to live the good life without much effort on their part.

As to the competition between Russia and China for the leadership of Africa's "revolution," Peking now seems to have a slight edge over Moscow. This has resulted mainly from Red China's support of the Africans' clamor for greater representation in UN organs, in the face of Russia's opposition to any revision of the UN Charter. Yet both the Soviet Union and Communist China have committed the grave mistake of extending the Communist cold war to Africa and trying to involve the Africans in that conflict. Neither of those Communist powers has appreciated sufficiently the strength of the Africans' neutralism and their stress on the "African personality." The Africans want to evolve according to their own culture and interests, and are strongly opposed to copying any foreign model.

"TITOIST" COMMUNISM

Yugoslavia exemplifies the third brand of communism introduced to the Africans. Guinea, Mali and Senegal have diplomatic and trade relations with Belgrade, and Dahomey and Niger have signed agreements of economic cooperation with the Yugoslavs. Sékou Touré, Mamadou Dia and S. M. Apithy (then vice-president of Dahomey) have visited Belgrade, and early in 1961 President Tito made a rapid visit to West Africa, where he was warmly received. Of all the Communist leaders, Tito is probably the most popular with

French-speaking West Africans, who admire his nationalistic independence and neutralism. They have no reason to fear Yugoslavia's interference and would welcome closer contacts. At present, only a few Yugoslav technicians are working in Guinea and Mali, and in 1961 Tito offered Sékou Touré a $5 million loan. Yugoslavia is too poor, however, to provide large-scale aid to Africa, and therefore cannot take advantage of African good will to extend its influence there.

Generally speaking, communism's aims in French-speaking Africa are the same as elsewhere in the world, but both the Soviet Union and Red China realize that conditions there are not propitious for founding Communist parties and installing wholly Marxist governments. Consequently, they have concentrated on wooing and indoctrinating the youthful radical Africans who, they hope, will be the future rulers of their respective countries.

Relations with the West

FRANCE

Of all the Western countries, France has long been and still is by far the most important to the French-speaking Negro African lands. The nature and closeness of this relationship varies from country to country, but it is generally strongest and most extensive with the U.A.M. states and weakest with Guinea and Mali. Its most widespread impact is in the cultural sphere, for French is still the official language throughout former French West and Equatorial Africa, as well as in Cameroun and Togo, and the prestige of French culture remains high. The relationship is most limited in the field of politics and administration, where the Africans are especially eager to take over and feel competent to do so.

Paradoxical as it may seem, the number of Frenchmen living in Negro Africa has increased since independence, although the composition and distribution of the resident French community have undergone marked changes. In 1962 laws defining nationality were adopted by all the French-speaking West African governments except Dahomey. As a result, all Frenchmen have now resigned from the legislative assemblies to which they were elected. Senegal and Ivory Coast, however, retained French cabinet ministers. By and large, French civil servants have been replaced by Africans, but many have been persuaded to stay on as advisers to the African administrators. French troops have been evacuated from Guinea, Mali and Upper Volta, but France still maintains some West African military bases (the most important being that of Dakar), and French officers are training most of the new national armies of former French West Africa.

French businessmen have been leaving those countries that have been rapidly nationalizing their economies and from which the transfer of foreigners' funds is permitted. Even in Guinea, however, more than 1,000 Frenchmen are still employed by the Fria company. Naturally Senegal and Ivory Coast, which are the most prosperous of the French-speaking West African states and still offer considerable scope for private enterprise, have attracted the greatest number of French businessmen, but Guinea as well now has an investment code designed to appeal to foreign capitalists. Moreover, in 1963, Guinea and France signed an agreement for technical cooperation and trade. Although Guinea withdrew from the franc zone in 1960 and has been doing business mainly with the Eastern-bloc countries, about two-thirds of the foreign commerce of all the other French-speaking West African countries is with France.

Most of the French now living in Negro Africa are teachers, technicians and businessmen. France cannot keep up with the demand for teachers, so much needed by its former African dependencies, including Guinea and Upper Volta, both of which have established their own educational systems. Africans seeking higher training usually try to enter a university in France or that of Dakar, which is ranked as the eighteenth French university. French technicians, like French teachers, are greatly in demand, both because many of them have had long experience in Africa and because they speak the foreign language best known to their African employers. The French traders and industrialists who have remained in Africa since independence or have gone there in recent years are those best able and willing to adapt themselves to the new conditions that prevail in France's former colonies. In fact, a growing proportion of the resident French community consists of young men not identified with the colonial period, who have come to Africa simply to earn good salaries and who take for granted the inevitability of their eventual replacement by Africans. In short, relations between France and French-speaking Africa now rest largely on a practical, apolitical basis.

This changing and mainly cooperative relationship has been facilitated by internal and international developments. It was made possible in the first place by the peaceable manner in which independence came to all the sub-Saharan French territories except Guinea, whose break with France in 1958 was marked by bitterness. Even the Guineans, however, did not have to fight to attain sovereign status. Except in the case of Guinea, French West African independence was largely a by-product of events in other African countries and of French West Africa's own moves toward unity; independence had not been their primary goal. After Morocco, Tunisia, Ghana and Guinea had become independent and had joined world organizations, the French-speaking sub-Saharan countries that had voted to join the Community became restless and impatient. They showed increasing sensitivity to the charge that they were still dependencies of France, and feared that such accusations might result in their being refused admission to the U.N. Yet they did not want to break openly with France, whose aid they still badly needed and whose culture they greatly admired. General de Gaulle, wiser for the failure of his policy to isolate Guinea after it had chosen independence in 1958, had the statesmanship to understand their dilemma and not force them to choose between independence and continued French aid. France helped the Mali Republic financially even after it had flounced out of the Community, demanded the evacuation of French military bases in Mali, and created its own currency. In the spring of 1962, when Guinea tried to mend relations with France, General de Gaulle agreed—even though very slowly—to negotiate with the aim of placing Franco-Guinean relations on a more cooperative basis.

Nevertheless, France's aid has been reserved chiefly for the U.A.M. countries which, with some important exceptions, have supported French diplomatic moves and continue to trade very largely with France. At the same time, the course of events elsewhere in Africa has helped to strengthen Franco-African relations. The relatively more stable situation in the ex-Belgian Congo, the cessation of French aboveground nuclear testing in the Sahara, the evacuation of France's base at Bizerte, Tunisia, in 1963, and above all, the end of the Algerian war in 1962 have eliminated the chief causes of Franco-African conflict or disagreement. Those issues, and particularly the Algerian crisis, had not only divided "revolutionary" from "reformist" Africa, but had split the U.A.M. group. With Algeria's independence, there was no longer any question of a UN-supervised referendum in that country or of African Negro troops serving in the French army there.

French-speaking Africa's dependence on France remains its outstanding characteristic but shows clear signs of decreasing—and by mutual consent. The African states have been trying to lessen this dependence financially by diversifying and increasing their sources of external aid, either from Western or Communist countries or both. France, although still willing to provide them with aid on a generous scale, and anxious to retain and even expand French cultural influence, no longer looks upon its former African territories as an exclusive French political or economic preserve. However, France is understandably concerned to safeguard French investments in Africa.

As for African diplomatic support in the U.N., France has less need of this since the end of the Algerian war. Then, too, General de Gaulle's new policy, announced in February 1964, of granting more aid to former French Indochina and to Latin America means that there will be less concentration on Africa, which for many years has received by far the largest share of French funds granted to underdeveloped countries. Moreover, through the agreement signed in 1963 between the Common Market and its associated African members, larger investment funds will go to them from France's five European partners. This will mean that their economies will become more diversified, as will the sources of their imports and the markets for their exports. In other words, France, within the foreseeable future, will cease to be virtually the only source of aid for French-speaking Africa and the principal focus of its foreign trade.

For so long as General de Gaulle remains in power, he will undoubtedly continue to wield great influence over the

French-speaking African leaders, among whom he has many personal friends and enjoys undiminished prestige. Yet even during his lifetime, it is likely that an economic disengagement will follow the political disengagement that has already taken place in Franco-African relations.

COMMON MARKET AND OTHER COUNTRIES

West Germany is the only member of the Common Market other than France which has made an effort to offer substantial aid to French-speaking Africa and to promote trade with that area. Belgium has done no more than enter into diplomatic relations with the U.A.M. countries, partly because Brussels is also the main center of Common Market activity. Italy has exchanged ambassadors and good-will missions with a number of African states, but it was not until 1962–63 that the Italians offered to help develop Senegal's shipping and processing industries and to make improvements in Ivory Coast's ports and roads. The sole gesture of the Netherlands has been to advise and help Dahomey with truck gardening.

As a matter of fact, a number of Western-bloc countries not members of the Common Market have shown more interest in French-speaking Africa than have most of France's Common Market partners. Great Britain, as might be expected, has channeled most of its aid to its own former colonies, but it has invited some French African leaders and technicians to visit London and to study in English universities. Canada has helped to develop mineral resources, Switzerland has signed an aid-and-trade agreement with Senegal and has been assisting Dahomey to organize cooperative societies, and even Spain has agreed to participate in the expansion of Mauritania's fishing industry. Nevertheless, only the Bonn government has displayed real initiative and zeal in promoting closer relations with the former French African dependencies, and not exclusively with those that are pro-Western and also associate members of the E.E.C.

The Malian leaders, even two years before their country gained its sovereignty, entered into negotiations with West German businessmen. The West Germans cooperated with a will and reaped a rich harvest of contracts for supplying Mali with trucks after the railroad to Dakar was barred at the Malian frontier late in 1960. As of 1963–64, two German experts have been organizing Mali's statistical service. It has been Guinea, however, that has received most of the West German aid. In 1959, the West Germans gave the Guineans hospital equipment and invited Sékou Touré to pay a state visit to Bonn. Their enthusiasm for helping Guinea, however, was soon dampened by Touré's insinuations that the West Germans were helping France to develop an atomic bomb in return for oil concessions in the Sahara, and even more by his move to establish diplomatic relations with East Germany. After Touré had recanted on East Germany, the West Germans again became friendly and helpful. President Heinrich Luebke of West Germany visited Conakry early in 1962, and there agreed to lend Guinea 50 million marks ($12,500,000). West German manufactured goods seem to be popular in Guinea, as are the 30 or so German technicians who are helping to improve its roads, install a water-distribution system in Conakry and establish a small fishing industry to supplement agricultural production.

West Germany has also been a source of loans, gifts and technicians for Senegal, Ivory Coast, and to a lesser extent Dahomey. This has paid off well in terms of African goodwill and of increased trade between these countries and West Germany, which has produced a commercial balance decidedly favorable to West Germany.

UNITED STATES

In French-speaking Africa, the United States has so far played only a minor role, although the winning of independence by the West and Equatorial African states in 1960 spurred the U.S. to become more active in those areas.

The United States, in trying to establish closer relations with the new African states, has labored under several handicaps. To begin with, it knew little about the region, having had only a consul at Dakar as the sole official representative in either French West or French Equatorial Africa until 1958. For their part, the French-speaking Africans were mostly uninformed about the United States, and their impressions were not wholly favorable. They admired or were awed by American wealth, power and technical knowledge, but were alienated by reports of this country's treatment of its Negroes. They were also afraid that American aid and the presence of Americans—even the Peace Corps workers—in Africa meant that the United States was trying to win them over to its side in the East-West cold war.

Extreme nationalists among the French-speaking Africans had still other complaints against the United States. They reproached Washington with supporting French efforts to put down the Algerian revolt and favoring the "enemies of African emancipation" in the former Belgian Congo. In this respect, the history of American-Guinean relations is instructive. Washington was slow to recognize Guinea's independence and ignored a Guinean request in December 1958, through the good offices of Liberia, for a shipment of arms. Then, when Washington—alarmed by the Communists' inroads at Conakry—got around to offering limited aid to Guinea, a year of hard negotiating was needed to induce the Guineans to accept an agreement for such aid. Although Sékou Touré made an official visit to Washington late in

1959, the year 1960 was marked by a series of unhappy incidents. In March, Washington was asked to close its Information Service in Conakry; in September, the Guinean press played up the story of a traffic dispute in New York's Harlem between a policeman and a member of the Guinean delegation to the U.N.; and in November, Touré asked two visiting American warships to leave after some of their crew had been accused of misconduct in Conakry.

A change for the better in Guinean-American relations began, however, in 1962, partly as a consequence of Guinea's disillusionment with Soviet economic aid and annoyance with Soviet political interference. New agreements were signed, a mining concession was granted to an American company, the Peace Corps was admitted to Guinea, and Americans were allowed to help form a school of public administration. As the Soviet Union's stock went down, that of the United States rose, and Americans working in Conakry were actually praised for their efficiency and technical skill. Sékou Touré again visited the United States, and commended President Kennedy for his efforts in behalf of southern Negroes.

In the conduct of its relations with Mali, the other "revolutionary" French-speaking African state, the United States has profited by its experience in Guinea. When the Mali Republic was proclaimed in September 1960, Washington immediately recognized it and sent an envoy who offered aid of all kinds and assured the Malian leaders that they would not be abandoned by the West. Modibo Keita was in general more receptive to such overtures than Sékou Touré had been, although he, too, censured the United States for supporting France in Algeria and for failing to back Lumumba in the Congo. Moreover, like Touré he demanded the closing of the United States Information Service in his capital city, Bamako. He was nevertheless more tractable than Touré about accepting U.S.

aid and technicians, and expressed warm appreciation of President Kennedy's "good will."

With the U.A.M. countries, the United States has made comparatively little effort to form closer relations and provide assistance. To be sure, Lyndon B. Johnson (when Vice-President), G. Mennen Williams and Robert F. Kennedy have visited Dakar or Abidjan, or both; the United States has given some financial and technical aid to the Entente states' development plans; and there has been more private American investment in Senegal and Ivory Coast than in Mali and Guinea. However, American aid to the U.A.M. has been small in comparison with that given to Southeast Asia, and much less than Communist-bloc assistance to French-speaking West Africa. The heads of some African states have been invited to Washington, as they have been to Moscow and Peking, but the other Africans asked to visit the United States have been of different caliber than those who have received invitations from the Communist nations. The Africans selected by Washington are usually cabinet ministers or heads of technical services on study missions, whereas the Communists more often invite youth and labor leaders to big congresses.

As a rule, the timing of French-speaking Africa's requests for American aid has worked against them. United States interest in French-speaking Africa began to grow only after this country had become somewhat disillusioned by the results of its efforts to help the newly independent states of Asia. In addition, Washington has not wanted to tread on French toes or to cause France to cut back its own aid to Africa. Consequently the United States has usually sent food surpluses to be sold for local currency—the proceeds to be applied to national development projects—and the flow of dollar funds has been relatively thin. In some cases the Africans, who expected greater financial assistance, have frankly expressed disappointment, and a few of them, notably the Malians, have succeeded in raising the amount. They regret that American aid has apparently been given in proportion to the supposed danger of Communist penetration, and that those countries most favorable to the West, such as the Entente states, have been the least generously treated. Their disappointment, however, has not prevented them from seeking further American aid and investments, nor has it affected the generally friendly relations they maintain with the United States government and its local representatives. Only time will tell whether the American impact on French-speaking Africa may make more of a dent in the future than the small one it does today.

Foreign Aid

Economic independence, to give reality and strength to their political independence, has become the goal of all the newly sovereign French-speaking African countries, but they cannot win it solely through their own efforts.

The lack of capital funds and of technicians in those countries is so great that all of their leaders readily admit their need for foreign aid on a huge scale. In carrying out their national development plans, the French-speaking African states can themselves supply little more than "human investment"—the more or less voluntary unpaid labor described in Chapter VII—and a few raw materials. For the bulk of the financing and technical expertise required for carrying out their plans, they must rely heavily on outside assistance. Logically, this should make them turn first to the industrialized nations best able to supply what they need. In some cases, however, this is difficult or impossible because of the attitude of African leaders.

As a general rule, the French-speaking African leaders are suspicious of foreign aid lest political strings be attached to it. All of them favor a policy of non-alignment with either the Western or the Communist bloc, and fear to jeopardize their countries' new-found independence by committing themselves deeply to one or the other as a source of aid. Mauritania represents the most extreme example of this cautious attitude, for its government has refused to seek aid from either the United States or the Soviet Union. Elsewhere the ideology—or lack of it—of the countries' leaders has influenced their attitude toward foreign aid. It is a matter of principle for the leaders of Guinea and Mali to accept aid from both the Western and Eastern blocs in quantities that roughly counterbalance each other. The Ivory Coast government, however, has let it be known that it would refuse aid from any Communist country. Between the extremes just described are the leaders of such states as Dahomey, Niger and Upper Volta, whose countries are so poor and whose principles are so elastic that they welcome assistance from any quarter that offers it.

Since attaining sovereignty, the French Negro states have been besieged by offers of aid from many parts of the world. But time has proved these offers to be less lavish and varied than they first appeared to be, and African leaders have grown so wary about the political implications of accepting them that the choice is actually quite limited. Guinea, for example, found that West Germany would grant it no aid if it established diplomatic relations with East Germany, and Senegal learned that it could not pursue a "two-Chinas" policy. From the outset many of the Africans have much preferred trade to aid, but in order to sell many of their products they had to make barter agreements which later turned out to be highly unsatisfactory. The United States has not loaned or given them the millions of dollars they hoped for, but has preferred to offer other forms of assistance.

Among the nations offering aid to French-speaking Africa, Israel and, to a lesser extent, Yugoslavia have been very popular. The Africans believe that neither of those countries wants to interfere in their internal politics, and in any case has not the means to do so. Israel, in particular, has been generous in helping the Africans to solve the problems of water shortage and civic service, with which the Israelis themselves have had to deal. Nevertheless, the African lands that accept Israeli aid incur the wrath of the Egyptians, and those that accept Yugoslav assistance antagonize both Peking and

An Israeli expert on youth leadership with African trainees at the Camberine School in Senegal.

the strongly anti-Communist nations. Moreover, welcome as
are the Israelis and Yugoslavs in most African countries, they
can bring little more than their technical skills and cannot
provide any appreciable amounts of investment funds.

In some ways, the agreements worked out with the Common Market offer a satisfactory solution, although not on a
scale commensurate with African needs and desires. These
agreements make available investment funds for projects of
general interest, and also establish trading conditions ad-
vantageous to merchants both in Africa and in the Common
Market countries. In African eyes, however, the ideal source
of foreign aid would be a wealthy, highly industrialized
nation that would pay for all their exports in hard currency,
and would unconditionally provide almost limitless funds
and many technicians to work on projects chosen by the Africans. Disillusionment inevitably came, however, and the
African governments have now learned to their sorrow that
no such fairy godmothers exist and that all foreign aid has its
price.

To all the French-speaking African countries except
Guinea, aid from France has been essential to their survival
or their development, or both, and is usually the most acceptable to them. In the first place, French aid has amounted
to more than that from all other countries combined. The
sequel to this is that French trade holds a privileged position
in those countries, but they have not had either to pledge
diplomatic support to France or to permit French military
bases on their soil. Then, too, because they have been accepting aid from France for so long a time, it seems more natural
and less risky than aid from newer and untried sources. Inevitably this has created a relationship of dependence, but
now both France and the Africans are striving to find ways
to make the latter less dependent. The French would like to

spread their aid farther afield to include certain underdeveloped Asian and Latin-American countries, and the Africans want to diversify and expand their other sources of foreign assistance.

Both France and the African nations also agree on the need for a reorientation in the use of foreign-aid funds. The Africans are beginning to recognize that it is unsuitable to their sovereign status to let another nation pay their bills, and the French believe that subsidies to meet the operating expenses of African governments have served largely to maintain artificially high living standards for an already over-privileged minority of the African elite. In 1963, Mauritania and Upper Volta—two of the poorest of the West African countries—decided that thereafter they would balance their budgets wholly from their own resources, and use French aid solely for national development projects. More and more, the Africans are resorting to the formula of "companies of mixed economy," introduced by the French after World War II. Such companies are financed by a combination of foreign capital and African public funds, with the latter controlling the majority of shares.

The African leaders and the foreign nations supplying them with aid are increasingly turning away from the blank-check type of gift. In too many countries such gifts have had regrettable psychological consequences for the African people. They began to be regarded as a permanent crutch, so that the Africans have tended to feel that they need not work hard themselves to develop their country. The donor countries in such cases have often come to the conclusion that their money has been wasted. The present trend is toward using foreign aid for specific projects which are proposed by the African governments, but which must be approved by the nations providing the funds and technicians needed to carry them out.

United Nations

Not the least of the many reasons why, in the late 1950's, the French sub-Saharan territories began striving for independence was their desire to qualify for admission to the UN. They wanted a voice in the policy decisions of the world organization, especially on matters relating to Africa. Moreover, through representation in the UN General Assembly and various commissions, they hoped to make their countries better known to the rest of the world, which was largely ignorant of Africa and its problems.

By the end of 1961, all of the French-speaking states of West Africa were members of the UN, its specialized agencies, and commissions such as the International Labor Organization, the World Health Organization and the Economic Commission for Africa. They also had joined three groups that had been formed within the UN. The largest of these was the Afro-Asian bloc, the next largest the African group as a whole, and finally they belonged either to the Casablanca bloc or the Afro-Malagasy Union (U.A.M.). The expressed aim of each of these groups was to formulate a common policy on certain specific issues debated in the UN, and in this way to influence its resolutions and recommendations.

As African membership in the UN grew, so did its influence in the General Assembly, which included delegates of all the African states. At the same time, however, this rapid increase in the number of African members inevitably lessened their ability to form a united front. Their voting record reflected the division of the French-speaking West African states between the "revolutionary" Casablanca bloc and the "reformist" U.A.M., and even within those two groups, unanimity was not always reached. The outstanding divisive African issues were Algeria and the ex-Belgian Congo, and the minor ones were France's maintenance of the Bizerte base in Tunisia and nuclear testing in the Sahara. On these questions, the smaller Casablanca bloc showed greater cohesion than did the U.A.M., but it, too, was divided in regard to leaving African troops under UN command in the Congo. Indeed, disagreements concerning the UN's handling of the Congo crisis, more than any other single issue, caused policy discord among the French-speaking Africans and gradually led to a change in their attitude toward the world organization itself.

A few years earlier, the Africans had been inclined to refer their disputes to the UN for settlement. When the Mali Federation broke up in August 1960, President Modibo Keita of Soudan appealed to the UN in the hope that that body would send troops to punish Senegal for its "secessionism," but UN Secretary-General Dag Hammarskjöld refused to do so. Then, when the UN did intervene in an African crisis— the conflict in the former Belgian Congo—the Africans displayed varying degrees of dissatisfaction with the results. The Casablanca bloc was bitter and vehement in its denunciation of the UN's failure to support Lumumba, and Sékou Touré, to show his displeasure with the organization, refused to utilize all the funds and technicians which it had placed at Guinea's disposal. Even the U.A.M., which on the whole backed UN policy in the Congo, expressed disapproval of the "United Nations' unwarranted intervention in Congolese internal affairs." Thus the Africans were angered and disillusioned both when the UN failed to respond to their calls for support and when it did take positive action in African affairs of which they disapproved.

The reaction just described stemmed in part from the Africans' failure to create and maintain a common front on crucial African issues, and in part from the structure of the UN itself. The composition of the Security Council has inevitably made it difficult for the Africans to obtain satisfaction in that small but powerful body. France and Great Britain, two of its permanent members, having been the major imperial powers in Africa, have naturally opposed any moves to implement strongly "anti-colonial" measures. Another permanent member, the Soviet Union, has blocked changes in the Charter that might increase African membership in UN organs and also has attempted to make Africa an arena of the cold war. As for the General Assembly, where the weight of African membership can make itself felt, that body can do no more than adopt resolutions and recommendations. Moreover, the African members of the UN have acted in unison only on the issues of racial discrimination in South Africa, denunciation of Portugal's policy in its African colonies, and increased African representation in UN elective and appointive posts.

Yet even though the Africans' expectation that the UN would do more to help them attain their goals has been somewhat dampened, they still regard the organization as useful and convenient. The UN has sent a few technicians to Africa and has provided limited funds for the execution of specific West African projects. In a new category of activity, UN experts—at the request of Senegal and Gambia—are studying the problems posed by the prospective closer association of those two countries. An important consideration, too, for the Africans is that in its General Assembly and Security Council meetings the UN provides an international forum for the airing of African views and grievances and a convenient meeting place for African delegates. Such countries as Dahomey and Niger, which are too poor to maintain many embassies, can utilize the UN headquarters as a substitute site for their diplomacy. There, Africans can meet readily and at no extra expense to iron out their difficulties or discuss joint action. It was in the corridors of the UN, for example, that arrangements for the Monrovia group's conferences reportedly were made.

Creation of the Organization of African Unity at Addis Ababa in May 1963 has made it possible for the African states to by-pass the UN in dealing with some important inter-African disputes. The conflict between Morocco and Algeria over the delimitation of their common frontier in the western Sahara was brought before the O.A.U. rather than the UN, as were the army mutinies in East Africa. The existence of this new, wholly African organization has permitted African leaders to avoid the frustrations and delays they have often experienced in the past in getting UN debate and action on the issues that concern them most directly. Above all, it has enabled them to demonstrate actively their contention that African problems should be settled by the Africans themselves.

Nevertheless, as a source of impartial technical aid, as a means of making Africa's voice heard on great international issues, and as a sounding-board to influence world opinion on African problems, the UN remains of great value to the African states in this crucial period of their political, economic and social development.

Appendix

Summary of National Political Institutions

REPUBLIC OF DAHOMEY

Proclamation of independence: August 1, 1960.

Constitution adopted November 26, 1960; provided for a presidential-type regime. Superseded after coup d'état of October 27, 1963, by a constitution approved by popular referendum on January 5, 1964. It provides for a regime of semi-presidential type.

Election of the National Assembly and of the president (Hubert Maga): December 11, 1960. National Assembly dissolved October 27, 1963, after coup d'état; succeeded by an Assembly elected January 19, 1964. President Maga resigned after the coup d'état; power then passed into the hands of Col. Christophe Soglo, military leader of the coup, who became provisional head of state. A new president, S. M. Apithy, was elected January 19, 1964.

Political party: The original single party, the Dahomeyan Unity Party, formed in December 1960, was replaced in December 1963 by the Parti Démocratique Dahoméen (P.D.D.), or Dahomeyan Democratic Party, which holds all seats (42) in the new National Assembly. The only opposition party that survived after the P.D.U. was the Union Démocratique Dahoméenne, or Dahomeyan Democratic Union, which was dissolved in April 1961.

Administrative organization: six departments, each in charge of a prefect; 32 sub-prefectures; 45 *arrondissements* (districts). Each department has a council-general. There are numerous elected village councils.

Member of: Council of the Entente; U.A.M. (or Afro-Malagasy Union); O.A.M.C.E. (Afro-Malagasy Organization for Economic Cooperation); O.A.U. (Organization of African Unity); West African Monetary Union. Was a member of the Monrovia Group, now dissolved.

REPUBLIC OF GUINEA

Proclamation of the republic and of independence: October 2, 1958.

Constitution proclaimed November 12, 1958. Provides for a National Assembly, elected for five years, and a president, elected for seven years and eligible for re-election. Suffrage is universal, direct and secret. The president is also head of the armed forces, negotiates treaties and has the right of pardon. He is assisted by ministers named by him. The constitution can be amended—except as to the republican form of the state —by two-thirds majority vote of the National Assembly.

The Territorial Assembly elected in March 1957 for five years became the National Assembly on October 20, 1958. New elections were held in September 1963. The 75 deputies receive no salary.

President: Sékou Touré.

Political party: Parti Démocratique de Guinée (P.D.G.), or Guinea Democratic Party.

Administrative organization: 29 regions headed by governors named by the national government. The former *cercles* have been transformed into *arrondissements,* under commandants. Villages are administered by village chiefs, assisted by village committees of the P.D.G.

Member of: O.A.U.; was a member of the Casablanca Group, now dissolved.

REPUBLIC OF IVORY COAST

Proclamation of independence: August 7, 1960.

Constitution adopted October 31, 1960. Provides for a presidential-type regime. The president is elected for five years by direct, universal suffrage, and is eligible for re-election. He is head of the government, head of the administration and head of the armed forces. He also names his ministers, who may not be members of the Assembly and are responsible solely to him. The National Assembly (70 members) is elected for five years by direct, universal suffrage, and cannot be dissolved. The Economic and Social Council (advisory) is composed of representatives of industry, labor and the government, designated by the president for five years.

Election of the National Assembly: November 27, 1960.

President: Félix Houphouët-Boigny.

Political party: Parti Démocratique de la Cote d'Ivoire, section du Rassemblement Démocratique Africain (P.D.C.I.-R.D.A.), or Democratic Party of the Ivory Coast, section of the African Democratic Rally. It obtained 95.7 per cent of the votes cast in the legislative elections of November 27, 1960, and holds all seats now filled (65) in the National Assembly.

Administrative organization: five departments; 100 sub-prefectures. Each department has a council-general, elected for five years by universal suffrage; it votes the departmental budget.

Member of: Council of the Entente; U.A.M.; O.A.M.C.E.; O.A.U.; West African Monetary Union. Was a member of the Monrovia Group.

Republic of Mali

Proclamation of the republic and of independence: September 22, 1960.

Constitution adopted September 23, 1960; a revision of the constitution of the Mali Federation proclaimed January 31, 1959. Provides for a president of the council (chief of state) and a National Assembly, which is elected for five years. The president of the council is designated by the president of the National Assembly, and names the vice-president and the ministers.

National Assembly (formerly the Legislative Assembly of the Soudanese Republic, elected March 8, 1959). It comprises 80 deputies, all members of the Union Soudanaise, the single party.

Chief of State and President of the Council: Modibo Keita. He is also in charge of foreign affairs, defense and state security.

Political party: Union Soudanaise-R.D.A. (U.S.-R.D.A.), or Soudanese Union, section of the African Democratic Rally.

Administrative organization: six regions, comprising 42 *cercles* subdivided into 224 *arrondissements.*

Member of: the West African Customs Union; O.A.U. Was a member of the Casablanca Group.

ISLAMIC REPUBLIC OF MAURITANIA

Proclamation of independence: November 28, 1960.

Constitution adopted May 20, 1961; a modification of the first constitution, dated March 22, 1959. Provides for a presidential-type regime. The president is elected for five years by direct, universal suffrage, and is eligible for re-election. He chooses the cabinet ministers, who are responsible to him, issues decrees having the force of law, is head of the armed forces and ratifies treaties. He also proclaims laws and can decree a state of emergency. The National Assembly is elected for five years; it legislates on matters specified by the constitution, all others falling within the presidential powers of regulation by decree.

National Assembly (formerly the Legislative Assembly, elected May 7, 1959). It comprises 40 deputies. The deputies, formerly members of four political parties, are now all members of the single (fusion) party, the Party of the Mauritanian People.

President: Mokhtar Ould Daddah, elected August 20, 1961.

Political party: Parti du Peuple Mauritanien (P.P.M.), or Party of the Mauritanian People, formed on December 25, 1961, by the fusion of four parties.

Administrative organization: 12 *cercles,* each comprising one or more subdivisions.

Member of: U.A.M.; West African Monetary Union; West African Customs Union; O.A.U. Was a member of the Monrovia Group.

REPUBLIC OF THE NIGER

Proclamation of independence: August 3, 1960.

Constitution approved November 8, 1960, by the National Assembly. Provides for a presidential-type regime. The president is elected for five years by direct and universal suffrage, and is eligible for re-election. He holds all executive power; names his ministers, who are responsible solely to him; is head of the administration and of the armed forces, as well as president of the council of ministers (i.e., premier); negotiates and ratifies international agreements; and holds other powers. The National Assembly (unicameral) is elected for five years by direct, universal suffrage from a national list of candidates (of the single party); with the concurrence of the president, it introduces laws drafted by government commissions; it votes laws and authorizes taxes. There is an Economic and Social Council (advisory), whose role is defined by the constitution.

Election of the National Assembly: December 14, 1958. Its 60 deputies are all members of the single party.

President: Hamani Diori, elected November 11, 1960.

Political party: Parti Progressiste Nigérien (P.P.N.), or Nigerian Progressive Party, which is the local section of the R.D.A.

Administrative organization: 16 *cercles,* most of which are divided into two or three circumscriptions (districts). Circumscription councils were elected in December 1962.

Member of: Council of the Entente; West African Monetary Union; West African Customs Union; U.A.M.; O.A.U. Was a member of the Monrovia Group.

REPUBLIC OF SENEGAL

Proclamation of independence: August 20, 1960.

New constitution of Senegal approved by referendum March 3, 1963. Provides for a presidential-type regime. The president is elected for four years by direct, universal suffrage and is eligible for re-election. He holds all executive power; appoints his ministers, who are responsible to him; can issue decrees having the force of law; is head of the administration and head of the armed forces; accredits ambassadors and negotiates and ratifies international agreements; and holds other powers. The National Assembly is elected by direct, universal suffrage for four years at the same time as the president; initiates laws, with the concurrence of the president; votes laws and authorizes taxes.

Election of the National Assembly: March 22, 1959 (under an earlier constitution of January 24, 1959, which provided for five year terms for deputies); new elections were held December 1, 1963.

President: Léopold Sédar Senghor, elected September 5, 1960; re-elected December 1, 1963.

Political parties: The majority party, which holds all seats (80) in the National Assembly, is the Union Progressiste Sénégalais (U.P.S.), or Senegalese Progressive Union. Two minority parties have existed: the Senegalese Masses' Bloc (B.M.S.), which was merged with the U.P.S. in late 1963, and the African Regrouping Party of Senegal (P.R.A.–Senegal), now inactive.

Administrative organization: seven regions, each headed by a governor, which are divided into 27 *cercles* and 85 *arrondissements*.

Member of: U.A.M.; the "renovated" Franco-African Community under agreements signed June 22, 1960; West African Monetary Union; West African Customs Union; O.A.U. Was a member of the Monrovia Group.

REPUBLIC OF UPPER VOLTA

Proclamation of independence: August 5, 1960.

Constitution approved by referendum November 28, 1960, and proclaimed November 30, 1960. Provides for a presidential-type regime. President is elected by direct, universal suffrage for five years, and is eligible for re-election. He appoints the members of the government (cabinet ministers), who are responsible to him, and is president of the council (premier); is head of the administration and of the armed forces; proclaims laws; accredits ambassadors and negotiates and ratifies international agreements; and holds other powers.

Election of the National Assembly: April 20, 1959. (Terms of the deputies then elected have been extended for five years from November 27, 1960.)

President: Maurice Yaméogo, elected December 8, 1960.

Political party: Union Démocratique Voltaique (U.D.V.), or Voltaic Democratic Union, local section of the R.D.A. It holds all seats (75) in the National Assembly.

Administrative organization: four departments, headed by prefects; these are divided into 39 *arrondissements.* In December 1960, 53 rural collectivities were established; their aim is to entrust to the local elites the management of such affairs as directly concern the villages grouped in the collectivity. Each collectivity is in charge of a council elected by direct, universal suffrage.

Member of: Council of the Entente; U.A.M.; O.A.M.C.E.; West African Monetary Union; West African Customs Union; O.A.U. Was a member of the Monrovia Group.

Summary of National Economies

DAHOMEY

Occupations (by percentage of population): Farmers, 76.5 per cent; fishermen, 7.7 per cent; herders, 4.2 per cent; other occupations, 11.6 per cent. Wage earners total about 29,000; as of 1962, more than 2,000 of these were unemployed.

Average annual income, per inhabitant: $70.

Principal products (with output in 1961):

Subsistence crops:	*Tons*
Manioc	1,235,380
Yams	614,174
Corn	219,713
Sorghum	61,200
Export crops:	
Palm kernels	42,893
Palm oil	35,050
Peanuts (in shell)	22,343
Coffee	1,954
Livestock (estimated):	*Head*
Cattle	350,000
Sheep and goats	750,000
Pigs	270,000

Minerals: No systematic prospecting of subsoil resources has been done. It is believed that Dahomey has deposits of phosphates, ilmenite and iron.

Foreign trade: Dahomey's trade balance is chronically unfavorable because 80 per cent of its exports are "poor" products (palm kernels and oil). Between 1955 and 1961 the approximate value of exports fluctuated between $11.2 million and $18.4 million a year, and that of imports, between $17.0 million and $25.4 million.

Industries: Unimportant in the economy, compared with agriculture; they include four palm-oil mills, one brewery, one carbonated-drink plant, a few soap factories and some cotton gins that operate at cotton-picking season. Dahomey has only two electric-generator plants, at Cotonou and Porto Novo.

Communications and transport:

Port: Cotonou. A deep-water port financed by the French agency, F.A.C., has been under construction at Cotonou since 1959.

Railroads: three lines, running from Cotonou to Parakou, Ouidah, and Porto Novo; total trackage is 362 miles.

Roads: 3,750 miles of roads and tracks, of which from 350 to 375 are paved.

Airports: Since December 1962, Cotonou's airport has been enlarged to handle jet planes and is now of international class. Airlines using it are Air Afrique, Air France and U.T.A. (Union des Transports Aériens). There are four secondary airports in central and northern Dahomey.

Motor vehicles: About 7,000.

GUINEA

Occupations: More than 80 per cent of the population are peasant farmers. Data on the remainder are not available.

Average annual income: No data available since independence (1958).

Principal products:

Subsistence crops (output 1960):	*Tons*
Rice	323,415
Manioc	433,519
Sweet potatoes	55,649
Fonio (a cereal)	43,967
Peanuts	10,648
Export crops (quantities exported 1961):	
Bananas	59,401
Palm kernels	18,652
Coffee	15,164
Peanuts	7,983
Pineapples	4,148

Livestock (estimated):   *Head*
  Cattle 1,500,000
  Sheep 339,000
  Goats 400,000
Minerals (exports, 1962):   *Tons*
  Iron ore 720,000
  Aluminum ore 351,577
  Alumina 458,000

Foreign trade: All exports except minerals are handled by a government agency. In 1963 there was some relaxation of state controls over imports and their distribution. There has also been partial restoration of trade with Western countries, which had been greatly reduced after 1958. In 1961 imports totaled, in value, about $7.3 million, and exports were valued at $6.2 million, of which minerals—including diamonds—accounted for two-thirds. Imports declined about 10 per cent and exports about 18 per cent in 1962.

Industries: Mining is by far the most important industry, and there are large reserves of iron and bauxite. Bauxite is processed for export by the Fria Co., which in 1962 produced 458,000 tons of alumina. Another alumina plant, to be run by a United States company, was planned for 1964. Other industries include sawmills, oil mills, pineapple canneries, and factories producing paints, metal building materials, bricks, soap and explosives.

Communications and transport:

  Ports: Conakry, a deep-water port with modern docks and equipment. Kassa, equipped for bauxite export. Minor coastal trading posts at Boké, Victoria, Boffa, and at Toboriah.

  Railroads: Conakry-Kankan (414 miles); and Conakry-Fria, a short line for ore export.

  Roads: About 3,500 miles of main roads and 2,700 miles of tracks. Only a very small percentage of Guinea's roads are paved.

  Airports: Conakry airport, of international class, and four

minor airfields at other towns. A national airline, Air Guinée, was started in December 1960.

IVORY COAST

Occupations: Of the active population totaling 1.7 million in 1962, wage earners accounted for only 197,000, of whom 29,000 were in government service and 168,000 in private employment.

Average annual income: $142.

Principal products:

Subsistence crops (output 1962):	*Tons*
Yams	1,900,000
Plantains (cooking bananas)	1,100,000
Manioc	860,000
Rice (paddy)	230,000
Corn	170,000

Export crops (output 1962 except as noted):	
Coffee, 1962–63 trading season	194,800
Cocoa, 1962–63 trading season	103,000
Bananas	139,000

	Cubic Meters
Wood (lumber and logs)	1,050,000

Livestock (estimated):	*Head*
Cattle	300,000
Sheep and goats	1,050,000
Pigs	95,000

Minerals (output 1962):		
Diamonds	carats	283,911
Manganese	tons	106,983

Foreign trade (other than coastal trade with West African Customs Union countries): In 1962, imports totaled, in value, about $15.7 million; of these, about $10.5 million worth came from franc-zone countries. Of total exports valued at nearly $20.0 million in 1962, more than 60 per cent went to the franc zone. Consumer goods accounted for more than half the imports. Coffee was by far the most important export commodity ($7 million).

Industries: Industrial enterprises totaled 207 in 1963. Building concerns and large-scale public works companies accounted for 73 of these. Of the other 134 enterprises, 41 were sawmills. These miscellaneous enterprises were engaged in food-processing, tobacco manufactures, oil milling, sawmilling (as mentioned above), manufacture of chemical products, automobile assembly, etc. A hydroelectric dam on the Bia River, with a potential output of 100 million kilowatt hours annually, accounts for 88 per cent of Ivory Coast's electric-power production.

Communications and transport:

Ports: Abidjan ranks second among ports of French-speaking Black Africa, after Dakar; it serves Upper Volta and Mali as well as Ivory Coast. Other ports are Sassandra and Tabou.

Railroads: The Abidjan-Niger (length, 716 miles) connects Abidjan with Bobo-Dioulasso and Ouagadougou in Upper Volta. It operates entirely on diesel power.

Roads: 500 miles of paved roads; 7,875 miles of earth roads; and about 11,800 miles of tracks (*pistes*).

Airports: Abidjan (international class A), and some small airfields suitable only for light planes. A national airline, Air Ivoire, was formed in 1963 to handle internal traffic.

Motor vehicles: 30,526, including 12,564 trucks and 15,526 private cars.

MALI

Occupations: 90 per cent to 95 per cent of the population are peasants, living in villages or, in the case of herders, isolated encampments.

Average annual income: Ranges from $60 to $80 a year.

Principal products (estimated output in 1962):

Subsistence and export crops:	*Tons*
Millet	850,000

Rice (paddy)	185,000
Manioc	180,000
Shea nuts	200,000
Peanuts (in shell)	120,000
Corn	65,000
Cotton (unginned)	18,000
Livestock (estimated):	*Head*
Cattle	3,862,500
Sheep and goats	8,159,000
Donkeys	336,000
Camels	157,500
Horses	119,000

Minerals: Mineral resources of Mali are almost unknown although Soviet technicians have been prospecting under auspices of Mali's Bureau of Mines. Phosphate, iron, copper, manganese and uranium deposits are thought to exist. Some gold is produced as well as salt and iron, the latter extracted from laterite by an ancient process.

Foreign trade: Officially, imports totaled about $46.0 million and exports about $10.1 million, by value, in 1962. However, if allowance is made for imports of equipment (Russian planes and German trucks) bought under long-term loans, for clandestine imports and exports, and for customs undervaluation by shippers, real imports amounted in that year to $41.9 million and real exports to $30.0 million. The government attempts to control and direct foreign trade, but it does not always succeed in doing so.

Industries: Mali's economy being basically rural, its industries are mostly related to the processing of agricultural products. There are three cotton gins, nine rice mills, two oil mills, 18 kapok-processing shops, and two beer and soft-drink plants. Others include three metal-construction enterprises, a glass factory and sawmill, a shipyard and a brick factory. Contracts have been signed with Czechoslovakia, West Germany, Yugoslavia and other foreign countries for the building of more factories (cotton yarn, oil milling, etc.).

Communications and transport:

Railroad: 400 miles of the Dakar-Niger line, between Kouli-koro and the Senegal border, via Bamako. Because of the closing of the border in August 1960, when the Mali Federation was dissolved, through traffic on the line was suspended until the summer of 1963. It was then reopened after negotiations between Mali and Senegal were successfully concluded.

Roads: Only two stretches of paved road exist, between Bamako and Bougouni (95 miles) and Bamako and Ségou (150 miles). All other roads and tracks are of earth.

Airports: Bamako has a class-B airport, usable by DC-7's, Constellations, and other piston-engine planes. There are five other smaller airports, near main towns, as well as small airfields at all *cercle* headquarters.

Motor vehicles: 6,599, including 2,506 private and business cars and 3,907 trucks.

MAURITANIA

Occupations: Three-fourths of the population, or about 800,000, are nomadic "white" Moors. Some 200,000 Negroes (Toucouleurs, Wolofs, Sarakolés) live as peasants in the Mauritanian part of the Senegal Valley. In 1963, wage earners totaled only about 18,500, but their number is steadily increasing with the growth of the mining industry. About 100,000 Mauritanians were living in towns in 1963, but with the creation of the new capital at Nouakchott and the mining and export of Fort Gouraud's iron ore, Nouakchott, Fort Gouraud and Port Etienne are growing rapidly. There is a serious shortage of manpower, which has been felt in building the railway from Fort Gouraud to Port Etienne (for iron-ore export) and in obtaining workers for the iron mines.

Average annual income: No data are available. Most of the population lives under a barter economy.

Principal products:

Subsistence crops (tonnages shown indicate only their relative importance; production may be as much as five times more or less than indicated, depending on years and regions):

	Tons
Millet	25,000
Dates	15,000
Niébé beans	5,000
Corn	3,000
Sweet potatoes	2,000
Peanuts	500
Barley and wheat	200

Export commodity: About 3,000 tons a year of gum arabic are obtained from wild acacia trees of central Mauritania, and are exported.

Livestock (estimated):

	Head
Cattle	1,500,000
Sheep and goats	10,000,000
Horses and donkeys	160,000
Camels	500,000

Fisheries: Above the continental shelf adjoining Port Etienne, an area of about 120,000 square kilometers of the Atlantic Ocean is one of the world's most important fishing grounds. Fishing fleets of many nations (Greece, Italy, Portugal, France, Japan, the U.S.S.R. and others) take about 150,000 tons of fish annually from the area. Of this amount, several thousand tons are landed and processed at Port Etienne for consumption in Africa and for export.

Minerals: Mauritania's economic development, present and future, depends very largely upon actual and planned production of its most valuable resources—iron and copper. In addition, however, prospecting for petroleum is going on in several areas, some salt is produced, and there are deposits of gypsum and ilmenite.

Iron: Development of Fort Gouraud's iron reserves was begun in 1960 by the Society of Iron Mines of Mauritania (abbreviated in French as "Miferma"), financed chiefly by French capital. The ore has a high average iron content (64 per cent), and reserves are estimated at 144 million tons. A railway from Fort Gouraud to Port Etienne (422 miles) to evacuate the ore was completed in 1963, and facilities for loading the ore on ships have been built at that port.

Copper: Reserves of this metal in the region of Akjoujt are estimated at 500,000 tons of smelted copper. It is hoped to extract yearly about 12,800 tons of concentrates containing 70 per cent copper and 640 kilograms (22,528 ounces) of gold. Specimens of the ore have been treated in the United States in furnaces developed by American engineers. If these tests prove successful, the Society of Copper Mines of Mauritania (Micuma) will try to persuade the Mauritanian government to grant it a special tax status, and begin mining operations. Exports of copper concentrates will move through the new port of Nouakchott, the capital.

Foreign trade: In 1962, general imports were valued at $75 million and consisted in large part of equipment brought in under the special regime granted to the mining companies, especially "Miferma." Exports were valued at about $1.6 million in 1962. Actual exports were greater, however, because statistics do not include cattle exports to Senegal and Mali, for example, nor goods shipped through Dakar, which are counted as Senegalese exports. Mauritania's balance of trade with the franc zone is highly unfavorable, but will be greatly improved when the volume of iron-ore shipments increases and copper exports begin.

Industries: Mauritania has no modern industry aside from the newly launched mining enterprises. Such industrialization as exists, other than the mines, is related to the processing of fish and other seafood at Port Etienne. Meat-processing is severely limited by lack of cold-storage and freezing facilities, and the animals (cattle, sheep, goats and camels) must be driven to the vicinity of consuming centers before slaughtering is done;

the losses caused by this are estimated at 30 per cent of the animals' value.

Communications and transport:

Ports: Port Etienne and Nouakchott.

Railroad: Port Etienne to Fort Gouraud (422 miles).

Roads: The principal road is the Transmauritanian (864 miles), which crosses the country from south to north via Nouakchott, Akjoujt, Atar and Fort Gouraud, ending at the Algerian border. Another road, which has been used by trucks carrying ore from Fort Gouraud to Port Etienne, coincides in part with the Transmauritanian. These roads are unpaved desert tracks. There are no paved roads.

Airports: Port Etienne and Nouakchott have class-B airports, served by U.T.A. and Air Afrique. In September 1962, a national airline, Air Mauritanie, was created for internal services.

Motor vehicles: As of January 1, 1961, there were 436 private cars and 1,517 commercial vehicles, including trucks.

NIGER

Occupations: Of the active population, which totals about 1.1 million, some 250,000 are self-employed and 850,000 are unpaid workers performing family or community tasks. Wage earners were estimated in 1962 at 18,350. Of the total population of some 3 million, about 20 per cent live in the desert regions of the north and are nomadic herders. About 77 per cent is accounted for by peasant farmers and by sedentary or semi-nomadic Peul herders, living in the southern regions.

Average annual income: No data are available. The population lives almost entirely under a system of barter.

Principal products, subsistence and export (1962):

	Tons
Millet	934,000
Sorghum	320,000
Peanuts (in shell)	205,370
Peanuts (shelled)	92,340
Corn, wheat and rice	15,500

Livestock (estimated) :   *Head*
   Cattle   3,500,000
   Sheep and goats   7,000,000
   Camels   350,000
   Horses   115,000

Minerals: Production has consisted only of cassiterite, of which 59 tons were produced in 1962. Some uranium exists, and this may eventually be mined by the French Atomic Energy Commission. Prospecting for copper, iron and petroleum has been done, but no important finds have yet been announced.

Foreign trade: Official statistics for 1962—which as indicated below do not reflect the true volume of goods exchanged—show imports valued at $27 million and exports amounting to about $14 million. Although their full extent is not known, actual quantities are much greater, because goods exchanged between Niger and neighboring countries of former French West Africa are not declared to customs and not entered in statistics. Also, there is much smuggling between Niger and Nigeria.

Industries: Industrial development is very slight, and the only enterprise in the country with modern equipment is a frozen-meat plant at Niamey. This sector of the economy (industry) accounts for only 2.8 per cent of the gross national product and employs only 2,830 persons, 2,360 of whom are employed on public works. Aside from the meat plant and 17 public-works construction firms, there are only such small, artisanal concerns as three oil mills, a cotton gin, a few furniture factories and a brick factory.

Communications and transport:

Railroad: None exists. In February 1963, the Niger and Dahomey governments asked the European Common Market to finance the prolongation to Dosso, in southern Niger, of the Dahomey rail line which connects Cotonou with Parakou. This would require the construction of 323 miles of track, at an estimated cost of $3 million. At the time of writing, no action had been taken by the Common Market on this request.

Roads: The road network, almost none of which is paved, includes about 4,500 miles of so-called national roads, local roads and tracks (*pistes*).

Airports: At Niamey (class A) and Tahoua, Agadés, Zinder and Maradi (class B). There are also 11 minor airfields. Airlines serving Niger include Air Afrique, Air France and U.T.A.

Motor vehicles: As of January 1962, there were 1,167 passenger cars and 2,312 light and heavy trucks.

SENEGAL

Occupations: Of the working-age population (estimated at nearly 1.4 million), about 1.2 million are engaged in farming, herding, and artisanry. Industrial workers total some 120,000, and wage earners in government service and .private business, 105,000.

Average annual income: Approximately $175.

Principal products:

	Tons
Agricultural (1962 season):	
Peanuts (in shell)	890,000
Exported	758,000
Millet and sorghum	360,000
Rice, unhusked	91,000
Manioc	133,000
Corn	29,000
Produce (truck-garden)	34,000
Niébé beans	15,000

	Head
Livestock (1961):	
Cattle	1,960,000
Sheep and goats	1,284,000
Donkeys	65,000
Horses	94,000

Tons

Fish, from maritime fisheries (1961) 104,728
Industrial products and minerals (1962):

Peanut oil:
    Unrefined 107,400
    Refined 45,800
Cotton yarn 602
Cotton cloth (unprinted) 1,124
Cement 183,200
Phosphate of lime 497,100
Phosphate of alumina (untreated) 141,400
Titanium-ilmenite 25,500

Foreign trade: Imports in 1962 were valued at $156 million and exports amounted to $125 million. Imports consisted in very large part of consumer goods, and France was the chief supplier (over $100 million worth). Peanuts accounted for about three-fourths of all exports, by value, and practically all peanut shipments went to France, Senegal's principal customer.

Industries: Senegal is the most highly industrialized country of West Africa and the one in which the total amount of investments has been greatest. Existing enterprises are diversified and too numerous to list here, but the products of some may be noted: farm machinery; tire-recapping, carbonated beverages; human and animal food products derived from peanuts; textiles; paper products; and fish products. Under the present four-year economic plan (1960–64), about $69 million are earmarked for establishing new industries. Out of this sum, $57 million are being used for seven large operations, construction of most of which has been started. These include an oil refinery near Dakar; a chemical-fertilizer plant; increased phosphate production; a fish cannery, with adjoining wharf and cold-storage plant; a textile mill at Richard-Toll in the Senegal Valley; an electric-power network throughout the country;

and a metals industry, including a scrap-iron treating plant and studies for a possible steel mill. Senegal's outstanding mineral resource is the phosphates at Taiba. Prospecting for petroleum was carried on for several years, but has slowed down because of disappointing results.

Communications and transport:

Ports: Dakar is West Africa's greatest port, its closest rival being Abidjan, Ivory Coast. River ports include Kaolack, Ziguinchor and Saint Louis. Kaolack's chief activity is the evacuation of peanuts from the Senegal Valley to the coast.

Railroads: (1) The Dakar-Niger, 804 miles long, connecting Dakar with Bamako and Koulikoro in the Mali Republic; this line has two short spurs to Kaolack (14 miles) and Touba (30 miles). (2) The Dakar-Saint Louis, 164 miles long, 44 miles of which consist of tracks of the Dakar-Niger line; from it branches a line to Linguère, 80 miles in length.

Roads: 6,785 miles of roads and tracks (*pistes*). Of this network, 437 miles of roads are paved.

Airports: 13 in all, one of which—Dakar-Yoff—is of international class. Saint Louis and Ziguinchor have class-B airports. The remaining ten are usable only by small planes. Among international airlines serving Dakar-Yoff are Air-Afrique, Air France and U.T.A.

Motor vehicles: On January 1, 1963, they totaled 40,146, including 23,286 passenger cars, 13,825 light and heavy trucks and 2,167 buses. Thirty per cent of all motor vehicles operating in former French West Africa are in Senegal, and nearly two-thirds of these are concentrated in Dakar and on the Cap-Vert peninsula.

UPPER VOLTA

Occupations: Almost 95 per cent of the population, or about 4.2 million, live in rural areas, and the vast majority are peasant farmers and herders. Of the working-age population, totaling some 2.3 million, wage earners accounted for only 27,417 in 1962.

Average annual income: Less than $45.

Principal products (1961):

	Tons
Sorghum	410,725
Millet	194,940
Peanuts (in shell)	110,350
Yams	82,530
Corn	74,985
Pois de terre ("ground peas")	74,341
Niébé beans	41,230
Fonio (a cereal)	15,528
Livestock (estimated):	*Head*
Cattle	2,000,000
Sheep and goats	3,650,000
Horses	100,000
	Ounces
Gold	201,864

Foreign trade: Upper Volta regularly has a highly unfavorable trade balance, although the deficit is usually offset to some extent by money sent back to their families by laborers who go as migrant workers to Ghana and Ivory Coast, where they earn wages on the plantations. In 1961, imports—about two-thirds of which were consumer goods—totaled $35 million. Exports, about half of which were live animals, were valued at $7.9 million. France was the chief supplier of imported goods and Ghana the largest customer for exports.

Industries: Industrialization has scarcely begun. There are 43 small manufacturing and processing enterprises, of which only three employ more than 100 workers. They include a combined oilmill and soap factory, two cotton gins, a rice mill, a brewery and various smaller plants. As indicated above, the only mineral produced in 1961 was a small amount of gold. Manganese prospecting in the northern part of the country has disclosed deposits of this ore, and plans to mine it are being made at the present time.

Communications and transport:

Railroads: 318 miles of the Abidjan-Niger railroad (whose total length is 716 miles) connect Ouagadougou with the Ivory Coast frontier, and freight and passengers are carried over it between the Mossi country and the seacoast at Abidjan.

Roads: There are 4,662 miles of roads, of which less than one-third are usable at all seasons. The only paved roads are streets in Ouagadougou and Bobo-Dioulasso, totaling about 40 miles.

Airports: Ouagadougou and Bobo-Dioulasso have international-class airports served by Air Afrique, U.T.A. and Air Ghana. There are 28 minor fields. The national airline, Air Volta, using single-engine planes, provides service over the internal network.

Motor vehicles: As of January 1962, Upper Volta had 6,687, including 2,234 private cars and 4,453 commercial vehicles and trucks.

Maps

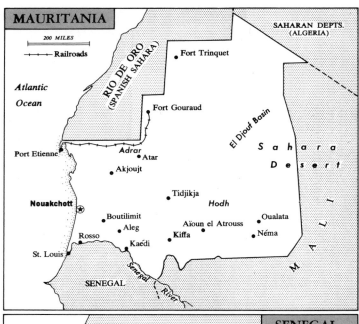

MAURITANIA

200 MILES

Railroads

Atlantic Ocean

RIO DE ORO (SPANISH SAHARA)

SAHARAN DEPTS. (ALGERIA)

Fort Trinquet

Fort Gouraud

Port Etienne

Adrar • Atar

Akjoujt

El Djouf Basin

S a h a r a   D e s e r t

Nouakchott

Tidjikja

Hodh

Boutilimit

Aleg

Oualata

Aïoun el Atrouss

Kiffa

Néma

Rosso

St. Louis

Kaédi

Senegal River

SENEGAL

M A L I

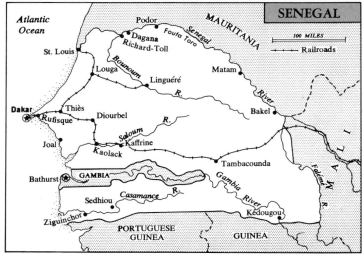

SENEGAL

Atlantic Ocean

Podor

MAURITANIA

Senegal

Fouta Toro

Dagana

Richard-Toll

St. Louis

100 MILES

Railroads

Louga

Bounoum R.

Linguéré

Matam

Dakar

Thiès

Diourbel

River

Rufisque

R.

Bakel

Joal

Saloum

R.

Kaffrine

Kaolack

Tambacounda

Bathurst

GAMBIA

Casamance R.

Gambia River

Sedhiou

Ziguinchor

Falémé R.

Kédougou

M A L I

PORTUGUESE GUINEA

GUINEA

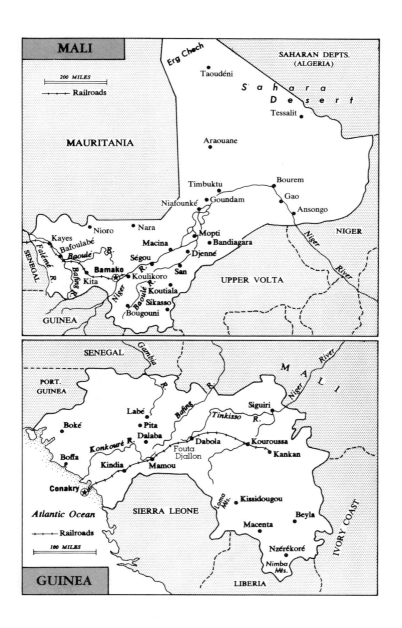

MALI

200 MILES

+ Railroads

MAURITANIA

Erg Chech

SAHARAN DEPTS.
(ALGERIA)

Taoudéni

S a h a r a
D e s e r t

Tessalit

Araouane

Timbuktu
Bourem
Gao
Niafounké • Goundam
Ansongo

NIGER

Nioro • Nara
Mopti
Kayes
Macina • Bandiagara
Bafoulabé
Baoulé R.
Ségou • Djenné
SENEGAL
Bamako
San
Falémé R.
Koulikoro
UPPER VOLTA
Bafing R.
Kita
Niger
Koutiala
Baoulé R.
Sikasso
Bougouni
GUINEA

GUINEA

SENEGAL

Gambia R.

PORT.
GUINEA

M A L I

Niger River

Bafing R.

Labé
Siguiri
Tinkisso R.
Pita
Dalaba
Konkouré R.
Boké
Dabola
Kouroussa
Kankan
Boffa
Fouta
Djallon
Kindia
Mamou

Conakry

SIERRA LEONE

Loma Mts.

Kissidougou

Beyla

Macenta

IVORY COAST

Atlantic Ocean

+ Railroads

100 MILES

Nzérékoré

Nimba Mts.

LIBERIA

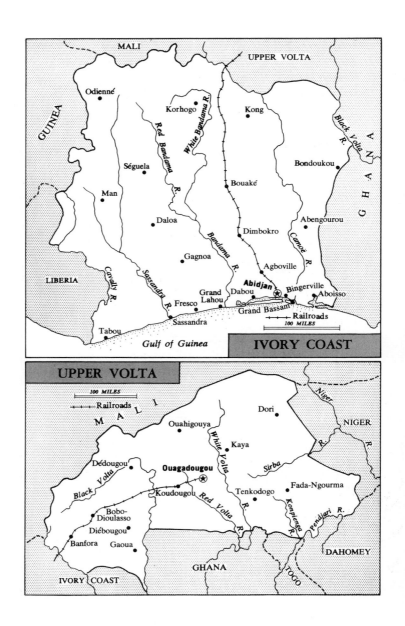

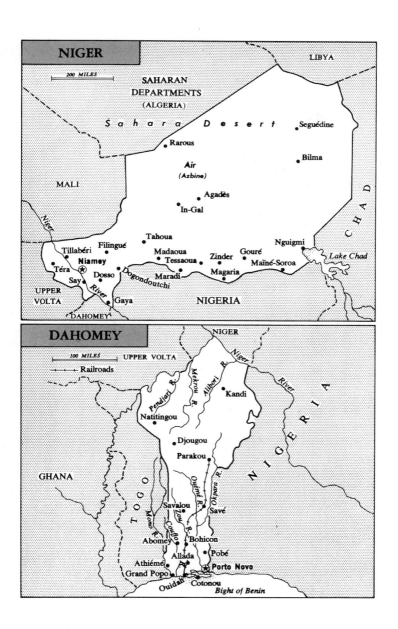

Glossary

animism (*an*-i-mism)—belief, prevalent among primitive peoples, that certain inanimate objects and natural phenomena possess living souls.

azalaï (*az*-a-lie)—camel caravans which carry salt from mines in the southern Sahara to markets in the sudanese zone, returning with foodstuffs and other goods for the desert nomads.

banco (*bank*-o)—sun-dried mud brick, similar to the adobe of southwestern United States; used in building houses, walls, granaries, etc., in the sudanese zone of Africa.

bellah (*bell*-ah)—Negro serfs, descendants of slaves, living among the Tuareg clans of West Africa, to whose chiefs they have ties of a feudal nature.

Berber—a member of the North African aboriginal population believed to be of Hamitic stock which migrated from Egypt in prehistoric times.

cercle (*sair*-cluh)—an administrative unit of former French African territories; it still forms part of the administrative structure of some of the independent French-speaking African countries.

corvée (kor-*vay*)—system prevalent in French Negro Africa during the colonial period, under which unpaid labor on public projects had to be done by adult males for a certain number of days annually; also called prestation labor.

coutumes (koo-*tume*)—fees exacted by West African chiefs from Europeans, before the French conquest, for the right to trade.

elite (aa-*leet*)—in Africa, a privileged class which formerly comprised only the traditional chiefs and the *notables;* under the French regime, a new elite was created on the basis of education.

erg (*airg*)—Sahara Desert areas consisting of shifting sand dunes.

fetishism (*fet*-ish-ism)—worship of, or superstitious feeling for, inanimate objects believed to have magical powers and to be animated by a spirit.

goumier (*goo*-me-aa)—an African desert policeman whose mount is a camel.

grigri (*gree*-gree)—an amulet or talisman, believed to have magical powers and associated with animist or fetishist beliefs.

griot (*gree*-aht)—an African minstrel-clown, who in former times was a member of a chief's retinue.

harmattan (*har*-mat-tan)—a dry, parching land wind which blows from the desert.

imam (*ih*-mahm)—the officiating priest of a Muslim mosque.

imrad (*im*-rahd)—low-caste Tuareg who are vassals of warrior nobles.

indigénat (an-*dee*-zhaa-nah)—during the French colonial period a native-status legal code under which administrators could impose certain penalties arbitrarily on non-citizen Africans for offenses punishable under law.

kapok (*kay*-pock)—fiber surrounding the seeds of an African tree which grows wild in the sahel zone; used in cushions and upholstery.

kola (*koh*-lah)—a nut, chewed as a stimulant; widely used by African Muslims as a substitute for alcoholic beverages, which are forbidden by their faith.

laterite (*lat*-uhr-ite)—a red, porous, iron-bearing rock formed by the decomposition of surface rocks under the action of intense sunlight and humidity.

litham (*lith*-ahm)—veil used by men of the Tuareg clans to cover the lower part of their faces.

loi-cadre (lwah *cah*-druh)—literally, a "framework law"; the French law of June 23, 1956, which authorized greater autonomy for the French African territories and other sweeping changes there.

marabout (mah-rah-*boo*)—a Muslim religious leader whose disciples revere him for his learning and piety.

méhariste (*may*-hah-reest)—a member of the camel-mounted desert patrol formed by the French Army in 1898.

monsoon (mon-*soon*)—a seasonal wind from the ocean which brings rain.

navétane (*nah*-vay-tahn)—a migrant African from western Mali who works as a seasonal share-cropper on Senegalese and Gambian peanut farms.

notable (no-*tah*-blah)—an African of high rank in his community or one who is treated with special respect for one reason or another.

pirogue (*peer*-ahg)—narrow canoe made of a hollowed log or of large sections of bark; usually propelled by an oar from a standing position.

piste (*peest*)—unpaved road or track.

polygamy (pol-*ig*-amy)—state of being married to more than one person of the opposite sex, whether male or female, at the same time.

polygyny (pol-*ij*-iny)—widespread African marriage custom under which a man has two or more wives at the same time (in contrast to polyandry: the custom of a woman's having two or more husbands simultaneously).

poular (*poh*-lahr)—language of the Peul tribe of West Africa.

reg—Sahara Desert plains regions strewn with rocks and gravel.

sahel (sah-*hell*)—geographic region of Africa lying between the sudanese zone to the south and the Sahara Desert to the north; its vegetation consists of sparse grass, spiny bushes and relatively few trees of drought-resistant types.

savannah (sah-*vahn*-nah)—plains region of West Africa north of the tropical-forest zone and south of the sahel; it has high grass, more trees and greater rainfall than the sahel, and is especially suited to agriculture. Also called the sudanese zone.

soudure (soh-*dyoor*)—period between seasonal food-crop harvests, often marked by famine.

taboo (tah-*bou*)—an animal or other object to which sacred significance is given in primitive societies and which it is forbidden to touch or harm. Comparable to the American Indian term, "totem."

tamachek (*tah*-mah-sheck)—language of the Tuareg nomads of West Africa; it is related to that of the Berbers of North Africa.

Tidjaniya (tee-*djahn*-i-yah)—a Muslim sect which is especially important in West Africa; it adheres rigidly to the precepts of the prophet Mohammed, and before the French pacification, was a brotherhood of warriors.

tifinar (*tee*-fee-nahr)—a Berber alphabet used in the written form of the Tuareg language, *tamachek* (see above).

zebu (*see*-bew)—humped cattle, usually with large, lyre-shaped horns; common in the sudanese zone of West Africa.

Bibliography

Although only books in English are listed here, it should be noted that the largest and most comprehensive body of publications dealing with former French West Africa consists of works in the French language, the great majority of which have not been published in English translation.

Berg, Elliot "The Economic Basis of Political Choice in French West Africa," *American Political Science Review,* June 1960
The role of French economic and financial aid in the political life of the French-speaking West African states analyzed in a very valuable study.

Bovill, E. W. *The Golden Trade of the Moors* New York: Oxford University Press, 1958
An interesting account of the trans-Saharan caravans and trade between North Africa and the Negro regions in the Middle Ages and later.

Burke, Fred G. *Africa's Quest for Order* Englewood Cliffs, N.J.: Prentice-Hall Inc., 1964 (paper)
A thoughtful recent study of the problems faced by emerging African states and of their social and political background.

Carter, Gwendolen M., ed. *African One-Party States* Ithaca: Cornell University Press, 1962
Six African nations, including Senegal, Guinea and Ivory Coast, are dealt with by various specialists. Stress is placed on the analysis of their single-party political systems.

———— *Five African States* Ithaca: Cornell University Press, 1963
A sequel to *African One-Party States,* mentioned above. Dahomey is the only French-speaking West African country included.

Carter, Gwendolen M. *Independence for Africa* New York: Frederick A. Praeger, Inc., 1960 (cloth and paper)
Political change in many areas of sub-Saharan Africa is studied by a perceptive observer who is a trained political scientist and has traveled widely throughout the continent.

Delafosse, Maurice *The Negroes of Africa* Washington: Associated Publishers, 1931

> Although published many years ago and not a good translation from the original French, this is a valuable description of tribal life and customs in French West Africa by a French administrator of the colonial period.

Delavignette, Robert *Freedom and Authority in French West Africa* London and New York: Oxford University Press, 1950

> One of the most authoritative studies of French administrative theory and practice in West Africa before World War II. The author is a retired governor of the colonial service in West Africa.

French Embassy Press and Information Service Six pamphlets on new states of former French West Africa, entitled *Republic of Senegal, Islamic Republic of Mauritania, Republic of Upper Volta, Republic of Niger, Republic of Dahomey, Republic of Ivory Coast* New York: 1960

> Brief, colorful descriptions, with many illustrations, of the political economic and social characteristics of the six countries.

Hailey, Lord *An African Survey—Revised 1956* New York: Oxford University Press, 1957

> A revised edition of one of the most authoritative studies of Africa, devoted largely to former British territories but containing also much useful information on former French West Africa.

Harrison Church, R. J. *Environment and Policies in West Africa* Princeton, N.J.: D. Van Nostrand Co., Inc., 1963

> Number 9 in the Van Nostrand Searchlight Books series.

Hodgkin, Thomas L. *Nationalism in Colonial Africa* London: Muller, 1956

> A well-written and astute analysis of African nationalism, based in part on first-hand observation in British and French West Africa.

Hodgkin, Thomas L. and Schachter, Ruth *French-Speaking West Africa in Transition* (International Conciliation Series, No. 528)

New York: Carnegie Endowment for International Peace, 1960 (pamphlet)

A concise account of political developments during the period just before the French West African territories became independent.

Howard, C. *West African Explorers* New York: Oxford University Press, 1951

Well-chosen excerpts from colorful first-hand accounts of travels in West Africa in the 17th, 18th and 19th centuries by a number of European explorers, including Mungo Park, Rene Caillie, and Heinrich Barth.

Kimble, George H. T. *Tropical Africa* (2 vols) New York: The Twentieth Century Fund, 1960; Anchor Books, 1963 (paper)

Penetrating studies of sub-Saharan Africa by an eminent geographer, which stress economic-geographic aspects but touch also on political and social questions. Authoritative and readable.

Schachter, Ruth "Single-Party Systems in West Africa," *American Political Science Review,* June 1961

An expert analysis of single-party government in certain West African states.

Segal, Ronald *African Profiles* Baltimore: Penguin Books, 1962; revised edition, 1963 (paper)

A study of newly independent African states which centers on the careers and personalities of their leaders.

Thompson, Virginia and Adloff, Richard *French West Africa* Stanford: Stanford University Press, 1958

This book's political analysis is now outdated as a result of developments since 1958, but it is otherwise useful for political background and for its description of economic and social-cultural aspects of pre-independent French West Africa.

Wallerstein, Immanuel *Africa—The Politics of Independence* New York: Vintage Books, 1961 (paper)

A searching and brilliant analysis of the aims and methods of African nationalism, deserving of close attention.

Credits

The format for *West Africa, the French-Speaking Nations* was designed by Robert Sugar. The cover was prepared by Leah Ice. The maps were drawn by Donald T. Pitcher.

For the photographs on the following pages we gratefully credit:

Index